(20) AR

RECLAIMING A RESOURCE

Papers From The

FRIENDS BIBLE CONFERENCE

Arch Street Meetinghouse
Philadelphia, Pennsylvania
Eleventh Month 10-12, 1989

Edited by
Chuck Fager

Kimo Press
Falls Church, Virginia

1990

ISBN #0-945177-06-2

Cover design by

Chroma Graphics and Communications,
Takoma Park, Maryland

Kimo Press
P.O. Box 1361
Falls Church, VA 22041
(703) 845-0427

Contents

Introduction

I

Like the Bible, this book is a richly diverse collection, and is intended to serve many purposes, some practical, others more reflective.

Suppose, for instance, you need a guide for a small group Bible study in your meeting. There are several here(e.g., the papers by Joe Izzo, Patty Levering and Joanne Spears, among others.) Complete instructions are included; the only other supplies you need are a group and some Bibles; and you're on your way.

Or say you're thinking about or planning for Bible study in your First Day School. You'll find a complete lesson plan by Mary Snyder; a consideration of the place of Bible study in religious education by Kate McCrone; Herb Lape's thoughts on whether Bible study can help kids cope with the onslaughts of our materialistic culture; and a survey of children's Bible music by Patricia McKernon.

But what if you're an activist, wondering whether the Bible is relevant to Quaker social concerns? Then consider Wallace Cayard's empathetic but clear-eyed survey of liberation theology; Jim Corbett on the biblical basis of the Sanctuary movement; Janice Domanik on ecology; several writers on feminism; and Elizabeth Watson on all this and more.

And if you want food for reflection and meditation, we have served up numerous rich and varied courses. To mention only a few: Cynthia Taylor on biblical Wisdom as a way of discovering the feminine side of God; John Yungblut's exploration of how insights from Jungian psychology can illuminate the scriptures, and be illuminated by them; Martha Grundy's examination of what Friends have learned from--and how they have struggled with--the Bible through most of our history; Carol Conti-Entin on the dialogue between the Bible without and the Bible within; and....

You get the idea. The range and variety of these papers reflects the surprising breadth and excitement of Bible study among unprogrammed Quakers in America today.

II

Did I say surprising? You bet. In fact, the whole Friends Bible Conference from which this book emerged was more than a surprise, it was in a real sense the result of a mistake: That's because a few years ago, I set out to write an article on how my sort of Quakers--the liberal unprogrammed kind--don't study the Bible enough.

I was ready with what were meant to be even-tempered laments over our neglect of the Scriptures, pointers to the potential spiritual value to be found therein, and gentle, nondogmatic coaxing to Friends to give the Good Book another look. To bolster this critique, I began an informal survey of what figured to be the few and paltry Bible study efforts that were underway among us.

That was when my mistake was revealed: The more I looked, the more Bible study turned up, in ever-more intriguing forms.

The point of the article that was ultimately written (in *A Friendly Letter* #59), was precisely the opposite of what I had started out to say: It celebrated the discovery that unprogrammed Friends were actually doing *lots* of Bible study.

And yet, there was an important element of truth in the original perception. While it was true that many unprogrammed Friends were studying the Bible--it was also true that practically none of us realized that anyone else was doing it. Most Friends I talked to felt isolated in their personal or small group study; they thought, as I had, that very few other unprogrammed Friends were doing likewise.

viii

Carol Conti-Entin, a member of Cleveland, Ohio Meeting, resonated to this last point, when we met at the 1988 Friends General Conference Gathering in Boone, North Carolina; she was leading a Bible study workshop in a room across the hall from mine. "But in fact," I said, "there's plenty of Bible study going on. You could fill a whole conference with it."

The next morning, Carol reminded me of this thought, and suggested we convene a meeting to see whether enough other Friends at the Gathering agreed with it to make something happen.

So we did, and the rest is, perhaps, history. At the very least, it produced the first formal Bible Conference for unprogrammed Friends since well before World War Two; and the book you are holding is the largest collection of writings on Bible study by and for unprogrammed Friends in at least as long.

Partly because it had been so long since any such gathering had been held, the Conference Committee chose to focus our attention on these efforts in a supportive setting, to share our excitement, start networking, and to build confidence in our own activities and concerns. Hence our theme, *Reclaiming a Vital Tool for Spiritual Growth.* This reclamation is already underway; we hoped only to highlight and reinforce it.

We were thrilled with the response, and hope through this collection to further extend and reinforce the enthusiasm and activity that filled Philadelphia's historic Arch Street meetinghouse for that brief weekend in 1989.

Whatever your particular Quaker interests, there should be something here for you. So browse, read, share, and above all use this book. Like the Bible, that's what it's for, Friend.

--Chuck Fager, Editor, and
Clerk, Conference Planning Committee

PS. Your comments on this book, and ideas for ways of pursuing Bible study among Friends, are welcomed. Write to Friends Bible Conference, %P.O. Box 1361, Falls Church, VA 22041.

Special Thanks To...

Many people cooperated to make the Friends Bible Conference happen. The planning committee members who saw the project through included:

Carol Conti-Entin, Cleveland Meeting, Ohio
Emma Engle, Mickleton Meeting, New Jersey
Chuck Fager, Langley Hill Meeting, Virginia
Martha Grundy, Cleveland Meeting, Ohio
Joe Izzo, Friends Meeting of Washington, D.C.
Dorothy Livezey, Woodbury Meeting, New Jersey

We also benefitted from the ideas of Courtney Bischoff at our initial planning meeting in Tenth Month, 1988, and from the hospitality of Pittsburgh Meeting, which hosted the session. Sam Prellwitz generously made the arrangements for that session.

At the Conference itself, our coordinator Jane Houser kept a multitude of details keenly and coolly in hand, like the pro she is. Bill Strachan assisted her ably, and Helen File, mistress extraordinaire of the Arch Street Meetinghouse establishment, expertly oversaw the logistics there. We were likewise assisted(bailed out might be a better term) by Lyle Jenks and the staff at Friends General Conference, who opened their office space when our registration total overflowed the available workshop space. And Esther Gilbert labored long and effectively to find housing for many Friends from afar, thus enabling us to keep the Conference costs down.

Our costs were further subsidized by generous grants from several sources. One crucial early donor wishes to remain anonymous; but among the others were:

Philadelphia Yearly Meeting Bequests Committee
The Ethel Reynolds Fund of Baltimore Yearly Meeting
Langley Hill Meeting Religious Education Committee,
    Virginia
Cleveland Meeting, Ohio
Central Philadelphia Monthly Meeting
Canadian Yearly Meeting Religious Education Committee
Stony Run Meeting, Baltimore, Maryland
Homewood Meeting, Baltimore, Maryland
Staten Island Meeting, New York
Kent Meeting, Ohio
Dorothy Stratton, Ashland, Ohio

We were also grateful for the committees and meetings which endorsed and helped promote the Conference, among them:

Friends General Conference Religious Education Committee
Lake Erie Yearly Meeting Religious Education Committee
Philadelphia Yearly Meeting Religious Education Committee
Central Alaskan Friends Conference
Chena Ridge Monthly Meeting, Alaska
Fayetteville Meeting, North Carolina
Manhasset Meeting, New York

Many of the 260 Conference participants made contributions beyond their registration fees to assist in meeting Conference expenses.

While Barbara Platt of Stony Run Meeting was prevented from attending the Conference, she still gave us significant help and advice at several points. Nor should we neglect the leaders of the twenty-seven workshops, who volunteered to prepare and lead their sessions, and most of whom whom then submitted papers on their workshop topics, which collectively make up this book.

xi

RECLAIMING A RESOURCE

1

The Bible And Liberation Theology

by Wallace Cayard

[Note: Wallace Cayard attends Pittsburgh, Pennsylvania Meeting. He spent forty years teaching religion at the college level.]

Friends can learn much about using the Bible from liberation theology, yet we need to recognize our differences and honestly state our criticisms. We shall concentrate on liberation theology from Latin America rather than from Africa or Asia, partly because Latin American liberation theology is the most influential in North America and partly because it emphasizes the Bible as a basic authority for theology.

To understand the role of the Bible in liberation theology we need to look at its assumptions about how to interpret the Bible. Liberation theologians emphasize that their approach to Scripture is from the bias of the poor. They criticize most North American and European theologians for not recognizing that they too are biased. The Latin Americans think that their bias is closer to the biblical revelation of what God is like, because they believe that God sides with the poor.

For Latin American liberation theology a living faith, a Christian commitment to the poor, comes before biblical interpretation and other forms of critical reflection. Gustavo Gutierrez of Peru, the most influential Latin American theologian, says that a commitment to the liberation of the poor is the first act of doing theology, and the second act is critical reflection on that experience, including the use of the Bible. (1)

Latin American liberation theologians either experience poverty directly or work with the poor in their daily lives. They live in a strong Catholic culture where there is widespread belief that the policies and practices of the United States are part of the cause of their poverty. Such personal and social experiences lead to the first act of liberation theology, a religious commitment to the poor, and these experiences color their critical reflection on the Bible.

The second act of liberation theology, critical reflection on the commitment to end poverty, involves three stages, according to Leonardo and Clodovis Boff of Brazil in their book, *Introducing Liberation Theology*. (2) The stages are: social analysis to discover why the poor are poor, biblical interpretation to discern God's way to overcome poverty, and practical interpretation to seek courses of action for liberation.

Social analysis as a form of critical reflection joins commitment to the poor as a second assumption of biblical interpretation. The social analysis perspective which liberation theologians develop is an attempt to secure a factual and theoretical understanding of the causes of poverty.

Gutierrez, like most Latin American liberation theologians, defends a Marxist social analysis of poverty. In his 1973 classic, *A Theology of Liberation*, Gutierrez says that a central fact of history is the class struggle between the oppressive rich owners of the means of production and the oppressed poor workers. (3) This Marxism is modified in the 1988 revision of his book where he agrees that not all social conflict is reducible to economic oppression of the poor classes by the rich. He now recognizes that he had neglected racial and sexual oppression. However, in agreement with most liberation theologians, Gutierrez still emphasizes class struggle as the primary form of social conflict. (4)

According to liberation theologians, their social analysis points to the need for a revolutionary change toward a socialist economic system in order to promote justice for the poor. Liberationists stress the role of the church in the promotion of a more just society. They say the church should appeal to the oppressed, not the oppressors, to stimulate and educate their necessary part of working for peace. Friends working for peace too often have been primarily negative, against war, and not positive enough for justice, a foundation for peace. We can learn from the liberation theologians to work for justice, including changing our foreign policy away from economic, political or military oppression of the Third World. And the liberation theologians can learn from Quakers that the root of justice is love and reconciliation, a recognition of that of God in everyone.

Liberation theologians agree with the prophet Amos' emphasis on justice. Speaking for God, Amos said:

"...let justice roll down like waters,

and righteousness like an overflowing stream." (12)

Quakers agree with the prophet Hosea's emphasis on love. Speaking for God, Hosea said,

"...I desire steadfast love and not sacrifice,

the knowledge of God, rather than burnt

offerings." (13)

Liberation theologians and Quakers should combine these emphases and agree with the prophet Micah who said,

"...what does the Lord require of you

but to do justice, and to love kindness

and to walk humbly with your God?" (14)

NOTES

1. Gustavo Gutierrez, *A Theology of Liberation*, Revised Edition, (Maryknoll: Orbis, 1988), pp. xiii, xx-xxviii, 9.

2. Leonardo and Clodovis Boff, *Introducing Liberation Theology*, (Maryknoll: Orbis, 1987), p. 24.

3. Gustavo Gutierrez, *A Theology of Liberation* (Maryknoll: Orbis, 1973), pp. 272-279.

4. Gutierrez, *A Theology of Liberation* (1988), p. 64.

5. Quoted by Gutierrez (1988), p. 64.

6. Craig L. Nessan, *Orthopraxis or Heresy: The North American Theological Response to Latin American Liberation Theology* (Atlanta: Scholars Press, 1989), p. 41.

7. Exodus Ch. 1-15.

8. Matthew 5:3, 6.

9. Luke 6:20, 21, 24, 25.

10 Gutierrez (1988), p. 8.

11. Precritical, critical, and postcritical interpretations are discussed by John Barton in "Reading and Interpreting the Bible," *Harpers Bible Commentary* (San Francisco: Harper and Row, 1988), pp. 2-13.

12. Amos 5:24.

13. Hosea 6:6.

14. Micah 6:8.

II

Using The Written Bible
To Hear The Bible Within

Carol Conti-Entin

[Note: Carol Conti-Entin does computer consulting for Oberlin College, and is a former musician. She attends Cleveland, Ohio Meeting, is the author of Improvisation and Spiritual Disciplines, (Pendle Hill Pamphlet #288), and she survived being Registrar for the Friends Bible Conference.]

What is the role of the written Bible in our spiritual journeys? If we have read some early Quaker history, we know that the answers Fox and Barclay gave to this question were jarringly at odds with those given by representatives of the various Protestant denominations. Each side was convinced that the other devalued the Scriptures by using them wrongly.

Rather than quote early Friends, however, I wish to turn to contemporary experience, because the end result is theologically equivalent. To set the scene for this, please imagine with me that you and I live not in a nation which claims to value the Bible but in a country (Albania, as a self-declared atheistic state, will do nicely) in which we have had no access to the Hebrew and Christian Scriptures and may not even know they exist. We may not have the written Bible, but we still have the Living Word of God--the Inward Teacher--Sophia--the Cosmic Christ who is before Abraham was. Under the circumstances we are unlikely to call this guiding force by any of those names, but we do, individually and communally, have encounters with the divine, inexplicable in rational terms, akin to those of the Israelites. Just as our spiritual predecessors did, we seek to name such experiences and to meditate upon them.

For some of us the written Bible might as well have been inaccessible, since we ignored it, perhaps for years. When the time came to discover or rediscover it, however, we found that the divine guide which we had already encountered dwelling within us suddenly had a most remarkable ally. Not only were we reading the Scriptures, but they were reading us! The spiritual experiences of the protagonists of the written Bible helped us reflect more deeply upon numinous events in our own lives. A new jigsaw puzzle piece would fall into place, making it easier for us to welcome God's next work within us. As we continued to ponder our accumulating body of spiritual experience, we shared our insights with others, thus participating in the same tradition which gave rise to the biblical canon.

Our Quaker mode of spirituality prepares us unusually well to engage with the written Bible. We know that it is not necessary to rely upon trained experts: God's word for us reaches us whenever we open ourselves to that same Spirit which inspired the biblical authors. Various "helps" such as interlinear translations, dictionaries, and commentaries can indeed increase our understanding of passages we have already allowed to search us. But God always could, and still does, send a prophetic message to and through an unschooled messenger. If we are led to obtain formal training, its fruitfulness is dependent upon how readily we continue to allow the Inner Light to come in and sup with us.

An important skill we have acquired through our Quaker practice is the ability to meditate upon queries which are themselves the product of deep inner searching. This empowers us to formulate the kinds of questions about a biblical passage which prevent us from being content with superficial observations and easy answers. Indeed, when we read the Bible with a yearning to know and obey God's voice, probing queries often emerge spontaneously.

Is there a pattern to the way in which reading the written Bible helps us to hear the Bible within? If by pattern one means an ordered sequence of steps by which each subsequent passage influences us, then in my experience there isn't. When I examine my own history of encounters with Scripture, I find that the process has been more like that of watching a photograph develop. During the first read-through, a few passages became vivid. During subsequent readings, as those initial foreground events intensified, a somewhat larger collection of passages took on shape and color. Gradually, over time, more and more details began to emerge from the formless void, and I came to see that my own spirituality also had a detailed topography to it.

Perhaps because the Bible is an entire small library, spanning hundreds of years and incorporating many literary styles, some passages invite passionate engagement, others lingering meditation, still others no more than a casual perusal--at least for the time being. Whether the next portion of Scripture one encounters is capable of furthering one's spiritual growth depends in large part upon the extent to which one seeks first to understand and evaluate the experience being presented as its authors understood and evaluated it.

This process and its companion, applying the insights thus gained to one's own current situation, welcome the involvement of one's total creative being. Any artistic or kinesthetic form may be called into play. Since the changes one thus undergoes invariably affect what one can bring to the next passage one meets, there is no end to the written Bible's ability to help one hear the Bible within.

A personal example will clarify why I recommend allowing the passage itself to reveal how one is to approach it. During one stage in my life I kept noticing the parallels between the disciple Peter's traits and experiences and my own. I found myself compelled to reread all four Gospels as well as all later references to Peter and to attempt to piece together a chronological biography of this forthright disciple. But then I came to the passage in Luke (22:61-62) which immediately follows the scene in which Peter denied that he even knew Jesus of Nazareth:

"And turning, the Lord looked at Peter, and Peter remembered the word of the Lord, as he told him, 'Before a cock sounds today, you will deny me three times.' And going outside, Peter wept bitterly."

At that moment I could do nothing else but gaze into the face which had looked at Peter and was now looking at me--into those patient, forgiving, searching eyes.

That particular example illustrates the movement from written to inner experience during one stage of one individual's life. Were you to have been led to meditate on those same two verses, I doubt that you would have seen exactly the same face that I did; who we are and the choices we have made in our lives to date affect the lessons we need to learn at any one moment.

But imagine the impact upon us if you, I, and several other earnest seekers are studying that passage together and doing our best to articulate what we understand to be its effect upon Peter--as well as what we are experiencing as its effect upon us!

Communal engagement with the written Bible, then, can amplify individual engagement (and vice versa). How can such a creative group process be begun and maintained? What if no candidate for the new group has already undergone a significant spiritual transformation through encounters with the written Bible?

In that case I can from experience recommend the method Joanne and Larry Spears describe elsewhere in this book. It enables anyone to facilitate and requires only one hour per session, yet it provides a fertile setting for growth.

The remainder of this essay is addressed to the person who has already had significant encounters with Scripture and who feels led to enable others to experience the transformational potential of the written Bible but does not know how to translate this desire into group process.

I strongly recommend that you start by reading a book by Walter Wink entitled *Transforming Bible Study: A Leader's Guide* (Abingdon Press). He begins with a convincing plea for a Bible study process which engages both hemispheres of the brain. The book includes transcripts of actual workshop sessions which illustrate the kinds of queries and creative exercises which bring engagement to fruition. But Wink rightly urges the would-be leader to avoid examining others' queries and techniques until one has formulated and experienced one's own.

It may well be that you notice a possible curriculum taking shape of its own accord. Perhaps the current state of the life of your Meeting has revealed a need, and you have found yourself drawn to relevant passages during recent months. Be forewarned that starting from scratch like this is very labor intensive: the preparation needs to be a labor of love over an adequate period of time. In order to prepare a particularly concentrated sixteen hours of material for the participants of one workshop, I dedicated my daily Bible reading time for a year.

Now that I am more experienced at leading such groups, I find that the formulation of suitable queries and exercises happens more quickly, but at this stage there is a new danger: Can I reuse old material without its coming across as stale? If a passage does not stimulate any additional queries, it may be a tipoff that I have rendered myself immune to its transformational ability. Although new insights could still arise from the assembled seekers (this is the most thrilling part of leading each such group), I would be better off using a different passage, one which is intensely present to me.

The danger of staleness is not necessarily present if you decide to use a curriculum designed by someone else. Here the preparation consists of "wearing" the curriculum designer's ideas long enough to ascertain which ones already fit you well, which require alteration, and which should be abandoned in order to make room for the ideas which have occurred to you during this time of preparation.

If you would like to explore adapting such an existing curriculum, the Religious Education Committee of Philadelphia Yearly Meeting has published several fine ones. Dorothy Reichardt's *Finding Our Way in the Bible: A Bible Course for Adults* is a survey designed for unprogrammed Friends. *Spiritual Journeys in the Bible* contains units by seven individuals (Dorothy Reichardt, William Taber, Rose Ketterer, Phillip Mullen, Kenneth Henke, Samuel Caldwell, and Hannah Gosling). If you would like to make the Gospels your focus, obtain Mary C. Morrison's *Approaching the Gospels Together* (Pendle Hill Publications), the fruit of long experience.

Whichever route you choose, be assured that a unique role

awaits you. The particular workings of the Spirit within you, coupled with your earnest and humble desire to help others hear the Bible within themselves, are your certification. No one else can offer the same combination of creativity and experience as you can.

III

The Bible And Covenant Communities

Jim Corbett

[Note: Jim Corbett has been a college teacher, librarian and goat rancher. In 1985 he was indicted for breaking federal immigration laws as part of the sanctuary movement, but he beat the rap. Jim attends Pima Meeting in Tucson, Arizona.]

the historical dimension of group discernment

In our meetings for business, we Quakers often cultivate group discernment to an extraordinary level of awareness. Yet, we are also notoriously deficient in our practice of group discernment as a people--as a community that persists through its successive generations and that, as a people, has undertaken a task we can only fulfill in history, through our generations. These deficiencies in the Quaker community's historical coherence and continuity are closely related to our uncertainties about the role of scripture and outward community practices, in light of our rejection of the authority of all outward forms.

The Quaker rejection of Bibliolatry is concerned with a certain way of quoting or using the Bible; it is not a rejection of the Bible itself. Rather, the rejection of Bibliolatry clears the way for a genuine Biblical presence in Quaker faith-and-practice, which is essential if Quaker community is to have a historical as well as contemporary dimension. As a matter of historical fact, we are a people grafted onto the prophetic faith of ancient Israel, as recorded in the Bible.

During the first and most formative years of the Society of

Friends, the Bible was in the mind as well the hand of all "publishers of Truth," and much the same could be said of most Quakers down to the early Twentieth Century; the native language of Quaker ministry and discourse is Biblical. The historical taproot of the Society of Friends is the prophetic faith that has found its pre-eminent expression in the Bible, much the way that the religion of Bali is rooted in Hinduism as expressed in the Mahabharata and Ramayana.

To understand the idiom and mythology at our origins--that is, to understand the symbolic forms used by earlier Quakers--we need to know the Bible. For similar reasons, ethnic groups commonly study, teach, and revive their traditions in order to maintain their identity. The Bible is also our most important source of a shared idiom for ecumenical conversations and for outreach to other branches of the church. But our Biblical taproot involves much more than this, because the prophetic faith is distinctive, as a faith that is centered by the people's covenanted task rather than individual insight. If, as a community, we lose our historical dimension, we lose the prophetic faith; individuals and communities can practice this faith only as members of a covenant people.

Many religions are primarily concerned with the discovery of timeless wisdom, but at the center of the prophetic faith is a covenant that we are to fulfill in history. The Kaddish and the Lord's Prayer put it much the same way; the community dedicates itself to serving the Kingdom, that shalom may prevail on earth as it does in the high heavens, through our lives, and in our days, and through the life of the entire people. (The Kaddish--the pre-eminent Jewish prayer for the coming of the Kingdom--is to be said only by the community, when a minyan is gathered. The Mourners' Kaddish at the conclusion of the synagogue service also links the community to its dead.)

We Quakers may be among the last and least of the covenant peoples, but nonetheless our adopted mothers and fathers agreed at Sinai to become a holy people--a people through whom shalom may reign on earth. And in our gathered meetings we, too, stand at Sinai and renew this covenant.

Many of us find greater wisdom in the Gita and a higher

personal morality in the Dhammapada than in the Bible. The Bible is unambiguously patriarchal, and trying to fix it by calling YHVH "Mother" and dressing Him in liturgical drag is a joke. The God of the Bible is also a zealous warrior who commands genocide to safeguard His cult and to create Lebensraum among the Canaanites. As timeless wisdom, many Biblical passages are worse than questionable.

--But where else should we start, to turn humanity in all our diversity toward the task of becoming a people that hallows the earth? The covenanted task concerns us as we actually are, unreduced, in all our historical specificity. "I am the LORD, and there is no other," Isaiah's God proclaims. "I make light and create darkness; I fashion shalom and create evil. I, the LORD do all these things". (Isa.45:6-7) The prophetic faith has no place for the Babylonian dedication to serving good by destroying rather than redeeming what is seen as evil. It also has no place for Hellenistic speculation about evil-free otherworlds to which a spiritual elite might escape. The Bible certainly makes no claim that any people anywhere has completed the covenanted task.

The rabbis of the Talmud criticized Noah for just obeying orders instead of arguing with God about the flood, the way Abraham argued for Sodom and Gomorrah. If the first-born of the covenant peoples can insist that the faithful must argue for justice, as Abraham and Job did, even against God himself, it's certainly no breach of the prophetic faith to argue with the Bible, wherever it promotes what we see as injustice. But Bowdlerizing the Bible to fit our views is another matter.

For example, in the few years I've been taking the Bible seriously, I've learned to see that the key roles of the sabbath and blood sacrifice can't be expurgated without losing sight of much that is essential to the practice of the prophetic faith. Yet, at first, I considered the Biblical emphasis on sabbath and the sacrificial cult to be superfluous as well as misleading; as the Bible's editor, I would have deleted them. To take the Bible seriously often requires that we argue with it and, with regard to many of its prescriptions, reject its guidance--but also that we learn to listen attentively to what its ancient voices actually say in their own way.

If we are attentive, the Bible preserves their presence as members of our community. We certainly have no calling to 'fix' the Bible for future generations, so that our successors will hear us in the Bible instead of its ancient voices. In using our own morality to winnow down to what we consider to be its timeless wisdom, we winnow out its historical presence. Winnowed Biblical wisdom ceases to be an aspect of torah; ahistorical wisdom detached from our past lacks the sense of direction we need to guide us as a people.

torah: the law of liberty

Different peoples living through their own unrepeatable histories develop distinct covenants that are then bequeathed to their descendants and that link them, as a people, to the primal Covenant. This is also true locally, among basic communities.

For example, a Quaker Meeting agrees on its specific understandings about its faith-and-practice in the form of minutes that are then bequeathed to future business meetings and all new members; these written minutes constitute the point from which any new agreement about the Meeting's faith-and-practice must start.

Different Meetings as well as different denominations are distinguished by their unique histories as well as different doctrines. Each community's covenant distinguishes it, in its historical specificity, from other covenant communities. Yet, our many visible branches constitute one visible church by virtue of the primal Covenant in which our diversity is rooted.

In common with other covenant peoples that have branched out of Christianity, Quakers also have a special relation to the Covenant's first-born; we are grafted onto Jewish roots that continue to sustain Judaism. From our beginnings as a religious society, notable Quakers have, in various ways, insisted that all who accept the yoke of the Covenant in spirit and truth are of one church. But notable Quakers have also said a good deal about the replacement of the Covenant at Sinai by the Law of Love.

Some Christians say that they have entered into a new covenant that is radically different from the old covenant and is free from all law. Free from community discernment and obligations, this new covenant tends to become a radically individualistic relation between the believer and God; the new covenant is then about a taskless faith (as belief) in the salvation of individual souls; it tends to divorce itself from the dedication of a community to becoming a holy people.

This reading of the New Testament--that is, the 'Books of the New Covenant'--has generally been rejected by Quakers, even during their most quietistic periods. ("He is not saved who's saved alone; that soul is lost that seeks its own.") For that matter, no branch of Christianity has cut itself off from its roots in the 'Old' Covenant and lived, in spite of repeated attempts to do so, from Marcion to Harnack.

Instead, Quakers have generally understood the gnostic passages in the Gospel of John, which are used as the primary source for separating Christianity's new covenant from the old covenant, to be rooted in what James calls the 'law of liberty':

"He who looks into the perfect law, the law of liberty, and perseveres, being no hearer that forgets but a doer that acts, he shall be blessed in his doing". (1:25)

"The peaceable sow peace and harvest justice" (3:18).(1)

The First Letter of John elaborates:

"Beloved, I am writing you no new commandment, but an old commandment which you had from the beginning; the old commandment is the word which you have heard. Yet, I am writing you a new commandment, which is true in him and in you, because the darkness is passing away and the true light is already shining. He who says he is in the light and hates his brother is in the darkness still. He who loves his brother abides in the light, and in it there is no cause for stumbling". (2:7-10)

"But if anyone has the world's goods and sees his brother in need, yet closes his heart against him, how does God's love abide in him? Little children, let us not love in word or speech but in deed and in truth". (3:17-18)

The new covenant turns out to be the primal Covenant continuing to reveal itself, a light shining in the darkness throughout the Creation, from the beginning.

Reading the Hebrew and Greek books of the Bible as an indivisible whole, Quakers have commonly taken Jeremiah's 'new covenant' passage (31:31-34) as their key concerning the old commandment made new, in the ever-present light of love:

"Behold, the days are coming, says the LORD, when I will make a new covenant with the house of Israel and the house of Judah, not like the covenant which I made with their fathers when I took them by the hand to bring them out of the land of Egypt, my covenant which they broke, though I was their husband, says the LORD. But this is the covenant which I will make with the house of Israel after those days, says the LORD: I will put my law within them, and I will write it upon their hearts; and I will be their God, and they shall be my people. And no longer shall each man teach his neighbor and each his brother, saying, 'Know the LORD,' for they shall all know me, from the least of them to the greatest, says the LORD; for I will forgive their iniquity, and I will remember their sin no more."

The concern here is to renew the broken covenant, not to foretell the institution of a radically different covenant. The Letter to the Hebrews quotes Jeremiah's new covenant verses twice (Chapters 8 and 10) and speaks polemically of a new covenant that replaces the old covenant, but the distinction actually drawn is between the priestly and the prophetic understandings of torah, with an insistence on the decisive supersedure of the sacrificial cult by the cross. (The letter is 'to the Hebrews'--a specific community for which religion is understood in terms of the sacrificial practices of the Temple cult.) The prophets repeatedly spoke to this cultic understanding of what it means to become a holy people.

"For in the day that I brought them out of the land of Egypt, I did not speak to your fathers or command them concerning burnt offerings and sacrifices. But this command I gave them, 'Obey my voice and I will be your God, and you shall be my people; and walk in all the ways that I command you, that it may be well with you.'" (Jer. 7:22-23).

In many passages, the New Testament does have a Hellenistic fixation on personal sin, punishment, and salvation that, when coupled with belief that the end of the world is at hand, cancels concern for the community's covenant, but the covenanted task remains the same, to become a people whose way of life hallows the earth.

--Nor is Jeremiah's 'new covenant' prophecy novel in proclaiming that the covenant will be found written on the hearts of those who choose to gather into or join a covenant people:

"It is not in heaven, that you should say, 'Who will go up for us to heaven, and bring it to us, that we may hear and do it?' Neither is it beyond the sea, that you should say, 'Who will go over the sea for us, and bring it to us, that we may hear and do it?' But the word is very near you; it is in your mouth and in your heart so that you can do it.

"See, I have set before you this day life and good, death and evil. ...Choose life...." (Deuteronomy 30:12-15,21) (2)

For the prophetic faith, covenant and torah are inseparable; the covenant community forms its faith into practice through torah --which could be translated as 'instruction' or 'guidance' as well as 'law'. As faith-and-practice, a community's agreed way of life is its law; the community's members count on one another to abide by the agreed way, that they may be a religious society in truth as well as name.

In this connection, Christian polemics against the Pharisees have been the source of considerable misunderstanding, not only concerning rabbinical Judaism but also concerning the nature of law. Rabbinical Judaism is always concerned with torah because torah forms the practice in a covenant people's faith-and-practice. Rabbi Jesus of Nazareth shared this concern; he sought to 'fulfil' the law rather than nullify it.

Some of the Pharisees were undoubtedly fundamentalists --that is, in their exegesis of Biblical jurisprudence, they were legal positivists--but fundamentalism never dominated Judaism, at least among the Pharisees, who insisted that revelation is continuous and all true insight is torah. (The Sadducees did anticipate the fundamentalist Karaites in this respect.) For example, the maxim that 'the sabbath is made for man, not man for the sabbath' is Pharisaic and Talmudic; it embodies a principle that is basic to observance of the law.

--Another, later example: The Ten Commandments were at the heart of Israel's liturgy from its beginnings, for more than a millennium, but to counteract Karaite fundamentalism that identified the letter of the law with the law, the rabbis expunged the Ten Commandments from the synagogue service.

Quakers, Ranters, and the gospel of liberation

Cromwell and other critics sometimes accused Quakers of being 'Judaizers' because of their emphasis on the practice of their faith. Quakers were said to be characterized by 'an outward legal holiness' (as John Bunyan put it) or 'a righteousness of the law' (in Lawrence Clarkson's words) that differentiated them from the Ranters. Otherwise, the Quaker and Ranter emphasis on the guidance of the inner light, unconstrained by outward authority, looked the same to many of their 17th-Century critics.

In 1654, George Fox thought the Ranters 'had a pure convincement' but then 'fled the cross'. Ranters would meet and speak openly, refuse hat honor and call the upper classes 'thee', and denounce the oath of fealty--until they were taken to court, imprisoned, threatened with fines, unemployment, or the loss of property, or otherwise put at risk. Then they would recant, give the pledge of allegiance, recite the required creed, bow and scrape, and go underground.

"Had not the Quakers come, the Ranters had overrun the nation," George Fox quotes Judge Hotham. "All the justices in the nation could not have stopped it with all their laws, because (said he) they would have said as we said and done as we commanded, and yet have kept their own principles still. But this principle of truth' said he, 'overthrows their principle, and the root and ground thereof.'" (3)

The insistence that the community practice its faith openly in the face of persecution would become an important issue once again in the Wilkinson-Story separation. In rejecting a double standard of truthfulness, 17th-Century Quakers were also rejecting a double standard of right--that is, of what is actually the law; there is to be no division of the law into higher and lower realms that separate religious profession from civil practice.

Some historians now claim that there never was a Ranter movement, that the Ranter threat to good order was mostly myth, invented by Episcopalians and Presbyterians to sound the alarm against the ungoverned congregational and individual practice of religion--a myth that was then further elaborated by Quakers to establish group discernment and internal discipline. (4)

No one questions, though, that there is a Ranter tendency; we know it first-hand in ourselves as well as our Meetings and can trace it as a perennial, unresolved tension throughout Quaker history. Sometimes it clears the way of established community practices that have become dead forms. Sometimes it simply throws off the covenant and revels in everyone's doing his or her own thing, unconstrained by any commitment to a community practice or task.

Because a community's outward practice of its faith does tend to become a fossilized form, our faith-and-practice would probably ossify and die without our Ranters and Ranter tendencies. Historically, Quaker faith-and-practice also seems to have been at its lowest ebb when our Ranter strain was weakest. Yet, when the Ranter strain prevails, we cease to practice any community faith.

At one extreme, uniformity replaces unity, and members are disowned for playing a fiddle. At the other extreme, we can't count on one another to stand fast as a community to maintain any standard or to abide by any agreement.

The interest of Anglo American Quakers in basic covenant communities is similar to the interest of Latin American Catholics in ecclesial base communities; we all want to cultivate a dynamic faith-and-practice that forms us into communities that are true to the covenanted task of hallowing the earth, particularly in the defense and protection of basic human rights.

But the ecclesial base community must establish its integrity in relation to Catholicism's hierarchical structure, while the basic covenant community must, among Quakers, establish its integrity in relation to our Ranter leanings.   As a result, the Catholic explanation and advocacy of basic communities scratches where few Quakers itch. Catholics must address the problems posed for church management by basic communities that go directly to the Bible to seek guidance; Quakers must address qualms about Biblical mediation and fixed forms that could and sometimes do supersede direct guidance.

One measure of the Biblical illiteracy common among unprogrammed Quakers is that many of us seem to think that the soul-saving, otherworldly escapism promoted by a prominent strain of Christian evangelism is Biblical rather than Manichaean or Cartesian, just because evangelicals of this kind are Bible-thumpers.

The Bible actually evolved to be an antidote to soul-saving religious autism and its companion, the divine right of rulers. Moses grew up among Egyptians who were obsessed with the hope of an afterlife, but for about a millennium after the Exodus the faith-and-practice of Israel was pointedly unconcerned with a personal life after death.

The Egyptians claimed the established social order had been created by divine mandate, but Israel insisted that rulers and ruled are equally bound by the Covenant and that the people sinned in asking for a king, to be like all the other nations.

Israel's authentic prophets proclaimed the covenanted faith-and-practice, in opposition to the creation theology of court prophets who preached unquestioning obedience to the 'divinely ordained' kingly power.

During and after the Babylonian exile, Israel's prophets struggled against the Babylonian dualism of good and evil, to maintain the integrity of the people's covenanted task--that is, the task of hallowing the creation in all its diversity, whole and unreduced, which is the service of the true God for whom there is no other and from whom no part of the creation can be irredeemably alienated.

In short, soul-saving evangelicals may preach self-centered escapism, but then they hand their listeners the antidote the prophets forged over many centuries and that has retained its integrity through two millennia of syncretism.

If the Gospel works to remove the mote of escapist individualism in the eyes of many evangelicals, could it also remove the beam of activist individualism and its organizational corollary, the politicized Gospel, in our unevangelical eyes? It should, if the Gospel really does fulfill the Law and the Prophets.

The Sermon on the Mount was one of the discussion pieces I happened to use in 1964, when I taught a freshman philosophy class in a junior college on the U.S-Mexican border. After the first class discussion, a young man who commuted from the other side came up to me, clearly upset.

"Did He really say that?" he asked, a hint of hostility coloring his incredulity. "I've been a loyal Catholic all my life, but they never said I had to be like that!"

The Sermon challenged everything he'd been brought up to think a man should be. It must have sounded much the same to Jews, Greeks, and Romans when it first came out of Galilee. Whether it comes from evangelicals or liberationists, it must sound much the same throughout Latin America today.

Many evangelicals accompany it with an insistence that one must obey those who hold power, even in support of militarism and torture. Many liberationists accompany it with some variation of Ernesto Cardenal's revolutionary gloss (borrowed from his friend, Sergio Ramirez), that "Christ forbade the sword, but not the machinegun." (5) (The point being that Jesus was really a Zealot who knew the time was not yet ripe for revolution.) Yet, the Gospel has a way of maintaining its radical vitality, sprouting wherever sown, in spite of all efforts by its goal-driven professors to de-activate it to serve their own purposes.

In 1982, a woman who was driving a family of undocumented Salvadoran refugees and me across Iowa, to reach sanctuary in Illinois, explained that the nuns who taught her to be an observant pre-Vatican II Catholic would be horrified by what she was doing--that is, in helping refugees who were 'illegals', she was committing what federal officials would consider a felony. "I guess those nuns taught me better than they thought," she reflected.

From what I've seen in Mexico, I think something similar will turn out to be true of the evangelical enthusiasms that have been sweeping through Latin America. When North American missionaries go home and the local congregation takes charge, the Bible remains, a common ground even for splits and spin-offs.

When foreign missionaries aren't in charge, the evangelicals of Latin America often become pacifist, communitarian, and anti-political, ready to share what they have with the needy and to take personal risks to protect the persecuted. The enthusiastic evangelicals I've known in Mexico have usually been women who played leading roles in community-established house churches. When asked about community problems that their religion empowers them to address, they talk of alcoholism, philandering, birth control, and family violence.

To many of Latin America's evangelicos, political violence looks like the same machismo they know as family violence. They don't blame it on foreign devils or other alien forces, and they therefore feel fully empowered by the Gospel to deal with it right where they are, with love and community cohesion rather than counterviolence. Liberationist pictures of Jesus as a campesino cutting down oppressors with his machete or machinegun just look like more macho obscenities, as drawn by student revolutionaries who have no feeling for the Gospel but know that many campesinos do.

Similarly, liberationists who want to conscientize campesinos and the urban poor into becoming a revolutionary proletariat are in a class with priests who take up arms, another reason to be evangelico rather than a Catholic or a progressive Protestant.

Talk with an evangelical grandmother dedicated to keeping a little house church going, and you're likely to find that pie in the sky isn't the only reason evangelical Christianity is sweeping through Latin America. The empowerment of women and local congregations, as illuminated by the Gospel vision of a loving, nonviolent alternative to machismo and revolutionary politics, may be equally important.

(The reason ecclesial base communities have flourished in Brazil, yet seem to wither into being the religious auxiliaries of politico-military organizations in much of Hispanic America, may also be related to the Brazilian bishops' emphasis on a nonviolent reading of the Gospel. "Helder Camara isn't really a liberation theologian," a Mexican priest who was a key organizer of base communities in Southern Mexico once explained to me, "because he doesn't believe in violence." The antipathies and sympathies of unprogrammed Quakers in all this are sometimes ironic, as though we, too, may be losing our feeling for the Gospel.)

personal remarks

There's enough in this background statement to fuel endless theological debate, but I'll follow Quaker custom (and try to keep my provocations from becoming an invitation to open-ended theologizing) by just indicating how I got this way.

I turned Quaker before attending a Meeting or knowing much about Quakers. In 1962, I experienced a turn-around and, from the little I knew about Quakers, guessed that I'd probably become one. Finding a Quaker Meeting to attend, I decided I had.

My turn-around involved a change of direction for me rather than a new set of beliefs. If I'd already belonged to another religious community within the prophetic faith, I would have had no reason to become Quaker. Yet, Quaker tolerance, in itself, didn't attract me. Quakers were the only group within the Christian tradition that I'd heard were indifferent to creed, yet I felt no need to be within the Christian tradition; Taoism and Buddhism both seemed to be equally tolerant of my continuing unbelief (6) and far richer in wisdom and personal guidance.

I sought out a Quaker Meeting because the new direction my life had taken could only be followed by a people--by a gathering that could hear itself addressed and also respond as a community. This is a distinguishing characteristic of a covenant-formed faith-and-practice, but I didn't know then about the prophetic faith in which Quaker ways are rooted, just that Quakers gather in stillness to be addressed as a community, not about spiritual secrets or arcane truths, but about the community's way of life.

If I'd known the Bible, I might have explained the practical, communitarian, down-to-earth mysticism I sought and sometimes found among Quakers by quoting the Torah: "The secret things belong to the LORD our God; but the things that are revealed belong to us and to our children for ever, that we may do all the words of this law". (Deut.29:29)

I didn't know about the prophetic faith because I thought I'd learned all I'd ever need to know about the Bible when I was nine, from a Southern Baptist preacher who tried to save my soul. I struggled to believe all the things he said I had to believe in order to live forever. I also read the Bible through, mechanically --with limited comprehension but enough understanding to be disgusted with many of its notables, such as Abraham, Jacob, Joshua, David, and God.

Deciding I didn't believe most of the things I was supposed to believe, and concluding the preacher was probably conning me about life after death, anyway, I shucked the whole thing. Until I turned Quaker at 28, I was contemptuous of all organized religion--and for almost twenty years afterwards. (Many Quakers do consider themselves to be outside organized religion. Meetings are organized for routine housekeeping, but we tend to think of our religious association as societal rather than organizational.)

After I turned Quaker, I sometimes winnowed the gospels or the First Letter of John for inspirational passages, but for about sixteen years I really didn't look to the Bible for guidance. When I did start taking the Bible seriously, it was because I'd begun to study Judaism to fill in the historical dimension that I missed in Meeting.

Then, the development of sanctuary led to my discovery of the fully ecumenical church, which in turn led to the integration of the historical and presence-centered dimensions of my faith-and-practice. Almost twenty years after recognizing that I'd turned Quaker, I sought membership in my Meeting.

I had to discover the church before membership in a Meeting could mean something other than--in fact the contrary of--a sectarian contraction of my Quaker faith-and-practice. I had to discover the church as a society of peoples before membership in a Meeting ceased to mean joining an organization.

Seeing the distinctive role of the sanctuary church, I could also see that membership in Meeting was the way for me to join the religious society constituted by the fully ecumenical church; before that, I'd seen it as a way to distinguish myself as a Quaker from the members of other denominations, which I had no desire to do. I wrote about this personal discovery at the time (and, when explaining sanctuary since then, have often quoted myself) as follows:

"...A place to stand with the dispossessed and serve the peaceable kingdom can only be found in a special kind of community that dedicates itself to such service. During recent weeks I've been discovering this catholic church that is a people rather than a creed or rite, a living Church of many cultures that must be met to be known. Out of these meetings, a meaning has opened to me that I'd like to share.

"...Recently, as I struggled to cope emotionally with having become a peripheral witness to the crucifixion of the Salvadoran people, a suspicion grew that the cross opens a way beyond breakdown--as revelatory depth meaning rather than salvationist egoism. This is the kind of meaning one discovers only in meeting those who share it, much the way a language lives among a people rather than in a dictionary's afterthoughts. It is also the kind of meaning that binds the generations and diverse cultures into one people and that is accessible to children and the unsophisticated, a meaning that is here among us, historically and communally, rather than being the invention of clever minds or the discovery of a gnostic elite." (7)

On one occasion in the late Sixties, when I'd begun making special efforts to get into Tucson to attend Pima Meeting, I noticed

that Pat seemed to be apprehensive about it, so I asked why.
"You're going to get into trouble again," she said. Most Quakers
know that gathering for worship is risky. Pat and I certainly knew
it from the time we first met, shortly after I'd become Quaker.

Yet, knowing nothing about the distinctive empowerment of
the covenant community, I'd always taken it for granted that the
social concerns and testimonies that germinate and are cultivated
when we meet for worship are then to be translated into individual
or organizational action. I would act, for example, through the
AFSC or the FOR--or maybe make a one-man stand of some sort.
Until the development of sanctuary and my discovery of the church
as a fully ecumenical society of peoples, I couldn't even see the
difference between societal and organizational social action.

--Which I suppose means that I was really a Ranter rather
than a Quaker, following my conscience individually and gathering
with others into social-action organizations that were defined by their
common causes rather than their common ground.

Actually, I knew of Quakers' 'righteousness of the law', at
the practical level, before I knew anything else about them, although
I didn't reflect on the reason Friends should be called a religious
society until after I'd been Quaker for about two decades.

When I was a student at Colgate University, the chaplain
was a Quaker, Ken Morgan. I avoided all religious services and
religion classes but knew Ken because he'd invite me to come to
dinner during the school-year vacations, when I was often the only
student on campus. I assumed Quakers were just another variety of
Christian and never asked him to explain, since I thought (as he
knew) that it was all nonsense anyway.

But during my last semester, when I became involved in an
effort to make the school's fraternities eliminate racial and religious
discrimination from their selection procedures, a friend made a
comment about Ken and the Quakers that remained in my memory.
Our campaign had been reported in the New York Times and was
beginning to pose an image problem for Colgate, so our support
among faculty and administration liberals was suddenly collapsing;
they didn't think Colgate should pay the price of being singled out

and identified with the racial discrimination practiced by Greek fraternities everywhere.

Ken was the chair of the key faculty committee that we needed to push the issue through to a decisive student referendum. I told my friend the faculty would probably drop the whole thing because we'd lost too many liberals. "Don't worry," my friend assured me (correctly, as it turned out), "Ken's a Quaker. He'll stick."

My friend was a neo-orthodox Christian and a religion major, so I didn't ask him why Quakers should be different from other Christians or liberals, but his comment came to mind several years later when I was cowboying in the Huachucas and heard on the radio that a Quaker couple in Tucson, Barbara and Vern Elfbrandt, were refusing to sign Arizona's loyalty oath.

The report included a few words of explanation from Barbara--calm, reasonable, gentle words that had no hint of the stridency and indignation I expected of a religious fanatic who would pay such a high price for an empty gesture.

It seemed silly--yet admirable somehow--that the Elfbrandts were willing to suffer financial hardship and public denunciations rather than sign a piece of paper that didn't really mean anything. (If I'd known more about Quakers, I probably would have formulated my question in terms of Ranter rather than liberal casuistry: Why should they take an empty form so seriously?) Out tending the cattle each day, I'd mull over the radio reports I heard during breakfast, which undoubtedly had a good deal to do with my ready recognition, when I experienced a personal turn-around soon afterwards, that I must have turned Quaker.

Quaker halakhah

Some of the boycott lists one sees posted on Quaker refrigerators would challenge the dedication of a halakhic Jew, but observances of this kind are, among Twentieth-Century Quakers, generally considered matters of individual conscience rather than community practice. In reaction to the rigid uniformities that many Meetings imposed on their members during the Nineteenth Century, most unprogrammed Quakers would probably now say that a

Meeting's members are really under no obligations concerning the community's agreed faith-and-practice, at least outside meetings for worship and business.

In addition to mentioning that unprogrammed Quakers have no required creed or rite, we often describe Quaker faith-and-practice as though it includes no obligatory observances. Yet, agreements about daily practice are a central concern for any covenant community.

Most of us would probably agree with halakhic Jews (and disagree with classical liberals) that "if religion is anything, it is everything," which for the prophetic faith means that there is no separation of religious and secular realms. (8) Yet, our ways as a religious society are generally in keeping with a liberal segregation rather than a halakhic integration of religious and secular concerns.

In the absence of any agreed-upon practice, there is neither a covenant community nor a religious society--just an assembly of individuals who may be wise, conscientious, generous, courageous, and socially involved but are powerless to do justice, to be the co-creators of any way of life, or to weave basic rights into the surrounding societal order. The prophetic faith's covenanted task, to become a people that hallows the earth, can be joined by individuals but can only be undertaken by a community.

Every kind of Quaker Meeting does regularly agree to continuing practices that obligate the community as a whole (sometimes as represented by volunteers whom it recognizes as doing its ministry). For example, sanctuary for first-asylum refugees is the practice of a community rather than separate individuals, and sanctuary volunteers (if they are, in fact, doing sanctuary work) are doing the ministry of the community. Yet, there may be no unprogrammed Quaker Meeting anywhere in the world that has, in recent decades, assembled and published the community obligations of this kind to which its members are committed and for which they are liable.

For most Quakers, any publication of covenanted obligations, as membership requirements, to be covered, for example, in clearness committee discussions with prospective members or to be available for review and reference by its membership, seems dangerously close to the formulation of a Quaker catechism. In the case of volunteers whom a Meeting recognizes to be acting on its behalf, the recognition of formal requirements for 'ordination' would be even more problematical.

The emergence of sanctuary in Tucson made certain agreements among sanctuary volunteers about their guiding principles and procedures unavoidably imperative:

If some of us agreed to be open and truthful about our activities, our practice of sanctuary couldn't mix with the activities of those who wanted to be clandestine;

If we would not politicize our practice of sanctuary to screen out refugees who wouldn't serve politico-military objectives, we couldn't integrate into a sanctuary network that did;

If our practice of sanctuary was a matter of community faith-and-practice that we would not subordinate to a vote, we could not become members of a sanctuary organization that did make decisions by voting;

If we would insist on a jury trial and refuse to plea bargain if indicted, the integrity of our sanctuary practice required that we exclude anyone who would plea bargain; and

If we would not permit coyotes (the slang term, for persons who smuggle refugees over the border for a fee) to tie into our sanctuary services, we could not be part of a sanctuary network that hires coyotes.

In Tucson, these agreements evolved into a written list, 'The Trsg [Tucson refugee support group] Principles and Procedures', which anyone who participates in Trsg deliberations and refugee-aid activities is required beforehand to agree to observe. The Tucson Ecumenical Council Task Force on Central America, which co-ordinates most sanctuary activities in Tucson, has also adopted it. Pima Meeting incorporated it into the job description submitted to Friends United Meeting's Quaker Volunteer Witness position.

Trsg, TEC, or congregationally-based border assistance that involves sanctuary communities from outside Tucson specifies agreement on the principles and procedures as a condition for joint action. This set of agreements has also been used to assure church networks in Mexico that their connection with our sanctuary activities will not compromise or subvert the integrity of their assistance for refugees.

A dispute over this last consideration illustrates how separations necessarily evolve out of a community's standing agreements about the way it will, as an active member of a fully ecumenical religious society, practice its faith. In a meeting last April with the parish priests of Mexico's Hermosillo Diocese (which covers most of Sonora), Father Ricardo Elford and I spent an entire morning describing the evolution of sanctuary in the United States and the principles and procedures that guide our practice in the Arizona-Sonoran borderlands. (Ricardo and I were there in connection with the Redemptorist Order's sanctuary program in the borderlands, which also adheres to the Trsg principles and procedures.)

One of the reasons that we needed to specify the principles and procedures we follow and to explain the separations that have occurred in the evolution of sanctuary in the United States was that, during the Arizona sanctuary trial, misunderstanding about our actual practice had blocked support for two Mexican defendants, Father Quinones and Socorro de Aguilar, by the Mexican bishops (apart from the Archbishop of Hermosillo, who gave his full public support and, after the trial, appointed Fr. Quinones Vicar for Migration).

The misunderstanding had its roots in an incident in 1984, when professional activists in the Eastern U.S. met, named themselves the National Sanctuary Movement, and decided their first National Action would target the Bishop of San Diego. When notice of the planned action came out, the sanctuary group in San Diego objected but was told the decision had already been irreversibly made by the Sanctuary Movement on the national level.

At the same time, the professional organizers who'd formed the NSM launched a concerted effort to bring sanctuary under a national directorate--that is, to form a goal-directed organization to fit the name they'd given themselves. In the borderlands, we immediately took steps to disassociate ourselves from the kind of sanctuary being organized by the NSM, and what came to be known as the Tucson-Chicago split occurred.

As it turned out, the Bishop of San Diego's close friend, the Archbishop of Tijuana, was the key person through whom any recommendations about the support of Fr. Quinones and Socorro de Aguilar would have to be routed to the Mexican bishops. Hence, when indictments were served five months after the NSM announced its first action, the word went out to the Mexican bishops that sanctuary was just a left-wing front that uses refugee concerns to support revolutionary movements in Central America. True, Father Quinones was being put on trial in the United States for ministry in Mexico that is (as the Archbishop of Hermosillo puts it) 'the natural vocation of the Church'. Yet, the Church couldn't allow itself to become entangled in the politicizing of its witness for human rights, especially by left-wing gringos.

Thus, in Mexico, what might have become a concern of virtually every parish for the natural vocation of the Catholic Church to protect human rights from U.S. intervention therefore remained almost entirely a media affair.

In discussing the firm commitment of Trsg, the Tucson Ecumenical Council Task Force on Central America, and Tucson sanctuary congregations to remain separate from all organizations that use the name 'sanctuary' but politicize refugee rights, I promised the Archbishop of Hermosillo that I would take special care to prevent the Mexican Church from being compromised, specifically mentioning a clear separation from the activities of the Alliance of Sanctuary Communities, the National Sanctuary Movement's latest incarnation.

To those who have no community covenants and personal promises to live up to, our hardline refusal to attend any decision-making meeting of the politicized sanctuary network is often considered rigidly doctrinaire, but it's just a matter of keeping agreements and maintaining the integrity of a completely catholic, unpoliticized, congregationally-based sanctuary movement, without which our fully ecumenical networking to provide sanctuary for first-asylum refugees would disintegrate.

This need to maintain the integrity of a covenant community's practice by being emphatically specific and open about differences and separations is just plain speech, but it goes against the Quaker grain. We usually prefer to gloss over differences while seeking the reconciling insight that opens the way to unity. This works fine when the community is seeking agreement, but leads to the violation of its already-covenanted obligations.

The recognition of practices that violate a community's covenanted principles and procedures is inseparable from the recognition of practices that are in compliance; each mirrors the other. But unlike ideological disputes, incompatible practices that distinguish one community or association of communities from another ordinarily cause no hard feelings, provided the communities are clearly separated.

For example, Jews and Quakers have no argument about whether Quakers should live according to the 613 commandments of the Shulhan Arukh or whether Jews should cease using fixed forms for worship; those arguments are just among Jews and Quakers, respectively. With regard to incompatible covenant community practices, entanglement rather than open separation stands in the way of true unity (which, unlike uniformity, depends on unreduced diversity).

In the Arizona-Sonoran borderlands, sanctuary for Central American refugees has evolved as what I call civil initiative, which is the way covenant communities that insist on a single standard of right can weave either human rights or earth rights into civil society. All of Israel's prophets insisted on a single standard of right, but civil initiative reaches to Quaker tradition and to Gandhi's satyagraha for the characteristics that summarize it as a procedure: Civil initiative is nonviolent, open (truthful), catholic, dialogical, germane, volunteer-based, and community-centered. (9) The key choices that a community must make in covenanting to practice civil initiative are enumerated by these characteristics; the alternatives in each case characterize community organizing or political jiu-jitsu. (10)

This fundamental choice between civil initiative and political jiu-jitsu differentiates direct action to establish a societal order from direct action to establish a managerial order (an organization). For Quakers, it's the choice between being a free people formed by its covenant and being a subject people formed by (and therefore seeking) kingly power, "like all the other nations." (11)

This is also the difference between the "church" conceived as a pluralistically catholic religious society of which the Society of Friends is a branch and the "church" as a managed religious organization from which the Society of Friends would be excluded.

Notes on the Sanctuary Workshop

Workshop #4 will consider the Biblical continuities of civil initiative, as community covenanting, using the I-9 requirement of the Immigration Reform and Control Act as a case for consideration. The emphasis will be on the Gospel as fulfillment of the Law--the cross as the practical aspect of 'pure convincement'--that makes a Quaker community's faith-and-practice an indivisible whole.

Opportunities to question the issues raised by this discussion piece should come up in the course of considering civil initiative in relation to the I-9. Sample minutes about the I-9 (some of which have been approved by Pima Meeting and some of which are to be considered by Pima Meeting during the coming year) are appended to illustrate the choices that every Meeting in the United States now faces in deciding whether, for example, asking Meeting employees to make the I-9 attestation is consistent with the Meeting's understanding of its faith-and-practice.

At this point, few Meetings in the United States would be able to employ anyone new, not yet having decided, one way or the other, about the I-9 attestation. Meetings that have decided may also need to decide what obligations they should assume to support members and attenders (and also service organizations such as the AFSC) who suffer as job applicants or employers for refusal to sign, require, or file the I-9 attestation.

APPENDIX

The I-9 Attestation as a Concern for Quaker Meetings

general background

The Immigration Reform and Control Act of 1986 (IRCA) "requires employers to verify employment eligibility of individuals on [Form I-9: Employment Eligibility Verification]... Failure to present this form for inspection to officers of the Immigration and Naturalization Service (INS) or Department of Labor within the time period specified by regulation, or improper completion or retention of this form, may be a violation of the above law..."

The rule of law is nullified whenever the state reduces its subjects to involuntary servitude. Military conscription is the most familiar way that the relation of free citizens to government officials is forcibly changed to that of servant to master, but military conscription is by no means the only way governments try to reduce those who are subject to their police and military powers into vassals of the state.

Unfree peoples are forcibly held under state management, apart from any excepted rights such as those enumerated in the first eight articles of the Bill of Rights. The Ninth Amendment was therefore included in the Bill of Rights to emphasize that a free people never relinquishes the unnamed rights that distinguish it from unfree peoples. Freedom from being conscripted to serve the state is of special importance for a religious society, particularly when the required activity would constitute apostasy.

Because the I-9 requirement does seek to conscript every Meeting in the United States that employs anyone to be the direct agent for enforcing the policies of the INS, there is now a nationwide need for Meetings to decide what action is consistent with their faith-and-practice.

The following are several minutes that have been approved or are under consideration for approval, provided here as samples:

I. Pima Meeting's Minutes on Noncompliance with the I-9 and on Nondiscrimination against Undocumented Job Applicants:

As an employer, Pima Monthly Meeting of the Religious Society of Friends will not require, fill out, or file Form I-9 (Employment Eligibility Verification). In common with all other testimonies concerning faith and practice, the Meeting's refusal to require, fill out, or file Form I-9 will be open and public.
  [Approved, 5-14-89]

Pima Meeting will not discriminate against job applicants who are undocumented, either in hiring or paying them.
[Approved, 6-11-89]

II. Three Minutes Recommended by the Peace & Social Concerns Committee of Pima Meeting (to be considered for approval by the Meeting in 1989 and 1990):

[UNAPPROVED DRAFT]
(1) Meeting Support for Members and Attenders Who are Coerced into Acting against Conscience:

Many among us who have been employed by the government have already signed affirmations of fealty that were against conscience, even if not so directly connected as the I-9 attestation with the implementation of human rights violations. Pima Meeting recognizes that some members and attenders will, for example, decide on the basis of family obligations, career objectives, or material needs to attest that they are not aliens excluded from employment, in spite of their conscientious opposition to doing so. We also recognize that we are not yet able to assure a viable alternative for the job seekers among us whose conscientious objection to collaborating with the INS is overbalanced by other obligations or is overwhelmed by basic needs. We will therefore undertake the development of livelihood and service alternatives through which our members and attenders can fulfill their personal obligations and meet their material needs without being forced to betray their faith. In doing so we will also seek to open ways for every member and attender to be true to our professed faith through the Meeting's practice, even if we are sometimes unable to be faithful in our personal and familial practice.

[UNAPPROVED DRAFT]
[UNAPPROVED DRAFT]
(2) Pima Meeting's Reasons for Refusing to Comply with the I-9 Requirement:

Treating no one as a violable enemy, alien, or inferior is fundamental to the practice of our faith. IRCA's I-9 requirement mandates that employers, with the assistance and signed attestation of job applicants, become agents of the INS in denying employment to the undocumented. Because Pima Meeting is a sanctuary covenant community that has assisted Central American refugees since 1981, many of our members know from extensive experience that the INS systematically violates the basic rights of undocumented refugees from El Salvador and Guatemala. In seeking to force Pima Meeting to be an agent of the INS in implementing these policies, the I-9 requirement violates the Meeting's right to the free exercise of religion.

Our conscientious objection to complying with the I-9 attestation reaches beyond the INS violation of refugee rights. When the landless poor are excluded from the market for their labor, they are prevented from making a living. Being prevented from making a living violates a person's right to life. With respect to this basic right, no human being is an alien.

"The Creator of the earth is the owner of it. He gave us being thereon, and our nature requires nourishment which is the produce of it. As he is kind and merciful, we as his creatures, while we live answerable to the design of our creation, we are so far entitled to a convenient subsistence that no man may justly deprive us of it." (John Woolman, *A Plea for the Poor*)

Apart from threatening a specific practice of our faith, the I-9 requirement would forcibly conscript us, as a religious community, to act as an agent of the state. This also constitutes a threat to our free exercise of religion, to which Pima Meeting will not submit.
[UNAPPROVED DRAFT]

[UNAPPROVED DRAFT]
(3) On the Nonsectarian Nature of Pima Meeting's Refusal to Comply with the I-9 Requirement:

Quakers are among the least numerous of the peoples who covenant to hallow the earth. We know the communion of these peoples as the Church, which is limited by no credal, ritual, sacramental, or organizational forms. The Church as we know it includes all who covenant as communities to treat no one as a violable enemy, alien, or inferior. Our testimony concerning the I-9 attestation is no Quaker peculiarity but simply a matter of faithfully building the Church, as a sanctuary for all life.
[UNAPPROVED DRAFT]

NOTES

1. "Los pacificos siembran la paz y cosechan la justicia"--La Biblia, Edicion Latinoamerica. The King James translation renders James 3:18 to the same effect but more elaborately: "And the fruit of righteousness is sown in peace of them that make peace."

2. See also Deuteronomy 30:6; Ezekiel 11:19-20; 36:26-27; Joel 2:28-29; Jeremiah 24:7; 32:38-40.

3. See Christopher Hill, *The World Turned Upside Down*, Penguin, 1975, pp. 210, 236-238, 257.

4. See J.C. Davis, *Fear, Myth and History; the Ranters and the historians*, Cambridge University Press, 1986.

5. See Ernesto Cardenal, *The Gospel in Solentiname*, vol. 4, (Orbis, 1982), pp. 194-197.

6. I don't believe in a substantial self that survives death, and I consider any conceivable God to be an idol.

7. For more about this discovery of the church, see *The Sanctuary Church*, Pendle Hill Pamphlet #266, 1986.

8. Refusal to segregate religious from secular concerns challenges the way liberals have usually separated church and state. For a

particularly good explanation of the way the prophetic faith does it without advocating a theocracy, see Solomon Schechter, *Aspects of Rabbinic Theology,* Schocken, 1961. The quotation is from page 142.

9. For a brief explanation of these characteristics in relation to sanctuary, see *The Sanctuary Church,* pp. 23-24. For a much more extensive explanation of the way a single standard of right can guide a covenant community in its relation to civil society and a legal system, see *Sanctuary on the Faultline* (Pacific Yearly Meeting - Social Order Series, 1988), which also goes into more detail about the relevance for the covenant community of the distinction between societal and organizational order.

10. 'Political jiu-jitsu' is outlined and advocated by Saul Alinsky in *Rules for Radicals,* Vintage, 1972.

11. Consult I Samuel 8 & 12.

IV

The Bible and Care of the Creation:
Being Stewards of Our Environment

Janice Y. Domanik

*[Note: Jan Domanik teaches biology at McHenry County College in
Crystal Lake, Illinois; her dissertation dealt with the sex lives of fiddler
crabs. She has been a stalwart of the Friends General Conference
Religious Education Committee for many years, and she attends Illinois'
Lake Forest Meeting, where she makes sure no styrofoam cups are
used. Asked how she became so interested in ecology and recycling, she
points to her mother, who is a descendant of the Pennsylvania Dutch,
a people who never threw anything away, even when the landfills still
had plenty of room.]*

Historically Friends have used the Bible to support their
spiritual growth and development. The study of the Bible during the
various stages of our faith development can provide guidance on
issues confronted in our daily lives. This is true with reference to
the environmental crisis which is occupying many of us today.

The environmental problem has its seed in Genesis 1: 26-28.

"Then God said, 'Let us make man in our image,
after our likeness; and let them have dominion over
the fish of the sea, and over the birds of the air,
and over the cattle, and over all the earth, and
every creeping thing that creeps upon the earth.'
So God created man in his own image, in the image
of God he created him; male and female he created
them. And God blessed them, and God said to
them, 'be fruitful and multiply, and fill the earth

and subdue it; and have dominion over the fish of
the sea and over the birds of the air and over every
living thing that moves upon the earth'." (RSV)

In this passage is the statement that people will have dominion over
the earth and subdue it. While some have considered this passage
and concluded that dominion means to care for, or to have
stewardship over, and others consider that in the image of God
means we should care for the creation as God would. These are not
the widely accepted meaning of the passage. Those who are
concerned with the environmental problem must wrestle with this
passage so that the conflicting messages from God about the
environment in early Genesis can be revealed and used to resolve
the apparent message to use/abuse every living thing.

Genesis 6:18-21 and Genesis 7:2-3 seem to conflict with the
idea that people are to be all powerful over other living organisms.
In these passages God instructs Noah to take two of every living
thing aboard the ark whether they are clean or unclean. The
message here is that Noah is to be a steward over these pairs of
organisms. While there will be a great flood, there is a provision for
the continuation of every species.

These latter two passages appear to be in conflict with the
earlier passage in Genesis. In addition these latter passages may have
a message for today with regard to the problem of biodiversity.
While there is not necessarily a "great flood" coming, there is the
problem of the conflict between people subduing the earth and the
survival of the diverse species on this planet.

In Isaiah 5:8-10 the Lord instructs us not to join house to
house until there is no more room. If we do, then there will be
empty homes and the land will yield poor crops. What does this
passage say with regard to caring for the land? Are there examples
in modern times when the disregard for the land has resulted in the
loss of valuable topsoil through wind or water erosion? In the Noah
story we are charged with caring for all of creation but in this
passage are we being told that we do not care for the creation by
being greedy? What is the implication of this with regard to
converting farm land into subdivisions?

Exodus 23:10-11 and Leviticus 25:1-7 instruct us about proper use of farm land. We are to allow the land to rest for a year after it has been used for six years. In these passages there is again the message about caring for the land. Is this a way of further fulfilling Noah's charge to care for all the creatures? As we care for and protect the land are we also protecting the species which inhabit the land?

Leviticus 25:23-4 says that the land belongs to the Lord and we are sojourners on the land. Today we are confronted with the buying and selling of lands. Often there are conflicts which arise between people over the issue of land sales. As we decide how to handle these problems we must remember Leviticus 25:23 and also the letter which Chief Seattle sent in 1852 with regard to the United States Government wishing to purchase tribal lands. In this letter he says:

> "This we know: the earth does not belong to man,
> man belongs to the earth .... Man did not weave
> the web of life, he is merely a strand in it.
> Whatever he does to the web, he does to himself."
> (*The Power of the Myth*, p. 34)

Considering these advices can we use/abuse land in order to make profits or are we charged with the preservation of land for future generations? Mustn't we always remember that we are sojourners?

In Mark 12:1-11 there is a parable about a landowner who sets up a vineyard and wine press and goes away to another land. He leaves it to his tenants to care for everything. He sends a servant to get fruits from the vineyard. The tenants beat him. Many others are sent and all, even the landowner's son, are beaten or killed. As with all parables it requires several readings and meditation to extract a full lesson. Was this landowner being an effective steward of the land? Was the landowner only interested in the profits? What does this parable say to us about our responsibility to the planet earth?

Galatians 6:7-10 is the passage which says we reap what we sow. Today as we are confronted with ever-decreasing amounts of landfill space are we not reaping what we have sowed? Are we fully aware of the environmental implications of the way we live?

Finally let us examine I Peter 4:10:

"As each has received a gift, employ, it for one another, as good stewards of God's varied grace:" (RSV)

What are the implications of this passage with regard to how we approach the environmental issues which confront us in 1990? Does this passage challenge us to use our gifts to serve the "Planet"? Does this passage allow us to sit back and be passive as others disregard the health of the planet or does it push us to become active in changing our lifestyle and encouraging others to do the same so that everyone becomes a responsible global citizen?

As you open yourself to these passages keep the image of planet earth in your thoughts. This image should be of a colorful planet with blue waters and reddish-brown landmasses. The colorful planet should be surrounded by darkness. Can you see boundaries between nations? Can you identify deserts or rich lands or do the landmasses look the same? If you were closer could you identify different kinds of lands? Does the mixing of the land areas and the inability to distinguish national boundaries change the way these passages speak to you?

V

Divine Judgment and
The Near-Death Experience

Gracia Fay Ellwood

*[Note: Gracia Fay Ellwood teaches in the Department of Religious
Studies at California State University at Long Beach. Author of the
acclaimed feminist Bible study essay **Batter My Heart** (Pendle Hill
Pamphlet #282), She attends Orange Grove Mtg. in Pasadena,
California.]*

Since Raymond Moody coined the term "Near-Death
Experience" (NDE) in his 1975 book Life After Life, there has been
a groundswell of interest in these phenomena, and a Gallup poll has
revealed that at least eight million U.S. citizens have had them. The
image of death as the Grim Reaper has begun to be replaced by a
hopeful one of transcendent joy and beauty.

Among religious persons, two groups have been notable for
their reluctance to share the general enthusiasm. Evangelical
Christians have objected to the impression that all and sundry are
welcomed by an indulgent Divine Being, whatever their past deeds
or religious non-commitment. What has become of judgment or
sacrifice and salvation?

On the other hand, liberals, including unprogrammed
Quakers, seem to scent a return to pie-in-the-sky supernaturalism
that is likely to distract attention from the urgent missions of peace,
justice and planetary healing. The theme that these two contrasting
groups of dissenters have in common is the question of justice.
Judaism and Christianity affirm that God judges human behavior
and rights wrongs, some say, by supernatural acts of grace and

punishment, others, by means of human action in the world. Do the accounts of NDE's in fact subvert the need for judgment and justice?

It is my opinion that the NDE material presents remarkable insights into the reality of divine judgment. In this workshop we will sketch some of the biblical themes of judgment, overview the basic patterns of the NDE, and make comparisons. One of the early themes of judgment in the Hebrew Bible is the deuteronomic, which expressed a faith in this-worldly justice. If the people of God keep his covenant, shun the worship of other Gods and respect the rights of the poor, they will have long life and prosperity. If they break God's laws, they will suffer disease, famine and victimization by aggressor nations.

This theme received support from the work of the great prophets, who (fore-)saw the violent attacks of Assyria and Babylon against Israel as the threatened punishment for many longstanding breaches of God's laws. The theme of exodus, of God's repeated acts of deliverance of his oppressed people, shows such this-worldly judgment, as do the myths of the Fall and the Flood. However, the problems inherent in the deuteronomic conception eventually surfaced: on an individual level, it doesn't work, as both Ezekiel and the (poet) author of Job show. The righteous are often oppressed and slain, while the wicked flourish.

Partly in response to this critique, during a period of painful oppression, apocalyptic ideas developed. It was believed that God's judgment would come by an irruption of supernatural power from beyond history; it would overthrow the present world order via enormous calamities, and set up a new order of paradisal bliss for the righteous, and hell for the wicked. The righteous dead would be resurrected to share in the joys of paradise.

Jesus' sayings reflect apocalyptic expectations. Among them are some that show a profound conception of judgment as a present and future uncovering of the oneness of human hearts: "Judge not, that you be not judge...the measure you mete out will be the measure you get back"; "Love your enemies"; "Whatever you have done to the least of these...you have done to me." The exhortation to repent in anticipation of the Kingdom is a response to what is

simultaneously God's   extraordinarily severe demand and God's
unbelievable generosity.

For the first few decades after Jesus, the churches expected
the divine judgment to be realized soon, for all, with his return.
When this did not take place, expectation focussed on the
experience of the individual soul after death, facing heaven or hell.
In the Twelfth Century the idea of purgatory developed to cover
those who fell somewhere between. All the redeemed, in heaven, on
earth and in purgatory, were seen as united in a vast web of life,
able to assist in one another's transformation through prayer.

The idea of final judgment did not disappear, and from time
to time there was a quickening of expectation of the End.
Seventeenth-Century England saw one such time, with Quakers and
other radical groups combining mystical awareness on the oneness of
all hearts in God,   urgent   demands   for social justice, and
expectation of an imminent final judgment. Interestingly, in the
twentieth century we have the development of a secular apocalyptic
that is the reverse of divine judgment. The feared destruction of
civilization or even of all life by nuclear or ecological convulsions is
understood by many as eclipsing all values, rather than vindicating
God's justice.

One of the bases of the idea of divine judgment is theodicy,
the justification of God in a world of oppression and suffering. This
search for meaning is a necessary part of being human, but when (as
so often) it takes the form of interpreting massive calamities as
expressions of the just wrath of God, contemporary Friends and
other sensitive persons rightly demur. Such a theodicy supports an
image of God as a patriarch who demands obedience and becomes
violent when he doesn't get it; the image subtly encourages male
dominance and violence.

It does not follow, however, that rejecting this image means
we must reject the concept of divine judgment as well. The
Near-Death Experience offers new perspectives on this situation.
The "Moody-type" experience that has entered the popular
imagination, with its peacefulness, release from the suffering body,
dark tunnel, welcoming family and friends, life review and Being of
Light, is Good News, reducing the fear of death and leading often

to a transformation of life. But the evangelicals have a point: it does give the impression that wrongs and evils are reducible to useful occasions for soul growth.

However, there are NDE's of other sorts. Cardiologist Maurice Rawlings has uncovered a substantial number of negative, even hellish ones, and sees evidence from his own experience in resuscitating patients that there are many more that get repressed. Negative experiences tell of accusing faces, of descending to infernal realms, of flames and torture, even of the devil. They escape for various reasons, a principal one being rescue by a Christ-like figure.

Rawlings' discoveries have led him to a world view of hellfire and born-again Christianity. I call this the "Noah's Ark" approach. It is interesting that these cases often lead to transformation of life, just as the "Good News" cases do. But the world view is so constrictive and unappealing that it is not surprising that most major researchers dismiss these cases with a few paragraphs. I feel, however, that we must take them seriously, without necessarily seeing them as the key to divine judgment.

In a minority of cases, involving unusually deep NDE's, the life review appears in a highly developed form that offers much more promising insights into the concept of judgment. Moody in his second book *Reflections on Life After Life*, and NDE's Phyllis Atwater, describe total life reviews in which every deed, word and thought was relived, together with their impact on all that one had encountered, persons (even passersby on the street), animals and the environment.

This stunning expansion of consciousness supports Jesus' words on non-judgment and love for enemies, as well as the testimony of mystics about their experiences of oneness with all things. It is also a powerful incentive toward social justice and a deep support against burnout.

A further complication is to be found in what we might call "the Gray Realm." Some of Moody's NDE's, and notably George Ritchie, perceived spectral beings in angry, frustrating interaction with each other, and frustrated or parasitical interaction with living persons. Here we have support for the spiritualist conception of earthbound spirits, explored by thinkers such as Carl Wickland and Edith Fiore.

We have long considered ourselves too sophisticated to take spirit possession seriously, and may need to discipline our emotions to look at these data squarely. What do they mean? The picture given seems to undercut the idea of the life review as inevitable judgment. Could it be that some persons after death manage to evade the life review, escape its judgment, and perpetuate misery for themselves and others?

In trying to sort out these complex pictures, we can get some help from Buddhist ideas. One is the concept of the six realms: the physical human world, the paradise of the godlike, the realm of the titanic fighters, the limbo of the hungry ghosts, the hells of the tortured, and the physical world of animals. Analogs to one or another of these six realms appear in virtually all NDE's.

Another helpful Buddhist concept is that of the Bodhisattua, the compassionate being who goes down into the worlds of suffering on rescue missions. Still another helpful Buddhist conception is presented in the Tibetan Book of the Dead, where one sees an afterlife scenario including both paradisal and hellish elements.

Basic here is the Buddhist idea that I am one with what I experience; the psychedelic beauties and horrors are within me, and I project my own loves, fears and hates outward in the form of figures that delight or terrify me. The goal is union with the Light; if I understand the situation rightly, I can accept and affirm any of the figures I see toward that end. As Westerners we may or may not find such an outlook satisfactory, but we can learn from it much about the power of the human mind in shaping its own experience and, ultimately, judging itself.

VI

From Detoxification To Godwrestling:
Three Stages Of Bible Study

Chuck Fager

[Note: Chuck Fager attends Langley Hill Meeting in McLean Virginia. He publishes A Friendly Letter and The Friendly Bookshelf Catalog, and works for the U.S. Postal Service. He served as Clerk of the Friends Bible Conference Planning Committee.]

"What Canst Thou say?" is the perennial question for Friends, the question put by Fox to his earliest hearers, the question that echoes for us. I have worked in Bible study for several years, above all because I believe it can help find Friends discover our individual and corporate answers to that question.

While working among Friends on Bible study, I have watched many people, including myself, go through three distinct stages in their encounter with the Bible. Not everyone goes through them, and they are not presented here as an ideal to be followed; but I have observed them often enough to think a description may be helpful to Friends still unfamiliar with the Bible:

The first stage I call Detoxification, because many Friends come to the Bible with much negative baggage. This can range from a reaction against sentimentalized Sunday school images, to experiences of persecution at the hands of fanatics using the Bible as a weapon.

Early Friends knew about this oppressive use of the Bible too, from hard firsthand experience. For some among Friends today, such encounters have soured them permanently on the Bible; and who can blame them? But others eventually come to suspect that there is more to it, and they are now curious enough about the book to put some effort into understanding it.

Crucial to this detoxification stage is the finding of a supportive and nonjudgmental study environment. That, for example, is what we hoped to create at the Friends Bible Conference; and it is what a good self-directed Meeting study group can provide as well. In such a safe setting, it becomes possible to examine both the Bible and our notions about it, to see if there is any potential value in the text for us.

If we do find the right environment, usually the Bible is quickly shown to be very different from what we thought it was. It is a very diverse set of texts, sometimes appealing and sometimes repulsive, but more and more intriguing throughout. There is often a sense of discovery, and perhaps some anger at the teachers or authority figures who left us with an image of Scripture as a flat, narrow, cold or sinister document.

With this process of discovery we pass into Stage Two, which I call Uncovering a Resource. As study continues, a sense of the counterpoint and depth of the texts begins to emerge:

There are gripping stories here, and prophetic poetry that rings true and powerfully even after 2500 years; there is clear-eyed confrontation with the essential ambiguity of life and theological efforts to make sense of it; there are appealing characters--even Paul has his points, and then there is the enigmatic carpenter's son he came to call his lord.

And there is even the experience of seeing Scripture challenge and criticize Scripture:

In the Book of Jonah, for instance, the Israelite religious and cultural chauvinism is sharply challenged; in the New Testament there is a underlying tug of war between universalist and particularist interpretations of Jesus' message. Then again, the celebration of war and even genocide in some parts of the Hebrew Scriptures is clearly rejected by the teachings of Jesus and the practice of his first followers.

Even the predominantly patriarchal attitudes of much of Scripture are called into fundamental question, by many of Jesus' actions, in the Song of Songs, and elsewhere.

In sum, as the Bible is approached with open eyes, it is revealed as the enemy of the easy answers that so many of its purported champions seem to find in it. But this truth, among most "detoxified" Friendly readers at least, only enhances its appeal and usefulness. The Bible is useful in life because it is like life.

Furthermore, over time parallels typically begin to emerge between issues and stories in the text and aspects of our own lives. This outlook was well expressed by the Quaker theologian Robert Barclay in his *Apology* of 1676: "In the Scriptures God has deemed it proper to give us a looking glass in which we can see the conditions and experiences of ancient believers. There we find that our experience is analogous to theirs....This is the great work of the Scriptures, and their usefulness to us."

At some point, however, some of us have begun to realize that the Bible is taking on a deeper dimension for us. This typically does not happen quickly or dramatically, although it can; it is more like a slow dawn, or the sprouting of a plant.

Exactly what to call this new phase can be a problem, because often there is a reluctance to use traditional terms. I call this third stage Godwrestling.

It is based on a growing a sense that among these stories and images, with their many layers of meaning, are passages that seem especially directed at the reader--at you or me--texts which speak to our condition in a manner unlike, and deeper than, other written sources. This often takes the form of a conviction of being personally addressed or called through the medium of the text.

In this third stage, moreover, the traditional idea of the Bible as being divinely inspired begins to make a certain kind of sense. This idea of inspiration is similar to that set forth in such passages as Second Timothy 3:16 and Romans 15:4:

2Timothy 3:16: "All scripture is inspired by God and

profitable for teaching, for reproof, for correction, and for training in righteousness...."

Romans 15:4: "For whatever was written in former days was written for our instruction, that by steadfastness and by the encouragement of the scriptures we might have hope." (Both quotations from the Revised Standard Version.)

The first passage is a favorite of fundamentalists who favor the Inerrancy theory, according to which every statement in the texts must be factually correct. But the text actually makes no such claim; instead, it says that the inspiration of the Scriptures makes them "profitable." The Greek term here can also be rendered as "beneficial," "advantageous," or simply "useful."

But a text can be *useful* in many ways without being historically factual. This point was not lost on the biblical writers.

The thrust of the passage from Timothy becomes even more evident in Romans 15:4. Here Paul again describes the scriptures in almost a utilitarian way. But the utility of Scripture has a more tender emphasis here than in Timothy. These writings are not only for "instruction" in a pedagogical sense; they are a resource which is to be explored with steadfast attention.

The word here rendered as "steadfastness" has also been translated as "patience" and even "endurance;" in this Paul shows sensitivity to the inner difficulties and uncertainties that can beset a religious quest, especially one which is trying to make sense of the Bible.

The value of this effort is primarily internal, even existential. It yields "encouragement," which can also mean "comfort," or even "consolation." And from this patience and encouragement Paul says we can draw something even more important, namely, hope--the ability to find meaning and promise in a situation where they had previously been lacking.

To me, this second passage has a distinctly contemporary ring. After all, to many Friends today the debates over biblical inerrancy seem irrelevant and even silly; we don't come to scripture

looking for a science text or an error-free account of events more
than two millennia past.

Rather, especially in the second, resource stage of study,
what most Friends are looking for is much more personal: we're
seeking glimmers of light in a world which is too often outwardly
dark and inwardly uncertain. We come, that is, in search of
encouragement. We come in search of hope.

A very profound French theologian, Jacques Ellul, has
argued in his book, *Hope In Time of Abandonment*, that in our
nuclear age, the form that authentic religious faith takes is not so
much belief as hope; that is, it is shown more in the ability to find
and sustain a sense of meaning and promise in life, than in the
acceptance of doctrine.

I think Ellul is right, and his insight underlines the
importance of this sense of inspiration: It is what enables the Bible
to "speak to our condition"; the source of its ability, steadfastly
explored, to bring us encouragement and hope.

Seen this way the Bible does not become an answer book,
but rather an arena of ultimate engagement, even struggle, as well
as a source of comfort and reassurance. As Barclay put it, "[The
Scriptures] find a respondent spark in us, and in that way we discern
the stamp of God's ways and his Spirit upon them."

So this third stage represents a qualitative change in one's
relationship to the Bible. Scripture could now be described as a
vehicle of revelation, or some equivalent term.

But why call the third stage Godwrestling? I have borrowed
the term from a Jewish writer, scholar and activist, Arthur Waskow.
Waskow, long a secular leftist activist, wrote vividly of his own
journey along this path in a March 1, 1973 article in WIN Magazine:

"In the spring of 1968," he recalled, "I began an encounter
with Judaism, Yiddishkeit; in the winter of 1972, that encounter
deepened into one with God. The God of Abraham, Isaac and Jacob
--especially the God of Jacob, who became Israel, the God-wrestler."

Waskow is referring to Genesis 32:24-30, in which Jacob spends a night wrestling with a mysterious figure, who is unable to overcome Jacob, even after dislocating his thigh. The figure tells Jacob to let him go, but Jacob says he won't let go until he receives a blessing.

The blessing he gets is a name change: "Your name shall no longer be called Jacob, but *Israel*...." (Gen 32:28) And the name Israel means "the one who has wrestled with God," or the Godwrestler.

Although it is only a few verses, this is a seminal passage in the Hebrew Scriptures. For one thing, in Hebrew life and religion, a name is a clue to essence and meaning. And it is no accident that in his new identity, Jacob/Israel becomes the ancestor of the "children of the Godwrestler", and later the nation of the Godwrestler, and still later the people of the Godwrestlers; and today even have the State of the Godwrestlers.

For Arthur Waskow, his own pilgrimage began quietly enough, with learning Hebrew and studying the Jewish Scriptures. How did Waskow know when he had made this transition?

"I knew how sharp a turning it was when I realized that for the first time in my life, I was writing poetry."

And this was not greeting card verse, either. Consider these lines from one of his earliest poems (Waskow, WIN, Ibid.):

"Wrestling feels a lot like making love."
Why did Jacob wrestle with God, why did the others talk?
God surely enjoyed that all-night fling with Jacob:
Told him he'd won,
Renamed him and us the Godwrestler,
Even left him with a limp to be sure he'd remember it all.
But ever since, we've talked.
Did something peculiar happen that night?
Did somebody say the next day we shouldn't wrestle? Who?
We should wrestle again with our Comrade sometime soon.
Wrestling feels a lot like making love."

This, then, was what one man could say as a result of his own passage through these stages. Waskow's continuing spiritual journey led him to become part of a Jewish renewal group in Washington, D.C. called Fabrangen, which tackled the Bible in just this way regularly in its Sabbath services. As Waskow puts it in a book called *Godwrestling*:

> "...Every Shabbos morning, the Fabrangen wrestles God. Ourselves, and each other, and God. We do not simply accept the tradition, but we do not reject it either. We wrestle it: fighting it and making love to it at the same time. We try to touch it with our lives."

For me, Waskow's key sentence bears repeating:

"We do not simply accept the tradition, but we do not reject it either."

Such an ambivalent relationship to Bible the would hardly satisfy a fundamentalist; but it is a familiar one to most unprogrammed Friends. While such ambiguity and uncertainty have their price, the freedom they make possible is no small benefit.

Another crucial benefit of the Godwrestling image is that it brings into the open and legitimizes a task which I believe anyone who studies Scripture with their eyes open must tackle, namely confronting the Dark Side of the Bible. The issues raised there, the justification of oppression, the righteous cruelty, and the spectre of meaninglessness in life, are not simply literary or historical curiosities; they are very much part of life today.

Coming to grips with them is, I believe, part of what serious Bible study is all about. And when we do that, we join a company of honest Jews and Christians who have wrestled with them for centuries; and we will also find that some of the deepest, most searching of these struggles take place in Scripture itself.

One further potential benefit of wrestling with the Dark Side of the Bible is that it can help keep us humble about our own interpretations of the texts. The writers, even while talking with God, remained human and fallible, and so did their writings. Are we any better? I doubt it. As Paul admits in one of his humbler moments, "we have this treasure in earthen vessels." (2Cor.4:7) Humility is appropriate even as we are obliged to stand up for our convictions.

Can we find examples of Godwrestling in our Quaker tradition? Well, take another look, for instance, at the early chapters of George Fox's *Journal*: the years of wandering, questioning, and struggles with despair depicted there sound an awful lot like an extended bout of Godwrestling. And throughout these years, remember, the Bible was Fox's constant and main companion, and the realm in which this long match was played out.

The contemporary British Friend and religious scholar John Punshon, in his book *Encounter With Silence*, tells of picking up the New Testament shortly after his father died. He too was thoroughly familiar with the text, having read and studied it often. Yet when encountered outside his conventionally religious and intellectual frame of mind, in the flush of his very personal loss, he suddenly found the gospels speaking to him directly, in a way that took hold of him and permanently altered his understanding of himself as a religious person.

To reiterate, not everyone who begins Bible study goes through these same stages of Detoxification, Uncovering a Resource, and Godwrestling, and in describing them I do not mean to set up an ideal pattern to which everyone ought to conform.

But as you pursue your own course of Bible study, George Fox's ancient challenge to his early audiences will remain: what, as a result of encounter with the Scriptures, canst Thou say?

If, as I believe along with Robert Barclay, there is something in the Bible that can strike "a respondent spark" in the human soul, then if you study the Scriptures with the steadfastness called for by Paul, it ought to be of use and encouragement to you in discovering what *you* can say; and when the time comes, it can help you to stand up and say it.

FOR FURTHER READING

Coleman, Richard J. *Issues of Theological Conflict.* Grand Rapids, MI: Eerdmans, 1980. A very illuminating survey of the divisions between liberal and evangelical Christians, with much emphasis on Biblical issues. Quakers who think they are above such squabbles are usually kidding themselves.

Ellul, Jacques. *Hope In Time of Abandonment.* New York: Seabury, 1973. A stunning example of how seriously evangelical faith, and devotion to Scripture, can also be politically trenchant and culturally revealing. A landmark. And if you like this book, don't miss:

Ellul, Jacques. *False Presence of the Kingdom.* New York: Seabury Press, 1972. The best, most telling critique of religious social activism I ever read, made all the better because it is not at all conservative in its underlying outlook.

Ellwood, Gracia Fay. *Batter My Heart. Wallingford, PA: Pendle Hill Pamphlet* #282. I doubt if a feminist perspective/critique of Scripture has ever been put so pungently and concisely. A mistresspiece, not to be missed.

Fager, Chuck. *A Respondent Spark: The Basics of Bible Study.* Falls Church, VA: Kimo Press, 1984. My own modest contribution to the field, designed to equip Friends new to the Bible with the tools needed for beginning self-directed Bible study.

Freiday, Dean, ed. *Barclay's Apology In Modern English.* Available from Barclay Press, Newberg, Oregon. Although this basic Quaker theological treatise is over 300 years old, there is much in its sections on the Bible that so-called "modern" biblical scholarship is still trying to catch up with. Still radical after all these years.

Punshon, John. *Encounter With Silence.* Richmond, IN: Friends United Press, 1987. While about more than the Bible, this account of a modern Friend's ongoing religious pilgrimage shows how important a resource the Bible can still be.

Soulen, Richard N. *Handbook of Biblical Criticism, New Expanded Second Edition*. Atlanta, GA: John Knox Press, 1981. This is a detailed dictionary of technical Bible scholar's jargon, which will make for much easier sledding if and when you begin to wade into heavyweight Bible scholarship.

Swartley, Willard H. *Slavery, Sabbath, War & Women*. Scottdale, PA: Herald Press, 1983. A probing, enlightening examination by a Mennonite scholar of how several crucial issues have been treated in the Bible **and** by Bible interpreters through the centuries.

Waskow, Arthur. *Godwrestling*. New York: Schocken, 1978. First class; a Jewish perspective on the Bible that no Christian should be without.

Bibles and Commentaries:

The New Catholic Study Bible, Catholic Bible Press, has probably the most progressive theological perspective, includes the important Deuterocanonical books which Protestant Bibles leave out,(to understand more about why these books are important, see Cynthia Taylor's essay on Sophia elsewhere in this book) and presents all in the easy-to-read Todays English Version.

The Master Study Bible, Holman, packs the most helps between two covers(including an 800-page biblical encyclopedia) and its commentary, while conservative, is not mindlessly so.

The Interpreters Bible, Abingdon, is the old reliable commentary among non-fundamentalist scholars, and rightly so. Its twelve volumes and 10,000 pages may look formidable on the shelf, but it is easier to use than you think, and is loaded with illuminating historical, theological, textual and linguistic information. Its $300 price tag is steep for a personal collection, but no Friends meeting library should be without it.

VII

Plenary Address

How Early Friends Understood The Bible

Martha Paxson Grundy

[Note: Martha Paxson Grundy, "Marty" to most Friends, has recently finished a doctoral dissertation in Quaker history for Case Western Reserve University. She is also raising a family and attends Cleveland Meeting, where she has been part of a Bible study group for several years.]

It was in 1649, three years before the vision on Pendle Hill, and the gathering of the Westmoreland Seekers, and the visit to Swarthmore Hall. George Fox was passing Nottingham one First Day, with Friends, on their way to a meeting. From the top of a hill he could see the great steeplehouse, and the Lord said to him, "Thou must go cry against yonder great idol, and against the worshippers therein."

So after attending meeting, a meeting in which the "mighty power of the Lord God was amongst us", Fox got up and went to the steeplehouse. The priest was expounding on this text from Peter, "We have also a more sure word of prophecy, whereunto ye do well that ye take heed, as unto a light that shineth in a dark place, until the day dawn, and the day-star arise in your hearts." The priest explained that this was referring to the scriptures which were the final authority by which all doctrines and religions should be judged.

We read in Fox's Journal, "Now the Lord's power was so mighty upon me, and so strong in me, that I could not hold, but was made to cry out and say, 'Oh, no, it is not the Scriptures', and was commanded to tell them God did not dwell in temples made with hands. But I told them what it was, namely, the Holy Spirit, by which the holy men of God gave forth the Scriptures, whereby opinions, religions, and judgments were to be tried [or tested]; for it led into all Truth, and so gave the knowledge of all Truth." (1) As Fox continued to explain this basic Quaker position, officers came and led him off to gaol. So the very first Quaker imprisonment had to do with the issue of biblical authority.

Robert Barclay, trained by both Calvinists and Roman Catholics, systematized early Quaker beliefs as much as anyone did. His *Apology* examined thoroughly most of what was at issue between Quakers and the major contemporary denominations. (2) Barclay concluded that because "it is only by the Spirit that we can come to the true knowledge of God, and...it is by the Spirit that we are led into all truth and taught all things, then the Spirit--and not the scriptures--is the foundation and the basis of all truth and knowledge." (3)

People crave certainty. The Roman Catholic Church found it in its institutionalization. Protesting against that, Protestants found it in the Bible (as interpreted by their favorite prelate). But it was opened to Fox and the early Quakers that those attempts to find certainty depended on the letter--which killed. They were directed to the Spirit--which gives life.

Friends grasped the eternally radical insight that the ultimate authority is the Spirit. This is radical because the Spirit is not under the control of humans. We cannot point to a written law or tradition or body of writing and therefore prove that we are right and our misguided opponent is wrong. We must, instead, humble ourselves, and open ourselves to the possibility of change and instruction, to patient listening and obedience to the Divine Guide.

This is risky because God might not tell me what I want to hear. God might not throw out or punish those I see as rascals or sinners, or at the very least, as inconvenient stumbling blocks to my happiness. Instead the Spirit might tell me that I am to love these annoying, wrong-headed people, even as God has loved me.

Oh! Give me a nice clear-cut set of rules any day. Don't give me an open-ended instruction to love, to change myself to fit God's commonwealth. I'd much rather have a book in which I can find verses which suit my needs, and bolster my opinions, and prove me justified and righteous, even self-righteous.

Because early Friends saw that the Bible was not the final authority, and because we have seen it misused and abused, and know that it is steeped with the patriarchal culture out of which it sprang, can we then ignore it? Is it an outmoded book, doing more harm than good? Are we really living in a post-scriptural Society of Friends?

George Fox and the seventeenth century Friends did not reject the Bible. They read and reread and meditated on it. They were steeped in its language and ideas. They couched their arguments and their openings and understandings in its words. They used it devotionally, for preaching, and as ammunition for controversy. (4) But they did not use it like other Christians of their day. Only now, some 340 years later, are theologians of other denominations coming to understand what was revealed to Fox. And, ironically, many Quakers are now ignorant of our rich heritage.

We can thank Lewis Benson for helping Friends rediscover the original message, and thank Douglas Gwyn for putting it into new language and tying it together so provocatively and powerfully. (5) In particular I want to draw your attention to Gwyn's brilliant explanation of the way in which the Spirit opened the Book of Revelations to Fox. The Second Coming is not to be understood in terms of a distant "rapture" but as happening now; whenever an individual allows the Christ Spirit into his or her heart and is transformed by it, at that instant God's commonwealth breaks into history.

The key to Fox's understanding of the Bible is his plea that it must be read in the power of that same Spirit which gave it forth. But what do those words mean? Other 17th Century Protestants used similar formulas: that we are dependent on the Spirit of Christ to explain the Bible's meaning to us. But Fox imbued the words with richer meanings.

The breakthrough understanding for Fox, it seems to me, was that the Bible should be applied to my own inner work. (6) What is the story of Cain about? A story of jealousy and murder against one whose sacrifice was acceptable to God. What does that have to do with me? Nothing if I insist on viewing it as a story of someone thousands of years ago who murdered his brother.

But if I allow the Light to show me, deep within myself, those areas of jealousy against someone whose spiritual life seems going better than mine, there is immediate value to me, important lessons to heed.

What do the stories of Esau, David, the walls of Jerico, Jonah's reluctance, the exodus, have to teach me? When I open my soul and invite the Spirit to show me how they apply to me, I learn a great deal, indeed.

It was this point that Fox meant when warning against those "people, who in reading Scriptures, cry out much against Cain, Esau, and Judas, and other wicked men of former times, mentioned in the Holy Scriptures; but do not see the nature of Cain, of Esau, of Judas, and those others, in themselves. And these said it was they, they, they that were the bad people; putting it off from themselves: but when some of these came, with the light and spirit of Truth, to see into themselves, then they came to say, 'I, I, I, it is I myself that have been the Ishmael, and the Esau', etc. For then they came to see the nature of wild Ishmael in themselves, the nature of Cain, of Esau, of Korah, of Balaam and of the son of perdition in themselves, sitting above [i.e. superior to] all that is called God in them." (7)

Robert Barclay, amongst his 19 pages justifying and explaining the Quaker's assignment of the scriptures to a secondary place, adds a single paragraph describing the scriptures as "a looking glass in which we can see the conditions and experiences of ancient believers. There we find that our experience is analogous to theirs." (8) By observing the way God watched over them, the snares that trapped them, the ways in which they were delivered, we can learn and move towards righteousness ourselves.

In addition to seeing individual characters and episodes as

metaphors, what Fox called "figures" for our own inner struggles, Fox saw the whole sweep of the Bible as a pattern for the development of an individual's faith. He condemned people who saw only the ancient historical/theological events, which he grouped as death reigning from Adam to Moses, the law and prophets reigning from Moses to John, and then the coming of "the kingdom greater than John's".

In that quaint seventeenth century language, that some of us love and others find a real stumbling block, Fox urged people to look within themselves and discover death reigning inside from "the entrance into transgression" until they came to "the ministration of condemnation which restrains people from sin that brings death". Then after the "ministration of Moses" is passed through, the ministry of the prophets can be read and understood, which "reaches through types and figures and shadows until John, whose ministrations prepare the way of the Lord". And as this ministration is passed through, "an entrance comes to be known into the everlasting kingdom".

How does this translate into modern English? What Fox is talking about here are stages of faith development. What could be a more exciting and timely topic for the late 20th century? (9)

M. Scott Peck sketches four levels of the development of faith. (10) They are simplistic, and therefore do not adequately explain any specific individual's spiritual journey. But as a crude diagram of the way we work, it is at least as useful as Freud's diagram of psychological growth, or Gesell and Ilg's description of the development of a child. (11)

The first, beginning level for Peck is chaotic. Peck places this in early childhood; as a mother, that is not quite what I observed. It may be more helpful to think of times of chaos in our present lives, rather than to assume it is safely passed long ago in childhood. Divorce, for example, is a real time of chaos. Going off to college can be such a time. Whenever I get caught up in society's wrong values, I feel chaos rushing in like a tidal wave. This sounds very much like Fox's "death reigning from Adam to Moses". But within the chaos are seeds of growth.

Moses received the Law from God and passed it on to God's people. Peck describes the movement from level one to level two, which he calls the Formal Stage, by an acceptance of religion, often by a "born again" conversion experience.   Such a person enthusiastically adopts the rules and mores of the institutionalized church. This corresponds to Fox's understanding of the acceptance of the Mosaic law, which shows what is sin, and by obedience to the law, keeps chaos at bay.

This is a real step forward, a positive acceptance and understanding of the way God's rules work, and a beginning understanding of how God's commonwealh functions.   It also contains the seeds for further growth. Just as the chaos of divorce, the terror of a new situation away from the familiar safety, can, if rightly handled, bring new growth, so, too, can level two begin to grow beyond the strictures, the confining rules as understood at the time.

Peck's third level is based on the Enlightenment: our skepticism of the institutionalized church, of other people telling us what laws to obey, of the hollowness of professing but not possessing all that is promised by Christ.   The third level turns outward and often passionately works to bring peace and justice to the world's downtrodden.

But the Enlightenment had not yet happened when Fox was preaching.   So his third level speaks of the "ministry of the prophets". And what was the message of those prophets? To do justice and love mercy and walk humbly with God.

The problem is that level threes tend to leave out the humble walk with God. Fox's description is not the same as Peck's skepticism, but it does share one important element, that of social action. It seems to me that level three is where most unprogrammed liberal Quakers are now.

But again, like the first two levels, this level has within it the seeds for further growth. There comes a time when we become skeptical of our own skepticism.   It doesn't answer the hard questions which confront us in the long cold night. It doesn't answer the queston of why bad things happen to good people--or to anyone else. Burnout slows and embitters the activist. Gradually one seeks for more.

The fourth level, which Peck calls the Mystic Stage, comes about with a gradual disillusionment with skepticism and rationality, and a rediscovery, at a far deeper level, of the spiritual truths we had embraced as level twos. But now one knows that one cannot do justice and seek peace in one's own strength; one experiences the walk with God, and grows in it, and finds there the instruction and the empowerment to live in God's commonwealth, now.

Fox describes this as coming "by the Spirit and power of God to Christ who fulfills the types, figures, shadows, promises, and prophecies that were of him", in other words, coming to experience all the promises of a mature spiritual life with Christ. Fox concludes that only then, "led by the Holy Ghost into the truth and substance of the Scriptures, sitting down in him who is the author and end of them, then are they read and understood with profit and great delight." (12)

What is the point of this digression into levels of faith development? One, that I find it fascinating that back in the 17th Century Fox apparently was able to see that the sweep of the biblical narrative correlated with the general steps by which an individual grows in relationship with God.

Second, I think it is important because it helps me articulate what I see as the mission God has given to late 20th century Friends. This mission is, simply, to help people move from level three to level four. Other organized churches are very good at helping people move from level one to level two. They have the rules and know how to teach them. But they get quite uncomfortable with questioning skeptics.

On the other hand, most people who come to Friends are already level threes. We are leery of rules, of institutions; we are very much into social action. Our great weakness is that there are so few level four Friends that some meetings have no examples of what the totality of Quakerism really is about. We think that our small piece, where we attach to the Quaker vision, is all that there is to the Society of Friends.

So we are full of hyphenated Friends. Our glory is that we accept that. We are a gateway group. We welcome the battered and bruised, those beat over the head and shoulders by misusers of the Bible. Our tragedy is that, in too many cases, we have lost the vision of radical Christian Quakerism that fired and empowered our spiritual ancestors.

So what was the importance of the Bible to early Friends? Barclay proclaimed that Friends "acknowledge that the scriptures are holy writings which possess more than earthly beauty, and whose use imparts strength and hope and is very necessary for the church of Christ." (13) Barclay meets the question of authority head on, by insisting that Friends "freely disclaim all pretended revelations that are contrary to the scripture....In other words, we distinguish between a revelation of a new gospel and new doctrines, and new insight into the established gospel and doctrines. We plead for the latter, but we utterly deny the former." (14)

The letter to the Governor of Barbados included this statement:

"Now concerning the Holy Scriptures, we do believe that they were given forth by the Holy Spirit of God through the holy men of God, who spoke, as the Scriptures of Truth saith, 'As they were moved by the Holy Ghost' (2 Peter i.21); and that they are to be read, and believed, and fulfilled, and he that fulfills them is Christ; and they are 'profitable for doctrine, for reproof, for correction, for instruction in righteousness, that the man of God may be perfect, thoroughly furnished unto all good works' (2 Tim. iii. 16, 17) and are able to make us wise to salvation through faith in Christ Jesus. And we do believe that the Scriptures are the words of God,....So that we call the Scriptures, as Christ and the apostles called them (viz.) the words not word of God." (15)

Early Friends assumed that the Light would not only lead them into unity with each other, but would lead them into unity with scripture. There is always a danger if one depends on the Spirit as the ultimate authority, that one may be mistaken and go off into Ranterism. Unity with the faith community and unity with scripture were--and are--two checks against Ranterism.

But is the Bible a clear statement of Truth? We are all well aware of its internal contradictions, and of the multiplicity of interpretations to which it has been subjected. Chuck Fager has suggested that one way out of the impasse presented by scriptural passages that do not fit with current understandings, is to embrace the ambiguity of the Bible as part of the biblical message. Rather than accept the interpretation of the Bible as given by your choice of evangelical preachers, acknowledge the contradictions which are in it, and declare that the authentic biblical stance is to reject an unambiguous view of "truth".

This stance insists on as much openness and toleration as we can stand, within the context of, and in dialogue with, the scriptures as a "looking glass" and model of faith and growth.

But although Barclay was aware of the contradictions in scripture, early Friends do not seem to have come to this solution. To get a sense of how earlier Friends dealt with the difficulty we will look back over our history and see what happened when Friends felt the Spirit was leading them in a direction that was not scriptural. I can identify at least seven issues over the past 340 years (among unprogrammed Friends) in which this seems to have been the case.

Because when one is trying to live a life of obedience to God the question of authority is so crucial, I'll briefly review some of these instances. How does Quakerism work out the tension between the Spirit and the Bible when they appear not to agree?

The first instance is the position of women. Fox was clear that women and men were spiritually equal and should be given equal opportunities to exercise their spiritual gifts. The dominant culture of the Seventeenth Century read Paul's stricture that "women should keep silent in church" and said the Quakers were unbiblical. The Spirit opened to Fox a different interpretation of Paul's prohibition. Margaret Fell's pamphlet on *Women's Speaking Justified* pointed to other passages which indicated that women had played an important part in the early church.

So in this case, it appears that under the guidance of the Spirit, Friends reinterpreted the troublesome verse and pointed to other passages which supported their position. (16)

The second instance was in the abolition of the outward ceremonies of baptism and communion. Here, it seems the Friends were on somewhat shakier biblical ground. The Spirit showed Fox that the true church experienced internal, spirtualized baptisms and communions, and that once Friends had experienced Christ alive within, the outward symbolic acts should be eliminated.

Canby Jones points out that where scripture deals with the actual experience of the Spirit of God, Fox insisted that "the life, the event, the faith experience" come first and scripture only serves to confirm it. (17) Here the biblical interpretation is a bit shakier than concerning the place of women, although I firmly believe that Fox heard it aright.

With the issue of slavery we can see the process at work. Although Friends quoted Bible verses at each other late into the night, the debate does not seem to be framed in terms of what Friends should do when there seems to be a difference between what the Spirit is saying and what the Bible says.

Instead Friends to whom the Spirit had shown that slavery was wrong, buttressed their message with reference to Jesus's Golden Rule. Friends who owned slaves had the weight of Biblical references on their side. Yet in the revolutionary decade of the 1770s, when everywhere in America people were talking about liberty and inalienable rights, yearly meeting after yearly meeting came to unity that slave owning was inimicable to God's will and contrary to the way God was calling God's people (Friends) to behave and demonstrate God's commonwealth.

Here we finally see the process at work. Although Jean Soderlund's excellent study of Philadelphia Yearly Meeting's struggle with the issue of slavery shows how mixed were our motives, and how reluctant we were to follow God all the way, still the general outline of the process is clear (18):

Friends did not couch the question as a conflict between Spirit and scripture. First a few, then increasing numbers of Friends acknowledged that the Spirit was leading them to denounce slaveholding. The Spirit pointed to places in the Bible where they could find confirmation of this position. But then the Yearly

Meeting, as the faith community, united on witnessing that God had called Friends to declare this new Truth. In other words, the question was not, how does one chose between Spirit and scripture? the question was, although unstated as such, what does the faith community hear the Spirit instructing us to do?

In other words, when the Yearly Meeting united on a new testimony, a new behavior which was required of Friends, and this was then put into the Book of Discipline, the question had, in effect, been answered. The faith community decided that the Spirit's new direction should be followed, despite the weight of Biblical references condoning slavery. (19)

In the first decade of the 19th Century the question was finally asked outright: what happens when the Spirit and the Bible disagree? Hannah Barnard from Hudson, New York, and Abraham Shackleton from Ballitore, Ireland, could not reconcile the loving God they had experienced, with the vengeful and violent God of the Old Testament who ordered the Israelites to destroy whole cities and every living thing therein. There was also some difficulty with the miracles, and miraculous conception of Jesus.

By this time many Friends seem to have forgotten Fox's breakthrough understanding that scripture could be used to understand one's own internal struggles. Too many Friends were caught up in the conflict which had captured most of the protestant denominations of the time between evangelicalism and deism. Barnard and Shackleton, although firmly in the ancient Quaker tradition, sounded too much like the hated and feared deists. They were disowned. (20) Those who held power in many Friends meetings chose to support an authority they could point to and touch rather than the radical and risky trust in the Holy Spirit.

The next issue on which Friends felt the lack of unity between Spirit and scripture was temperance. Although the Bible does not mention distilled spirits, the use of which Friends testified against first, clearly wine was an acceptable part of biblical reality. There are a few passages against drunkenness, but except for the Nazarites nothing implying total abstinence, and several verses actually advising drinking of wine.

Some staunch teetotalers tried to prove that the wine Jesus drank and created was really unfermented grape juice. In other words, efforts were made to squash the biblical record into the new mould. But that is not what made Friends accept total abstinence. As in the case of antislavery, Friends corporately came to see that the Spirit required a new testimony. When unity was reached, the testimony was included in the various Books of Discipline. It wasn't a question of reinterpreting the Bible. It was a question of discerning the Spirit's guidance, and obeying.

When we get to the 20th century, however, we have a quite different situation. Does anyone remember meetings wrestling with a new instruction from the Spirit that we should repeal the recent understanding on abstinence and go back to permitting drinking in moderation? Does anyone recall praying and waiting for guidance on rewriting the testimony to permit remarriage of divorced people? What is going on now?

It appears that yearly meetings have noticed that behavior has changed and therefore Friends need to change their Faith and Practice to keep up with the times. This is not the process by which we, as radical Christian Quakers, hear and obey our Guide.

I think we need to go home and discuss, and more importantly, pray over how we ought to go about changing our testimonies. We need to find, or rediscover, the right process.

As we look at what early Friends understood about the Bible, many of today's unprogrammed, so-called liberal Friends find ourselves grasping a two-edged blade. On the one edge we are pleased that the Spirit is the ultimate authority, and the Bible only points to it. We are delighted to discover that the Bible's incidents and characters can be taken to explain and illuminate our own internal struggles.

But the other edge is the definite understanding that the Spirit will not instruct us contrary to the Bible. Furthermore, it is very clear that early Friends knew themselves to be Christians. They felt they were living "primitive Christianity" rediscovered and restored. We cannot wish away that letter to the Governor of Barbados with its statement of beliefs that is even more orthodox than the Anglican Apostles' Creed.

What do we do with embarrassing facts or parts of our history which make us uncomfortable? As an historian, I cannot just ignore them. As a Friend, I must struggle to understand them. Perhaps understand, implying reason, is not quite the right verb. As a radical Christian Quaker, I allow the Spirit to work on them in me.

It seems to me that we are not called to answers. We are given a series of tensions. These are not meant to be stress tensions, but are more like the strings of a violin, taut, and capable of beautiful music. The Society of Friends has built into it a series of tensions. In the Seventeenth Century they made beautiful music. In the Nineteenth, Friends cut the strings in an effort to relieve the tension; we have never quite gotten the tune right since then. But let's go back and review what some of these tensions are, around the early Friends' understanding of the Bible.

There is a tension over the issue of authority, between the Spirit on one hand, and scripture and tradition on the other. If they are ignored, then there is a real possibility of going off in another direction, into Ranterism. When there is no conflict, the tension is nearly invisible: a low sustained background note. But when there seems to be a conflict, over, for example, same sex relationships, the tension increases, and the note becomes a shriek.

Another tension is between Christianity and what is often called universalism. Early Friends recognized elements of both, but kept them in harmony. Quoting John, Friends recognized not only that the Word, that was in the beginning, that was with God and was God, became flesh and dwelt among us, but also there was the Light that lighteth every one who cometh into the world.

We are all familiar with George Fox speaking with a native American and discovering that he, unfamiliar with Christianity, felt in himself a principle which reproved him when he did wrong and encouraged him when he did right. Fox identified this as the Christ Spirit. Building on Doug Gwyn's work, we could go so far as to suggest that the relationship between God and human has a name, and that name is the Christ Spirit. In other words, when a Buddhist or Sikh or native American or anyone has an experience of the divine, that relationship is Christ. (21)

Sometimes we try to domesticate God, we make God small and comfortable. But we forget. God is the creator, who made the entire infinite universe, who made the tiny perfect delicacy of an insect, who made the laws by which the whole thing fits together and functions. What can we do in the presence of such majesty but fall on our faces and worship? But that's not all.

One sunny day as I was about to throw my dirty laundry into the washer, the idea popped into my head that I should not do it. Not being experienced at naming these occurences, I ignored the nudge. But it turned out that the firemen were flushing hydrants that day and the white laundry came out rust-colored.

I came to realize that the stop I had felt came from God. The creator of the whole universe knew me intimately, and loved me, like a parent, a lover, a best friend. The creator of the whole universe loved me enough to help me with my laundry! What a God! The way God communicated with me, early Friends believed, was named the Spirit of Christ. How have you experienced this?

What happens if we do not recognize the biblical/Christian name, but call the contact the Inner Light? What happens? God graciously continues to reach out to us, no matter what labels we apply. Nowadays we do not disown or forbid membership to people who have not accepted Christianity--or to those who have. But it is clear to me that early Friends knew themselves to be radical Christians, and that throughout our history, the most God-centered, most Spirit-filled, most spiritually weighty and seasoned Friends were those who acknowledged their relationship to God through Christ.

At its center the Society of Friends offers this experience. Folks can back off, or can choose to experiment with it. We need to be an open doorway, encouraging and inviting--while not compelling. But we also need to acknowledge, I think, that therein lies the real power to transform our lives and thus the world.

Historians have argued with each other over what influenced George Fox. Clearly ideas he had were "in the air" of Seventeenth

Century England. But a close reading of his Journal indicates that
he did not accept currently popular ideas that he heard. He only
accepted an idea once the Spirit had "opened" it to him. Once God
instructed him that women, for example, were spiritually equal with
men, then Fox was led to passages in the Bible that corroborated
this Truth.

Other times, Fox was given the meaning of a passage which
then became a part of the gospel he preached. On rare occasions
I, too, have been given an understanding into the meaning of a
Bible verse. Late this summer, as I was working on this paper, the
following verse jumped into my mind: "I am the way, the Truth and
the life; no one goes to the Father except by me." (John 14:6) This
had always been a difficult verse for me because it seemed so
exclusionary.

But at the same time it came to me that, bumperstrip
slogans to the contrary notwithstanding, Jesus did not say "I am the
answer; only by accepting what the institutionalized church says
about me can you get into a relationship with God." An answer can
be tied up in a neat package; an answer can be nailed down. It is
pat and finished. The Way is a path, a process. It is open-ended
and continuing. Throughout the gospels, Jesus is calling us to a
process, to a relationship. He is quite definitely not into rules, for
the sake of rules.

But there is another part of this verse. The man Jesus could
only say "I am the Way" in that he was at that instant speaking as
God incarnate. Early Friends understood that their Way, their
process, had very much to do with the Christ Spirit. It had, once,
become flesh and dwelt among people.

Let me review again how early Friends saw this process.
Individually, Friends went through a series of steps, a process, a
qualification, which paralleled the sweep of the biblical narrative,
and was mirrored in a variety of biblical incidents, characters, and
verses. The Bible helped explain what they were going through, and
their experience helped them understand the Bible. Friends felt the
small nudges of the Spirit within, and responded by allowing,
encouraging, the Light to show them the dark parts of themselves
which were not in conformity with it.

The Light not only showed them what needed to be changed, it also showed them "the author of their salvation" --it brought them into a growing relationship with God through Christ. And it empowered them to make the necessary changes in their inward and outward lives. The Inward Christ Spirit was their guide and teacher.

Although there were lots of radical ideas floating around during the period of the English Civil War and Commonwealth, Friends did not adopt policies and practices because they seemed politically correct; they made them their own when led to them by their inner guide. It is this process, this Way, which it seems to me we Friends need to rediscover and reclaim today.

I want to conclude with the parable of the wineskins. These sayings appear in all three synoptic gospels, with great similarity. Jesus was responding to questions about why he did not fast, in other words, why he was not doing those things which it was expected pious people would do.

Jesus said that one does not pour new wine into old wineskins, because the new wine will burst the skins, the wine will pour out, and the skins will be ruined. (Mark 2:22, Matthew 9:17, Luke 5:37-39.) I understand the new wine to be the Spirit.

Remember on Pentecost, when the disciples were filled with the Spirit, and spoke in strange tongues, on-lookers accused them of being drunk? It is this new wine of the Spirit which can't be poured into old institutions. It needs the creation of new institutions. And since the wine is always new, the institutions must forever be open to being created anew.

I know some Friends to whom the old ways are so precious that they reject the new wine. They suspect that the new wine will bring radical changes which they do not want. Jesus seems to have foreseen this. Luke quotes him saying, ironically, I believe, "And no one wants new wine after drinking old wine. 'The old is better,' he says."

I know other Friends who have busily created a whole series

of fancy new wineskins, but have forgotten what it is that is supposed to go into them. They hang them there on the wall, like trophies, empty and useless.

And so, Friends, let us seek the new wine; let us invite in the Spirit. With courage and faithfulness let us embrace the healthy, creative tension between our ultimate authority, the Christ Spirit, and those witnesses to It: the Bible and our tradition. Knowing that each generation must work out its own salvation with fear and trembling, let us build up our faith communities, looking not for pat answers and rules, but for the Way, the Truth, and the life.

Suggested Questions for Worship Sharing

1. What experiences have you had of a nudge from God?

2. How has a Bible story, psalm, or passage helped illuminate an event in your life?

3. Can you share an "opening" you have received regarding a specific verse or passage in the Bible?

4. How has something in your experience helped you understand a Bible passage?

5. How am I as an individual and how is my meeting as a faith community living with the tensions inherent in Quakerism?

NOTES

1. *The Journal of George Fox*, ed. by John Nickalls, (Cambridge: at the University Press, 1952), p. 39-40.

2. Dean Freiday, ed., *Barclay's Apology in Modern English*, (Manasquan, N.J.: 1967) p. xx.

3. Barclay, *Apology* (Freiday ed.), p. 50.

4. T. Canby Jones, "The Bible: Its Authority and Dynamic in George Fox and Contemporary Quakerism", *Quaker Religious Thought*, IV, 1 (Spring 1962), p. 22. Jones adds a fourth use of the Bible by Fox: as the "chief source of his understandings." See also Joseph Pickvance, *A Reader's Companion to George Fox's Journal* (London: Quaker Home Service, 1989), pp. 1, 21.

5. See any of Lewis Benson's works and, especially, Douglas Gwyn, *Apocalypse of the Word: The Life and Message of George Fox*, (Richmond: Friends United Press, 1986).

6. For a contemporary approach, see John A. Sanford, *The Kingdom Within: The Inner Meaning of Jesus' Sayings*, rev. ed. (San Francisco: Harper & Row, 1987).

7. Fox, *Journal*, p. 30.

8. Barclay, *Apology* (Freiday ed.), p. 59.

9. Fox, *Journal*, pp. 31-2.

10. M. Scott Peck, *The Different Drum: Community Making and Peace* (New York: Simon & Shuster, 1987), pp. 188ff.

11. Arnold Gesell and Frances L. Ilg, *The Child from Five to Ten* (New York and London: Harper and Brothers Publishers, 1946), and others.

12. Fox, *Journal*, p. 32.

13. Barclay, *Apology* (Freiday ed.), p. 50.

14. Ibid., p. 63. See also Jones, "The Bible", p. 28.

15. Fox, *Journal*, p. 604.

16. Fox, pp. 24, 667-8; Margaret Fell, *Womens Speaking Justified: proved and allowed of by the Scriptures, all such as speak by the spirit and power, and how women were the first that preached the tidings of the resurrection....*(Amherst: Mosher Book and Tract Committee, New England Yearly Meeting, 1980); David E. W.

Holden, *Friends Divided: Conflict and Division in the Society of Friends* (Richmond, Ind.: Friends United Press, 1988), pp. 21-23.

17. Jones, "The Bible", pp. 28-9.

18. Jean R. Soderlund, *Quakers & Slavery: A Divided Spirit* (Princeton, NJ: Princeton University Press, 1985).

19. Holden sums it up, "Once a form of behavior was defined as being in the Light, it became part of the expectations imposed on all Friends." Holden, *Friends Divided*, p. 23.

20. H. Larry Ingle, *Quakers in Conflict: The Hicksite Reformation* (Knoxville: University of Tennessee Press, 1986), p. 9-10; Caroline Nicholson Jacob, *The Shackletons of Ballitore* (Friends General Conference, 1984), pp. 18-20; Rufus M. Jones, *The Later Periods of Quakerism* (London: Macmillan and Co., Ltd., 1921), vol. I, pp. 293-307; Holden, *Friends Divided*, pp. 51-3, 146. Not all Friends had forgotten how to use the Bible as "figures" for inner work. See, for example, John Comly, *Journal of the Life and Religious Labours of John Comly, late of Byberry, Pennsylvania* (Philadelphia: Published by his Children, 1854), pp. 249, 581-84, 586-8.

21. Gwyn, *Apocalypse*, Chapt. 4.

VIII

The Book of Job: An Allegory for Coping with the AIDS Crisis
and Other Sufferings

Joseph A. Izzo, M.A., M.S.W.

[Note: Biographical information follows this essay.]

On an autumn day in 1989, a freak storm swept up the East
Coast of the United States, spawning tornadoes that killed 19 people
in Huntsville, Alabama. Further north, winds from the same storm
caused the collapse of a tree, which crashed into the cafeteria of an
elementary school, killing eight children.

That same day, in El Salvador, an army death squad killed
six Jesuit priests, their house cook and her daughter. The priests
were regarded as part of the compassionate intelligentsia aligned
with the poor of El Salvador. They joined Archbishop Oscar
Romero, three nuns, a laywoman minister and 70,000 of their fellow
countrywo/men who had been slain in a decade-long civil war.

Thousands of lives were recently disrupted or destroyed by
Hurricane Hugo in South Carolina and the Loma Prieta earthquake
in northern California. Over a quarter of a million people
worldwide have been diagnosed with the Acquired Immuno-
deficiency Syndrome (AIDS). The pandemic may claim millions of
people by the end of this decade.

These are but a few examples of the natural and human-
created traumas that visit humanity on planet Earth. Accidents,
illnesses, storms, geological upheavals, environmental pollution,
poverty, famine, starvation, plagues and wars are not new to the
human condition. These evils and their attendant sufferings have
continually provoked poets, philosophers, theologians and ordinary
wo/men to ask the perennial question of "Why does a supposedly
loving creator of the universe allow such evil to happen?"

Some sagacious scribe of the 5th century, B.C.E., tried to answer this question in what we now know as the 42 chapters of the Book of Job found in the Hebrew scriptures. This essay will attempt to hear some of the responses made by that author and some of his/her 20th century "Seekers-of-Truth" who strive to know why bad things happen to good people.

Due to the length of the Book of Job, and the necessary brevity of this essay, this will not be a continuing commentary on each chapter and verse of the book, but rather, a cursory exploration of the major themes and issues the ancient author confronted. A bibliography at the end of this essay will allow the more energetic seeker to conduct a more detailed exegesis of Job. An attempt will be made to place the themes, theology and wisdom of Job into a contemporary context.

My personal interest in the Book of Job stems partially from an academic background in biblical studies (M.A., LaSalle University, 1978). I had been trained in the tools of biblical analysis. However, it was the pain and grief I have suffered over the last eight years as I have watched over three dozen friends and acquaintances succumb to AIDS that prompted me to look more deeply into the realities of suffering, evil and death.

The loss of young, vibrant women and men in their prime adult years, still ripe with promise, had shaken my faith and spirit to the core. Why would a benevolent God/dess permit such a microorganism as HIV to progressively deteriorate the immune systems of babies, children, teen-agers, young and old adults before many of them had been able to fully realize their dreams, talents and potentials? It seems so cruel, so unfair and so senseless, particularly since the illness can drag on for years. It was with these experiences that I encountered the Job story.

THE STORY AND THE TEXT

Job, the legendary patriarch of a Middle Eastern tribe, wrestled with the same dilemma and questions that confront all suffering people. Like the central character of the medieval morality play, *Everyman* (c. 1485), Job represents each of us in the struggle to accommodate the polarities of goodness and evil, bliss and despair, love and hate, joy and suffering, light and darkness. While the text of Job gives no pat answers, it courageously tackles the questions, rages against the dark night of the soul and submits in humble silence:

> *Behold, I am of little account; what can I*
> *answer you?*
> *I put my hand over my mouth.*
> *Though I have spoken once, I will not do so again;*
> *Though twice, I will do so no more.*

(Job 40: 1-5)

A likely dating of this book puts it in the post-exilic period (587-500 B.C.E.), as the nation of Israel began to sort out the meaning of their defeat and long exile at the hands of the Babylonian nation. Why did Yahweh permit such a wrenching experience to consume the chosen people? Yet the book explores the trials and suffering of the individual, not the collective nation. It is the experience of *one* person who struggles to find meaning in a sudden reversal of fortunes--a person who, throughout the book, hangs between anger and despair.

The literary genre of Job is that of a Middle Eastern folk tale, but within the Hebrew canon, it is classified as one of the Writings within the Wisdom tradition. It can also be considered a form of Lamentation, since it contains numerous "cries of pain" by the afflicted hero figure. There is evidence of other nonHebraic Job stories in Mesopotamian literature, so this one is not unique. Obviously, the issues raised in the book are both perennial and universal.

The language of the book is highly poetic and has caused considerable problems for translators. Additionally, the most ancient extant texts to which the scholars must turn contain highly corrupted (unintelligible) passages. In spite of some substantial problems for scholars, the book is a well-organized composition that follows an ordered format.

I.   Prologue (1:1-2:13)
          Background to the story of Job's plight

II.   Job's First Soliloquy (3:1-16)
           A lamentation that seeks the answer to the "Why?"
question.

III. First Cycle of Speeches (4:1-14:22)
           A. Eliphaz's first speech (4:1-5:27)
           B. Job's response (6:1-7:21)
           C. Bildad's first speech (8:1-22)
           D. Job's response (9:1-10:22)
           E. Zophar's first speech (11:1-20)
           F. Job's response (12:1-14:22)

IV.   Second Cycle of Speeches (15:1-21:24)
           A. Eliphaz speaks (15:1-35)
           B. Job responds (16:1-17:16)
           C. Bildad speaks (18:1-21)
           D. Job responds (19:1-29)
           E. Zophar speaks (20:1-29)
           F. Job responds (21:1-34)

V.   Third Cycle of Speeches (22:1-27:21)
           A. Eliphaz speaks (22:1-30)
           B. Job responds (23:1-24:25)
           C. Zophar speaks (25:2-6)
           D. Job responds (26:1-4)
           E. Zophar speaks (26:5-14)
           F. Job speaks (27:2-6)
           G. Bildad speaks (27:7-10; 13-23)
           H. Job speaks (27:11-12)

VI.   Poem on Wisdom or the Inaccessibility of Wisdom (28:1-28)

VII. Job's Final Soliloquy (29:1-31:37)

VIII. Elihu's Speeches (32:1-37:24)

IX.   The Yahweh Speeches (38:1-42:6)
           Job's responses to Yahweh (40:3-5)

X.   Epilogue

As can be seen from the above schema, the format of the book is a highly organized poem, in spite of the alterations in the Third Cycle. Scholarship has judged chapter 28, the Poem on Wisdom, to have been a preexistent text, separately written and stylistically different from the Job text. It appears to have been a later inclusion by some rabbi/scribe.

Likewise, the Elihu speeches are considered later interpolations. They add no new ideas to those already presented by Eliphaz, Zophar and Bildad. Rather, Elihu comes off as a young upstart and something of a "windbag." Perhaps a later editor wished to show that neither "old wisdom" nor "youthful wisdom" was capable of understanding the nature of evil and suffering posed by Job's condition. Neither the "mouths of babes" nor the insights of old sages could fully explain why Job suffered.

This, of course, leads us to the inevitable question of the book--Why does Job, the righteous patriarch, suffer such misfortune? The text itself presents a superficial explanation--the Satan negotiates with the God/dess to test Job's love and fidelity. "Is it for nothing that Job is God-fearing? Have you not surrounded him and his family and all that he has with your protection?...but now put forth your hand and touch anything that he has, and surely he will blaspheme you to your face" (1:9-11). It is obvious from the text that the Satan in this story is not that of Christian mythology. Such a dualistic understanding of good versus evil, God versus the Devil, had not developed in the Hebrew theology. John Sanford, in his *EVIL: The Shadow Side of Reality* offers this explanation:

> In the Book of Job Satan is represented as one of the sons of God dwelling in God's court with Him. Here Satan seems to be part of God's inner family and not yet a definite adversary to God's purposes; yet he is personified as different from God Himself and is able to talk with God as a separate being. It is because of the dialogue between God and Satan that the misfortunes come

upon Job.... It is to prove Satan
wrong that God allows him to
send misfortunes upon Job. We
can take Satan in the Book of
Job, therefore, as a kind of dark,
doubting thought in God Himself
which succeeds in producing a
good deal of mischief. (p. 26)

The Satan strips Job of his livestock, his slaves and his
children in a series of catastrophes. In grief, Job tears his clothes,
throws himself to the ground and says:

"Naked I came forth from my mother's womb, and naked
shall I go back again. The Lord gave and the Lord has
taken away; blessed be the name of the Lord." (1:21)

And the biblical narrator adds:

"In all this Job did not sin, nor did he say anything
disrespectful of God." (1:22)

Thus, the first trial fails to produce the effect the Satan
predicted. Job remains humbly faithful to God and God makes
note of Job's response to the Satan. A second challenge is offered
of "skin for skin." God succumbs to the gamble and permits the
Satan to afflict Job's person with severe boils from the soles of his
feet to the crown of his head. Enter Job's wife, briefly, to taunt
him to "curse God and die."

Nonetheless, Job remains faithful by acknowledging that if
"we accept good things from God; should we not accept evil?"
(2:10)

Thus, the stage is set in two chapters and in that short span,
the reader is forced to question the fairness and justice of God, who
is seen as permitting a sadistic test upon a good and righteous
person. From this point on, the drama unfolds according to the
rather neat format that has already been outlined.

Chapter three is an excellent example of lamentation--an

ancient expression of grief when a person is confronted by chaos, brokenness and confusion. Michael Guinan, in his commentary on Job, refers to a lamentation as:

> "...a loud, religious Ouch!" with two common features: 1) the repeated question "Why?" (see Pss. 22:2, 43:10, 43:2). While this implies, "I do not understand," it is a cry of pain rather than a request for theological or scientific explanation; 2) the focus is on the "I" (see Pss. 77:1-6). In the face of intense suffering, it is hard to look out-side oneself. Job looks to death...to bring him tranquility and rest. (p. 16)

Though Job refrains from cursing God for his fate, he curses the day on which he was born and the night he was conceived. He seeks relief and release from his suffering in a speedy death.

At this point in the narrative, we see and hear the parade of friends--Eliphaz, Bildad and Zophar--who are chagrined by Job's anger and refusal to accept his plight and by his demands for divine explanation. Instead of offering sympathy and consolation, they try to explain God/dess' action and serve as defense attorneys for God/dess against Job's attempt to force God/dess to explain and justify his/her actions.

Job will have none of their explanations or justifications and counters their arguments with a defense of his goodness. Though the arguments and counter-arguments get a bit repetitious throughout the three cycles of speeches (and especially with the young Elihu's long-winded diatribe against Job and the other "old men"), there is, nevertheless, a beauty and intensity to the poetry and momentary wisdom in this part of the book.

Job grows increasingly impatient with his friends, who continue to justify God's actions and are appalled by Job's questioning of God's judgment. He wants and demands explanation of the Almighty. He seeks an advocate who will represent and defend him before the heavenly court so his name and person will be cleared:

> "Oh, that I had one to hear my case, and that my accuser would write out his indictment!" (31:35) "My justice I maintain and I will not relinquish it; my heart does not reproach me for any of my days." (27:6)

There is a brief interlude in chapter 28, the Poem on Wisdom. As mentioned earlier, this poem is a later addition to the book and serves mainly as a pause, or an editorial aside, to allow the reader a rest from the dialogue of the three speech cycles.

With chapters 29 to 31, Job rests his case after enumerating all the ways in which he is not guilty and not deserving of the punishment he has received. He acquits himself of falsehood and deceit (31:5-8); exploitation of the land (31:38-40); lust and adultery (31:1, 9-12); violating rights of servants (31:13-15); hardheartedness against the poor and needy (31:16-23); idolatry (31:24-28); cursing and hatred of enemies (31:29-30); breach of hospitality (31:31-32); and hypocrisy (31:33-34).

Besides the calamities and losses he has endured, it is the accusations and withdrawal of his friends and the silence of God in not answering his soul-searching questions that are the source of Job's most intense suffering. "What are my faults and my sins? My misdeeds and my sins make known to me! Why do you hide your face and consider me your enemy?" (13:23-24) In the Hebrew text, this verse contains a pun--Job ('iyyob) is being treated as God's enemy (ôyeb). This loss of intimacy from the God/dess and friends is unbearable for Job or anyone who suffers.

Before Job receives a divine response to his questions, Elihu, son of Barachel the Buzite, has been biding his time to answer Job and the three older men. In chapters 32-37, Elihu concludes that God owes no one an explanation (37:23) and if an explanation were given, we would still not understand. Elihu emphasizes God's transcendence and inaccessibility to the human mind to know and understand. "Lo, God is great beyond our knowledge; the number of his years is past searching out." (36:26)

With the opening of chapter 38, God/dess surprises all of the characters and addresses Job out of the whirlwind. Instead of pro-viding answers, it is now God/dess' turn to interrogate Job and his friends--"Where were you when I founded the earth?" The Almighty continues with a litany of questions about nature, its creation and the inability of humanity to understand and control the natural order.

Job is humbled, as we see in Chapter 40:1-5 and again in 42:1-6--"I have dealt with great things that I do not understand; things too wonderful for me, which I cannot know."

Throughout the book, Job seeks for answers but only gets more questions. In fact, the Book of Job is a book of questions-- questions posed by the actors in the story and those posed by each reader of every generation.

This surfeit of questions and the paucity of answers leaves many readers of the Book of Job unsatisfied and starved for more definite guidance around the issues of the role of God/dess in the universe, the purpose of evil and suffering and God/dess' relationship to the dark side of life. What Job does is to toss the reader back into the abyss of mystery--a mystery at once awesome and consoling.

The true wisdom of Job is the absence of easy answers; in fact, it is the direct rejection of the easy answers posed by Eliphaz, Bildad and Zophar. The book challenges each reader to plumb more deeply into the nature of the deity, of evil and suffering, of faith, hope, patience and humility. We are forced to examine the nature of friendship and compassionate "presence" when someone is in pain.

Is it at all helpful to say, "It's God/dess' will; who are we to question it?" Is the universe dealing with a sadistic God/dess, or, as Rabbi Kushner suggests, a less than all powerful One who is incapable of altering the evolving course of the universe? Does the God/dess as the ground of being, to use Paul Tillich's phrase, subsume within her/himself what we refer to as goodness and evil?

If the God/dess is the all-in-all, the Alpha and Omega, does s/he not then possess both darkness and light? Can anything be said to be separate from or "other than" the God/dess? Are any of us really alone in our suffering, and how do friends and loved ones best serve us in our darker days? Where is the God/dess when we suffer?

SOME AFTERTHOUGHTS

To assist you in your own exploration of these "cosmic" questions, a bibliography and a reader/discussion guide has been appended to the conclusion of this essay.

While I do not wish to impose my insights from my own wrestling with suffering and my meditations upon the Book of Job, I would like to share some tentative thoughts I have gleaned from the text and the extra-biblical reading I have done.

As the Book of Job so eloquently states and restates, the ways of the God/dess cannot be fully known by human understanding. To question and search for answers is natural to the human person. As the *National Enquirer* says: "Enquiring minds want to know!"

Nevertheless, the mystery of the infinite God/dess confounds human, finite cognition/rationality. What Job discovers is that silence is sometimes, maybe always, the only legitimate response to human suffering. What Job finds in his silence is God/dess present to him in the whirlwind. Emmanuel--God/dess with us--the transcendent, yet immanent One, walks with us in our suffering.

A popular, contemporary poem, "Footprints," explains the agony of feeling alone in one's suffering with this concluding observation: "My precious child, I love you and I would never leave you. During your times of trial and suffering, when you see only one set of footprints, it was then that I carried you."

We, the offspring of Job, see in the Cosmic Christ, the God/dess fully present--at the crossroad of the suffering and incompleteness of the cosmos. As Paul so eloquently puts it in his letter to the Romans:

> The created universe is waiting
> with eager expectation for God's
> children to be revealed. It was
> made subject to frustration, not of
> its own choice but by the will of
> the One who subjected it, yet with
> hope that the universe itself is to
> be freed from the shackles of
> mortality and is to enter upon the
> glorious liberty of the children of
> God. Up to the present, as we
> know, the whole created universe
> in all its parts groans as if in the
> pangs of childbirth. (Rom. 8:19-
> 22)

The God/dess, too, experiences the suffering, incompleteness, tension, conflict and paradox of a creation still waiting to be born.

If, then, the answer to the "why" of suffering, evil, darkness and death eludes us, perhaps we need to focus on the "what." What is the human response to the unavoidability of suffering? To be who we are, made in the image and likeness of the God/dess, to be present to our own and others' pain in silent compassion, forgiveness, mercy and love.

Ours is not to judge, defend or explain the suffering to the afflicted person as Eliphaz, Bildad, Zophar and Elihu attempted. Rather, by being humbly present to the suffering servant (Isaiah 42-55), the Christ, we find the God/dess. For it is in suffering love (what Mohandas Gandhi referred to as "ahimsa") that the human and divine are joined and made one.

The timelessness/timeliness of the Book of Job lies in its ability to engage us in that perpetual struggle with the ultimately unanswerable question of "Why?"

It is my invitation and hope that this essay will motivate you to continue the lifelong wrestling with Job, yourself and your God/dess.

BIBLIOGRAPHY

The following books are a sampling of the resources available for your personal, scholarly and spiritual wrestling with the text and meaning of the Book of Job. Also check any general bible commentaries (Anchor, Interpreter's, Peake's, Jerome, etc.). Additional studies on the themes of suffering, evil, anger with God and wisdom are listed below the more explicit commentaries.

Cox, D., *The Triumph of Impotence: Job and the Tradition of the Absurd*, (Analecta Gregoriana), Universita Gregoriana Editrice, 1978.

Duquoc, C. and C. Floristan (eds.), *Job and the Silence of God*, (Concilium, No. 169), The Seabury Press and T. & T. Clark, 1983.

Eaton, J.H., *Job*, (Old Testament Guides), Journal for the Study of the Old Testament Press, 1985.

Gerber, Israel J., *Job on Trial: A Book for our Time*, Gastonia, NC: E.P. Press, P.O. Box 1172, Gastonia, NC 28052, 1982.

Girard, Rene, *Job: The Victim of His People*, Stanford, CA: Stanford University Press, 1987.

Gibson, John, C.L. *Job*, Philadelphia: Westminster Press (The Daily Study Bible Guide), 1985.

Glatzer, Nahum N. (ed.), *The Dimensions of Job: A Study and Selected Readings*, New York: Schocken Books, 1969.

Gordis, Robert, *The Book of God and Man: A Study of Job*, Chicago: University of Chicago Press, 1965.

Guinan, Michael D., O.F.M., *Job, Collegeville Bible Commentary*, No. 19, Collegeville, MN: The Liturgical Press, 1986.

Hone, Ralph E. (ed.), *The Voice Out of the Whirlwind: The Book of Job*, San Francisco, CA: Chandler Publishing Company, Inc., 1960.

Job, John, *Job Speaks to Us Today*, Atlanta, GA: John Knox Press, 1977.

Jones, Edgar, *The Triumph of Job*, London: SCM Press Ltd., 1966.

Sanders, Paul S. (ed.), *Twentieth Century Interpretations of the Book of Job, A Collection of Critical Essays*, Englewood Cliffs, NJ: Prentice-Hall, Inc., 1968.

Snaith, Norman H., *The Book of Job: Its Origins and Purpose*, Naperville, IL: Alec R. Allenson, Inc., 1968.

Vawter, Bruce, *Job and Jonah: Questioning the Hidden God*, New York: Paulist Press, 1983.

Zerafa, Peter P., O.P., *The Wisdom of God in the Book of Job*, Rome: Herder, 1978.

Studies

Burnell, S. Jocelyn, *Broken for Life*, London: Quaker Home Service, Swarthmore Lecture, 1989.

Fortunato, John E., *AIDS the Spiritual Dilemma*, San Francisco, CA: Harper & Row, Publishers, Perennial Library, 1987.

Jung, Carl G., *Answer to Job*, English Translation, Routledge and Kegan Paul, 1954.

Kahn, J.H., *Job's Illness: Loss, Grief and Integration, A Psychological Interpretation*, Pergamon Press, 1975.

Kushner, Harold S., *When Bad Things Happen to Good People*, New York: Avon Books, 1981.

MacLeish, Archibald, *J.B., A Play in Verse*, Samuel French, Inc., 1956.

Sanford, John A., *Evil: The Shadow Side of Reality*, New York: Crossroad. 1981.

REVIEW AIDS AND DISCUSSION TOPICS

Prepared by Michael D. Guinan, O.F.M.
Collegeville Bible Commentary #19
Copyright © 1986 by The Liturgical Press.
Reprinted by permission.

Introduction

1. The Book of Job is considered one of the masterpieces of world literature. What basis is there for this appeal?

2. Reading and studying an ancient writing can present problems to the modern reader. What problems would it be well to keep in mind?

I

Job 1:1-2:13 Prologue

1. Are there any dangers of reading later theological ideas back into our text?

2. What question does the Satan raise about Job? Is it a fair question? Why might God have gone along with this test?

3. Does Job's response strike you at all strange? Do his words and actions ring true to human experience?

II

Job 3:1-16 Job's Monologue: Lamentation

1. What is lamentation? Are we today comfortable with this dimension of biblical prayer, or are we more like Job's friends?

2. How did ancient mythology characteristically describe the forces of chaos and destruction? Do these symbols still

have evocative power (for example, Moby Dick, Jaws)?

3.   Do you find anything in Job's lament to be ^@too much"? Apparently the friends did; what might this be?

III

Job 4:1-14:22 First Round of Speeches

1.   In the first speech Eliphaz makes several points that will recur in the discussion. What are they? Does he strike you as a kind person? His speech shows elements typical of wisdom and some very atypical. What are they?

2.   The friends share a view of human nature. What is it? Does it seem to you to be adequate?

3.   Do the friends try at all to get into Job's shoes, or do they try to get him into theirs? What is Job's view of friendship? Do you agree?

4.   What view of the afterlife is reflected in the book? Do we face any danger if we read it with Christian eyes?

5.   Wisdom is based on experience--our own and that of others. Does Bildad show himself to be wise? Unwise? Both?

6.   Job uses extensive legal imagery. Does this tell us anything of his experience and disposition? Are there any problems with using this imagery in this situation?

7.   Job sharply rebukes his friends. (13:7-9) Do you think that we religious people today need to hear this as well? How might we err in this regard?

IV

Job 15:1-21:34 Second Round of Speeches

1.   A recurring theme in these chapters is the fate of the wicked. What do the friends say? How does Job respond?

2.   Feeling alone and forsaken, Job longs for someone to stand with him and vindicate him. (19:23-29) Has he felt this way before? Have you ever felt the same way?

V

Job 22:1-27:21 Third Round of Speeches

1.   Job is accused of particularly serious crimes. What are these? Are they still valid today? Do we evaluate them as seriously as the Old Testament does?

2.   The argument from creation is made in chapter 26. Does it occur elsewhere in the book? Does it have any validity? Does not a study of nature today (science) lead to atheism?

VI

Job 28:1-28 Poem on Wisdom

1.   What are the themes of this poem? Does it comment on the discussion so far?

2.   Where is wisdom and how do we begin to find it? Has Job been on the right path?

VII

Job 29:1-31:37 Job's Monologue: He Rests His Case

1.   Job has experienced God's blessing. What does this mean and how was it manifested? Are any cultural differences operating here? How might Job phrase it if he were speaking today?

2.   Lament frequently speaks of the self, to God and about enemies. How is this reflected in these chapters?

3.   In chapter 31 Job presents an impressive description of the moral life. Is anything important left out? Would you add anything? How might we phrase and apply these today?

VIII

Job 32:1-37:24 Elihu's Speech

1.   Have you ever met anyone like Elihu? How did you react?
        How do you think Job reacted?

IX

Job 38:1-42:6 The Yahweh Speeches

1.   Yahweh refers to the natural world and the animal world.
        What points are being made?

2.   Job modifies his stance from that in chapter 31. How?
        What does it mean?

3.   Do you think these speeches reply to Job's problem?

X

Job 42:7-17 Epilogue

1.   Do you think the epilogue is an anticlimax? Does it spoil
        the effect of the book?

XI

The Meaning of the Book

1.   What answers are offered for the suffering of the innocent?
        Do these contain any truth, or are they all oversimplified?
        Do you think that this is where the main emphasis of the
        book lies?

2.   How might we distinguish a problem from a mystery?
        Which is suffering? How does the idea of "relationship" fit
        in?

3.   Through the course of the book both Job and God change.

How? Might there be a sense in which God as well as Job
can be called "an innocent sufferer"?

4.   Job has been compared to both tragedy and to comedy. In
        what ways? Which relates more to the book we have?

5.   The issue of Job's speech has been constant throughout the
        book, and in the end he is praised precisely for his speech.
        What has he said to merit this? In what ways can he be a
        model for us today in situations of distress?

6.   What models of friendship are offered in the book? Could
        the friendship between God and Job have been maintained
        without Job's "correct" speech?

BIOGRAPHICAL SKETCH

Joseph A. Izzo has been a member of the Friends Meeting
of Washington since 1982. Formerly a member of a Roman
Catholic Brotherhood for seventeen years, he earned a Master's
degree in Religious Studies from LaSalle University in Philadelphia
in 1978. He also earned a Master of Social Work degree from
Howard University in 1989. For the last four years, he has been a
Health Educator with the Whitman-Walker Clinic in Washington,
D.C. In this role, he has been intimately involved with the AIDS
crisis as a counselor and prevention educator. In the summer of
1988, he was a plenary speaker at Friends General Conference in
Boone, North Carolina, where he addressed the topic, "Beyond the
Plague: Claiming Courage, Healing and Love in the AIDS Crisis."
It was partly as a consequence of that experience that he began to
reexamine the Book of Job and how it can speak to our present
condition.

IX

Dangerous Memory:
The Bible as a Cloud of Witnesses Claiming our Lives for God

Herb Lape

[Note: Herb Lape teaches at Friends Academy in Locust Valley, New York, and has been Clerk of nearby Matinecock Meeting. He was also a founding member of the Full Court Gospel Fellowship.]

I would like to begin by telling some family stories that I hope will help illustrate the theme of this workshop--"Dangerous Memory: The Bible as a Cloud of Witnesses Reclaiming our Lives for God."

Using a Biblical image, my family can best be described as a family of faith, not biology. My wife and I were both previously married, and she brought two children, a boy and a girl who were 10 and 6 when we married 7 years ago, creating an instant family. Three years ago we adopted a baby boy.

In many ways it was the Bible that brought my wife and I together, we both began to see in these stories a vision of the world that both made sense of the brokeness of our lives and gave hope about new beginnings. Sin and redemption, the crucifixion and the resurrection became truths that we saw being reenacted in our own lives. The numerous Biblical stories of broken families have sustained our faith and our family. The memory and example of Joseph as the ultimate stepfather has surely stengtened me in times of doubt.

Anyone who is a parent knows that you can't give your children religious faith, but you can give them stories, a Biblical memory, of heroic figures who have squarely faced the pain and tragedy in this world and yet kept their "eyes on the prize". You can hope that these stories will help them remember, in the words of Whittier, that "although the wrong seems oft so strong, God is the ruler yet". Through family prayer, Bible reading and required attendance at meeting for worship we try to give our children a religious memory and hopefully communicate the importance of God in binding together both our fragile family of faith and the fragile world at large.

The difficulty of this task, especially since the two oldest are now teenagers, was recently brought home again. Our youngest, the three year old, loves to have stories read to him. Of course, we use this love to occasionally pick out Bible stories, to supplement the secular classics of Curious George, Babar the Elephant and Dr. Seuss. He also loves music and frequently listens to the star of children's music, Raffi.

Not long ago, Nathan and I we were listening to Raffi sing his version of the spiritual "Daniel in the Lion's Den". I'm sure he has heard this song many times before, but this time it clicked. For this three year old, there is nothing scarier or more exciting, at least if you are securely sitting next to your daddy, than lions. The story of this man Daniel being thrown into a lion's den, praying to God and then having God send an angel down to lock the lion's jaw so they couldn't eat Daniel up, seized his imagination.

Again and again, I had to play the song as we sang along and learned it; and then, to avoid having to sing again, I asked him if he wanted me to read him the story. I opened our Children's Bible to the story and there was a great picture of Daniel in the den surrounded by scary lions.

His eyes popped-"read, Daddy read!!" And then the "why" questions as the three year-old mind tries to comprehend. Why was Daniel in the lion's den? Why did they throw him in? And then the usual moral sorting out of who's good and who's bad. (This is actually a little difficult in this story, since King Darius is good but forced to throw Daniel by his evil advisors in order to uphold his law. Try explaining this moral complexity to a 3 year old.)

Anyway, as three year olds are wont to do, he became

obsessed with this story for about a week. Everyone in the family had to read it to him again and again. The same questions over and over. And then since we were reading from the Children's Bible he became interested in other pictures and other stories.

I could tell that his teenage brother and sister were becoming a little uneasy with this fixation when they began suggesting that they read him more secular pieces like Dr. Seuss, but you know how three-year olds are about their reading material. He wanted nothing but the Bible. The older two are at the age where religion and the Bible are definitely not cool, which of course is a matter of some tension in our family since we still require them to attend meeting despite their sound arguments that this will only make them rebel and leave religion behind when they are free to decide for themselves.

The tensions came to a head at an evening meal during this period of Nathan's obsession. We alternate between a silent blessing, the Johnny Appleseed Song, and a spoken blessing as the spirit moves. This particular evening, my wife offered a vocal prayer and Nathan joined in! This was too much for the older two. I can't remember who spoke first, but it didn't matter since they were united in their testimony, "You are brainwashing him! He is never going to be able to grow up and think for himself. He's going to turn into a 'nerd' or become another Jim Bakker!"

It is a very serious matter in this culture to be accused of brainwashing and stifling a person's ability to think for himself. My response was an all-too-typical defensively flip parental reply-"Yeah! I'd rather have him brainwashed by us than by someone else."

I relate this story because it illustrates the focus of this workshop as well as my central concerns as both a parent and teacher of young people. Put crassly, it is this: Who is doing the brainwashing? We hear so much from our culture about how kids should be taught to think for themselves. Even more, kids hear this message so often that they all know well how to use it, and do use it with parents, teachers and other adults in their lives who ask them to do things that they would prefer not to do.

As parents we have tried to expose our children to Biblical

stories, images, and music that we believe accurately describe the world as it is--a beautiful gift from a loving God, broken by human sin and willfulness and yet redeemed by those heroic figures, like Daniel, who will not bow their knee to a man made god but work instead with God's help to make this world as it was intended to be in the beginning.

And yet as parents, shaped by this book, we have also been taught to see clearly that there are other stories, images, and music dedicated to very different gods and values that shape the imaginations of our kids which we can challenge but not eliminate.

Let me tell another family story that illustrates this point. Several years ago when my eldest son was around 13, my wife bribed him to attend a religious gathering, as a birthday present to her. It focused on the peer pressures that make it difficult for young people to keep their faith in a secular consumer culture.

The speaker was very good.   He focused on the development of a youth culture that seems increasingly dedicated to creating stories, images and music that stimulate universal passions of materialism, sex, narcissism, and immediate gratification of desire as the goal and purpose of the "good life."

We are all aware of this these stories. Beer commercials that portray a very seductive image of attractive young people having a good time with plenty of beer flowing. "The night was made for Michelob," we are told, and no party is complete without Budweiser's party animal Spuds MacKensie!

Is it any wonder that at our school, unchaperoned parties with lots of beer following, just like the commercial, have become the norm? And of course, Master Card proclaims that the end of boredom is a "carefree" spending spree. Ads consistently portray powerful images of expensive cars, clothing, entertainment, etc., that all seem to drive home a message that if you want to live the good life you are going to need lots of money.

The speaker also pointed out the powerful influence of music, which despite some positive influences also seems to promote the celebration and satisfaction of desire as the goal of life. For example, last year's Grammy-winning album of the year was George Michael's album, titled *Faith*.

That sounds even encouraging until you realize that the number one selling hit single from this album was a piece called, "I Want Your Sex".   Now that is a hymn to a different faith than that celebrated in the Bible.

One of the most thought-provoking parts of the presentation was how celebrities have replaced heroes in our culture. The Bible is full of heroes and heroines who set aside their own self desires in order to serve humanity. Their story inspires us to similar sacrifice and service, but our media is full of stories of the lifestyles of the rich and famous--celebrities who have dedicated their lives in many cases to the pursuit of personal desire--money, power, and sex.

Stand at the grocery check out counter and read about the excesses of the rich and famous, Lady Di's flirting, Rob Lowe's video exploits with teenage girls, and then realize that this dirt only adds to the fame and fortune of these celebrities. And of course Donald Trump regularly appears on the teenage list of most admired people.

In conclusion, our speaker urged young people of religious faith to realize that they lived in an alien and often hostile world in which they needed to support one another.

I am afraid that my son was a little too young to have gotten as much out of it as we had hoped, but the presentation had a big impact on me. At the end of the meeting we stopped at a local mall, so I could buy an all-too-typical last minute birthday present for my wife. I have never been a big fan of malls, but when you procrastinate as I do and have to get something in a hurry, I end up in the mall--the spirit is willing, the flesh is weak.

It is also important for the purposes of this story to know that I teach a Medieval history class in which I emphasize the importance of the medieval cathedral as the central public building in that culture, symbolizing its hopes and vision. In an effort to get my students reflecting on our own cultural values, I ask them to identify public buildings serving the same function today. Invariably they identify two types of buildings--the Mall and the sports arena.

As a result of these conversations, when students tell me that they hung out at the Mall over the weekend, I tease them with charges of idolatry--"You mean you worshiped at the cathedral of modern America; you sacrificed your dollars at the Temple of Desire."

Perhaps because of my overactive Biblical imagination, going to the mall has become associated in my mind with Canaanite Baal worship and fertility rites. And yet because of my poor planning and general laziness, here I was with my 13 year-old son going to the mall right after hearing an uplifting speech about the snares of the commercial culture and the need for people of religious faith to keep themselves pure.

Feeling guilty I was hoping to make a quick purchase so that neither God nor one of my students would see my weakness and accuse me of hypocrisy and idolatry.

Unfortunately, somebody had other ideas. As we entered Macy's department store an attractive young woman approached me with a free sample of a product she was advertising. "Would you like to try some 'Obsession' for Men"? she said innocently.

In another class that I teach on ethics, I get students to bring in advertising images. As a result I knew that this Calvin Klein product advertises itself with a photo of a flesh pile of naked female bodies with a simple picture of the fragrance bottle and its named 'Obsession for Men'.

I would like to say that I don't notice these ads, but I do-- again, "the spirit is willing, the flesh is weak". I have tried to get my students to question the blatant use of sex to sell products. While some respond, many shrug their shoulders and say that's the way things are. Sex sells and selling is the bottom line. It's moral if it sells in the market place. People do not have to look or buy if they are offended.

Anyway, back to the mall. Crisis of decision. Suddenly this no doubt innocent young woman, simply trying to make a few extra dollars, was transformed by my Biblical imagination into a Jezebel, a high priestess seeking to baptize me as I entered into Macy's, the inner sanctum, the holy of holies of this Temple of Desire.

I stood in stunned silence while images of prophetic challenge went through my mind. How would Isaiah, Jeremiah, or George Fox have responded? Isaiah went naked as a sign of Israel's spiritual poverty. Fox rolled up his pants and walked barefoot through the town of Litchfield in midwinter declaring, "Woe unto you Babylon ...."

Wasn't God calling me to make some similar response. Well....Nothing came, and as I continued to wait I could feel the alarmed presence of my son and a look on his face that had a much clearer message than any thing I could get from God. "Come on Dad," it said silently, "please don't embarrass me!!" It's a good thing that Fox and others did not travel in the ministry with their children!

Anyway, I simply told the woman no thank you and meekly walked off.

As a postscript, I was watching the TV a few days later and another perfume ad summed up my experience. It was a simple picture of a blue perfume bottle with the name 'Decadence' written on it. The voice simply said--"Decadence. Now at Macy's!!" Amen!!

I come back to the question of who is brainwashing the youth of America?--the Biblical stories of the various religious traditions or a powerful commercial culture of tv, movies, and rock music?

Put in less sensational terms--who is shaping the imaginations of our youth and thus shaping their sense of how the world is and to what ends are human actions oriented? Who are the role models? Talk to teachers, especially religion teachers, and they will tell you that few students have a Biblical memory. It's the commercial culture that shapes their vision of the world.

It is my thesis that we need to recover a living connection to the Bible because it can be a dangerous memory that calls the culture of this world into question. It can help us once again see that we have become slaves in the fleshpots of Egypt.

More importantly it can give us the faith to come out of Egypt and enter again into the wilderness, in the faith that our God will give us a cloud to lead us by day and a fire to lead us by night. We can become again as Abraham who left family, friends, job and culture behind to travel to an unknown land that God had promised.

Through this rich memory Fox and other early Friends were able to see the socio/political/religious system of his day as idolatry. In the even richer language of the Book of Revelations, he identified this system with the whore of Babylon, bedecked with jewels from draining the wealth of the poor, fornicating with the beast while drinking the blood of martyrs.

Fox and others frequently referred to the Quaker movement as the Lamb's War, fought of course with spiritual weapons, the shield of faith and the sword of the spirit, against this reincarnation of Babylon in 17th Century England.   Theirs was clearly a dangerous Biblical memory that turned the world upside down.

But we must be careful to recognize another less positive way that the Bible can be a dangerous memory. We know that its stories, memory and vision can be used to further tremendous evil and injustice in the name of God.   Religious intolerance, racism, sexism, homophobia, the rape of the earth and many other injustices have all been at one time or other been justified by appeal to Biblical memory.

One need only reflect on the image of the cross burning Ku Klux Klan, the Aryan Brotherhood's attempt to include *Mein Kampf* in the Bible as the key interpretive book, the Afrikaners' appeal to Hebrew stories of keeping oneself separate from the heathen Canaanites to justify apartheid, or Jewish settlers pushing Palestinians from the promised lands of Judea and Samaria, to understand and fear the use of Biblical memory for destructive ends.

Because of this type of destructive dangerous memory, the great modern temptation has been an attempt to construct a spirituality or philosophy of life that does not need a memory to help young people make moral decisions. This quotation from an advice column in *Seventeen Magazine* on sex is typical of this attempt:

"Deciding whether or not to have sex is a very personal thing--based on your and his unique feelings and values. Some people feel that they need to be fully grown up and independent before having sex. Some normal, loving people choose not to be sexually active until they are married. In any case it is a decision that requires careful consideration of your goals individually and as a couple." (December 1987)

But goals are very much related to vision and vision is shaped by images and stories. I think that evidence is becoming overwhelmingly clear that this kind of message of individual decision making is of little help when young people are surrounded by a commercial commercially exploitative sexual messages.

It should be clear to many that what I am saying about young people could also be said about a religious community like us. It is tempting to hope that we can construct a spirituality that does not need a communal memory of stories and images. As I have previously mentioned, a Biblical memory can be dangerous in a negative sense (divisive, rigid, etc.) but it should also be clear from what I have said that an even greater danger is to have no memory at all, and thus fall prey to having ourselves and certainly or children be shaped by stories that understand the 'good life' in very different ways than we would like.

In conclusion, I believe that the great task before us as Quakers is to recover our positive understanding of the Bible as a Dangerous Memory. I believe that we need to see our individual situation, that of our meetings, and that of the world in which we live through the vision that this memory reveals, and labor with one another to make sure that this memory is dangerous in the positive, not negative sense.

X

Four Aspects Of Productive Bible Study: A Summary

By Patty Levering

[Note: Patty Levering lives in Davidson, North Carolina, where she is assistant director of an enrichment program for black high school students. She attends Davidson Worship Group, which she helped found. Her curriculum, Disciplines For Discipleship, has just been published by the Christian Board of Publication, a cooperative program which includes Friends General Conference. In 1985-86 Patty was Meeting Ministries Secretary for Friends United Meeting. She is a graduate of Duke University and the Earlham School of Religion.]

ONE: ATTITUDES USEFUL FOR PRODUCTIVE BIBLE STUDY

1. Understand the author's worldview and look for what the author really says.

2. Avoid being critical of the author for not approaching the issue the way you would expect a writer to today. (The Bible does not conform to Twentieth Century historical or scientific standards!)

3. Understand the experience behind the ideas. The best way of understanding this may not be intellectual but experiential, connecting your own experience with that of the author.

4. Avoid the notion that there is one right way to interpret a passage. That is, what you learned about a particular passage in the past may not be the only way to understand that passage. If you can turn loose of a fixed idea about it, especially if the idea is one you can't accept, you may get new insights.

5. Interpretation is affected by our culture. Be aware of cultural biases. Bring questions from your experience and knowledge to see if there is something in the text that you may have not noticed before.

6. Let the text interpret you. Allow yourself to be challenged, to have your assumptions challenged, and to receive something new.

7. Read the Bible. Find out what is really there. See the complexity, the paradoxes, and the rich portrait of the reality of human existence with its ups and downs.

TWO: SOME APPROACHES TO UNDERSTANDING SCRIPTURE

1. Use "authorities," such as commentaries, Bible dictionaries, textbooks, scholarly articles, study guides that emphasize information. William Barclay's commentaries are particularly helpful in providing background information for non-scholars. The *Interpreter's Bible* has been a standard commentary for years, and *The Interpreter's Dictionary of the Bible* is a most informative source. The advantage of using this approach is that authorities provide background information, word definitions, and a scholar's carefully developed insights. Some preconceptions about the text may be modified and more openness to what the text has to say may develop from an effort to understand scripture through authorities.

The problem with authorities is that each one approaches scripture with questions that were important and assumptions that were held at the particular time the work was written. For example, commentaries written in the 1950s will not mention or consider the significant questions raised more recently by feminist biblical scholars. To use an authority also puts the reader in danger of thinking a passage has only one meaning.

2. Study, based on careful examination of the text, its words and context. (See "Bible Study Guidelines.")

3. Meditate on scripture. (See "Guidelines for Meditating on Scripture.")

4. Use of arts--crayons, clay, pipe cleaners, drama.

This approach has been developed and taught by Walter Wink, "Transformational Bible Study," and probably by others. Look for study guides that include these possibilities. The arts are particularly useful in studying story passages.

THREE: BIBLE STUDY GUIDELINES

1. Understand what the author is saying.

Put aside your preconceived notions about the text.

Look carefully at the words, relationship of words/ sentences/ideas.

Watch for repetition.

Compare translations.

Note context of passage.

Define key words.

Observe what the author is doing.

2. Interpret the author's meaning.

What was the purpose of the author?

For whom was the biblical portion written?

What are general truths and what are truths specific to a particular situation?

What is the relation of the truths found in a particular passage to the whole message of the Bible (or to a larger context within the Bible)?

How objective are you? Beware of cultural biases, personal prejudices, and too much reliance on what others have said the passage means.

3. Evaluate what the author says.
    What is the significance of the studied material?

    How does what the author says compare with your experience?

FOUR: GUIDELINES FOR MEDITATING ON SCRIPTURE

I. MEDITATING ON SCRIPTURE

1. Choose a passage. Read it over carefully, or have someone read it aloud to you. Choose a verse, phrases or a word that catches your attention.

2. Close your eyes and relax. Repeat the chosen verse, phrase, or word over and over and over until you are quiet inside. If the verse or phrase is too long, use a suitable portion of it to focus on.

3. After settling down with the scripture portion, begin to think about it in as many ways as come to you. (What are its possible meanings? Why did it catch your attention? What about it relates to what is going on in you or your life now? What experience might the writer have had that contributed to what was written? etc.) Let your thoughts flow freely and follow them where they go.

4. If you find yourself being distracted, let the distraction happen and then let it go. Don't worry about it. If you need to refocus, repeat the scripture again.

5. When you have thought about the scripture enough, simply let it go. Turn it over to God and get quiet. Let the Word speak to you and shape you.

6. Close the meditation period with a brief prayer.

7. You may want to carry the scripture in the back of your

consciousness for a while, especially if you think that it has more to reveal to you.

II. MEDITATING WITH THE IMAGINATION

1. Pick a parable of Jesus, another Bible story, or a passage that creates a scene.

2. Put aside all you have been taught about this passage. Expect to experience something new.

3. Pray that the Holy Spirit will speak to you through the passage.

4. Read the passage and listen for something you may not have noticed before. (Read it aloud, have someone read it to you, tape record it and play it back, or read a different Bible translation.)

5. Close your eyes and imagine that you are in the story or scene. Picture yourself as one of the characters in the story or as someone involved in what is being said. Picture yourself as that person through the whole story or passage. Let your imagination flow freely. If something that happens or is said in the passage catches your attention, you may want to stay with that idea or scene.

6. Remember that if something troubling occurs in your imagining, you may add a helper to what you are imagining. You may want to invite Jesus or Wisdom or the Divine as you experience it into your picture.

7. Ponder the story in your heart. Allow who you are to be shaped by the Word.

8. Return from your imagination to reality. Notice where you are and what is around you. Return to the present moment and what it calls for. If the story seems to have more to reveal to you, you may want to continue to let it come to mind off and an during the week as long as it continues to speak to you.

XI

Studying The Book Of Revelation

by David Martin

[Note: David Martin is the father of three children, married to Kate Mewhinney. They live in Winston-Salem, N.C. He is a member of Friendship Monthly Meeting, North Carolina Yearly Meeting (Conservative). He earns his living as a stonemason.]

The Revelation of John is the last book of the New Testament canon and a book that many avoid if at all possible. Some find it so difficult that they ignore it, while for many others it is used as a prooftest for their own views of the present and the future, to identify the Anti-Christ, to date the second coming of Jesus Christ and the end of the age.

Luther felt that the book should be excluded from the New Testament canon because few could understand it. Even some early Church fathers found it embarrassing after Constantine and wanted it excluded. But it remained and it is there for our use, reminding us of the days when the Church was under deadly attack.

The Book was probably written sometime around 95 AD, during the reign of the mad but shrewd Roman Emperor Domitian. Caesar worship had existed for a long time but had pretty much been ignored except during Nero's time. All subjects of Rome were required to go annually to the shrine of Roma and worship the emperor who had been deified. It was simple--you placed a pinch of incense on the glowing charcoal and simply said, "Caesar is Lord". For this you received a certificate stating that you had performed your duty.

It sounds so very simple, but believers of the Way could not bow their knee and declare someone other than Christ Lord.

It was a dangerous and deadly time. Your next door neighbor, while coveting your cattle or other property, might well turn you in. The member of the synagogue where you used to worship could slyly whisper in the ear of an official, and the next thing you knew they were at your door looking for this year's certificate.

Christians were fed to the lions, mothers were crucified with their live children hung upside down from their necks, all because they would not bow their knees and say three words. Terrible prices were paid for deep devotion and loyalty to Jesus Christ.

I would like to share with you how I came to lead this workshop and how I prepared for it. In First Month 1989 I was asked to lead a local bible study and told I could choose a topic. I chose the book of Revelation because I knew so little about it. I have always avoided the book, and when I tried to read it, at about Chapter Four my head started swooning and I set it down. Though I read the New Testament systematically, I could not remember anything save the "I stand at the door..." quote which I had memorized as a youth. It was like throwing myself into the deep end of the pool to teach myself to swim.

I purchased two very big notebooks and two Bibles, from which I cut out the last book. Then I pasted a page from Revelation upon the left hand side of each notebook, using the remainder of that page and the opposite page to the right for notes.

Then I started reading commentaries--eventually seven in all.

During all of this I was also reading the book of the Revelation to John, in various ways: I read it a chapter at a time, then two chapters at a time. I read it at one sitting, then moved to reading it meditatively. I read it slow, then fast, and then out loud. I bought a tape and listened to it, and had someone read it to me.

During all of this the Friends Bible Conference people were in touch and we agreed to deal with the Book of Revelation in Philadelphia too.

Now for me, the book is divided into three sections. First comes the greeting and the letters to the seven churches. The last section, the last two chapters, deals with the New Jerusalem. This leaves 17 chapters in the middle which I call the great conflict chapters.

In the first section, there are seven churches, as seven is the perfect number biblically speaking. Then we have seven letters to the Church as a whole. When reading these seven letters, think not so much about the specific church, but let the words speak to you: become the Church. Let these words speak to you.

Commentaries are nice and useful--how else could I feel, having read seven of them on one book of the Bible? It is helpful, for example, to know that Laodicea was a medical center that produced a world famous and much sought after eye ointment; that its citizens were noted for their beautiful woolen garments; and that as a banking center, coins were struck from the smelted gold there in the city.

Knowing this makes the statement in Rev. 3:17 that the Laodiceans are poor, blind and without covering more emphatic. That what they need is gold bought from Christ that they may be truly rich, and white garments that might cover their *real* nakedness. That what they need is to obtain from the lamb an ointment for their eyes that they might really see.

But having learned all of this and more I still had to ask myself If I was not lukewarm--neither hot nor cold but tepid. Tepid in a stylish way, surely, not to be singular for God's sake and appear peculiar to the world.

We are told that those Christ loves will be rebuked and disciplined. Is my demeanor such that will not let it happen--do I fear the love of God that brings with it correction and discipline?

I encourage thee, Friend, not to read those first three chapters as letters to seven churches that existed 1900 years ago--they are for thee and for me today. Read them in expectancy and wait to be opened to that.

Then we come to the middle section which I call the great conflict chapters. I would commend to you Douglas Gwyn's book *Apocalypse of the Word* and specifically Chapter 11. He will in turn lead you to Elizabeth Schussler-Fiorenze who has written at great length about these chapters and indeed the whole book. I would also recommend the Scotsman William Barclay, the current writer and commentator. These three people will do a much better job than I can in this short time in dealing with these chapters. But these few things I would share with you.

First was how it struck me so hard that it is GOD that is on the Throne. Was, is and always will be on the throne and at God's side is, was and will always be the Lamb, the victorious Lamb. If you are into God being dead and Christ as either a great mythical symbol or the ultimate in folklore imagery this will mean next to nothing. For those who were about to die in those early churches it must have been great and tender support to hear that still yet God is and was and will always be on the throne and at God's side is Jesus Christ.

Secondly it is the Lion of the Tribe of Judah, the Root of David, the Victorious Lamb that plays an active role. It is the son that loosens the Seals. Christ is an active force in the universe. Christ, the one who overcame, is an active player, not a possible observer.

And the last thing I want to point out is that God is not portrayed here as the celestial Mr. Rogers of the Divinities. God may love us just the way we are, but there are some expectations to measure up to, and if we choose to side with Babylon we will end up in big trouble--for instance the fiery pit.

I feel that this may be one of the reasons that current people have difficulty with this book. It does not say that you are OK and I am OK and that God is OK. If you side with Rome during the period of oppression you will not reign with Christ.

Accept your shortcomings and sinfulness, repent, lean on the active Christ; let him be your leading, kneel to the throne upon which God sits--period. This is not fashionable talk these days.

And now the last two chapters of the book. We could have a two day workshop just on these two chapters with forty eight verses. After the conflict in which God triumphs then comes down the new Jerusalem, the holy city. God dwells with God's people and will live with them. They will be God's people and he/she will be their God. There will be no more death, no crying, no Pain. God the holy parent will wipe the tears from their eyes. The old order is passed away.

Everything is made new. If you are thirsty and you have held firm in the faith--then water from the spring of life will be made available. For those who overcome God will be their Holy Parent and Christ the child. The actual quote in the KJV is, "I will be his God and he will be my son." (21:7) Not Moses, Abraham, Peter or Paul were called God's Son. Only David's son received such an honor (2Sam 7:24) and Christ Himself. (MT3:17)

But for the cowardly, the liars, the vile, the immoral, the sexually immoral there is the second death.

And in the last chapter we find the river flowing through the holy city and the tree of life for food and healing. When you read that, turn to Genesis 2:9: "And out of the ground made the Lord God to grow every tree that is pleasant to the sight, and good for food; the tree of life also in the midst of the garden...." We have come full circle and all that is missing is the tree of knowledge, for which now there is no need.

As well there is the throne of God and the Lamb that will be in the city and those who overcome and who held to the faith, the martyrs, will see God's face. "Blessed are the pure in heart, for they will see God." (MT5:8)

Well, there is much more but that much is up to you to deal with, for time is passing. Let me summarize my suggestions on how to study this most beautiful and precious book:

First you have to read and re-read it. Have it read out loud to you so that you can hear it as the first recipients did.

Then read some commentaries. Try *The Interpreter's Bible*,

available in most libraries.   I have mentioned Gwyn and do encourage you again to read his book. Read anyone and everyone; it will not hurt you.

Then quit, set aside the commentators.   Read the book again, through the heart and the soul. Wait upon the Lord to lead you in knowledge; then you will have opened to you what you need.

Now workshops participants noticed that I did not have my two big notebooks with me. Well, after at least six months of work, they were lost--maybe gone forever. In Philadelphia I opened my catalogue case which conveniently carried them and found, instead of the book of Revelation, annotated information bulletins on automotive fasteners.

Some poor automotive fastener salesman has at this time more information about the last book in the Bible than he would ever have wished for. They got switched on the airline.

After discovering this, the evening before the workshop, in some state of panic I walked through the cold late night. I sat down on a bench broken hearted. I just might fail, look foolish, not have anything to say, not be able to tell the participants what the golden lampstands are symbols of.

I must confess I had always a feeling of not completeness--like something was not quite full. But, horrors, here I was without my precious books that contained all the knowledge.

As I sat there in quiet expectant waiting I was filled with a presence that said to me--"I set before you at all times life and death--Choose life, though it may mean and will mean a death of one kind or another."

And there it was, the book of Revelation is about choosing. Which will it be, who will set upon the Throne?

Caesar worship is still alive today. The great conflict is not up there in the future, it is now, right around us. Will we side with Rome and Babylon, or will we be God's child doing God's will under the leadership of Christ?

The great conflict is now, in each of our lives, and the New Jerusalem is available here and now if we would choose. Christ has indeed come to his people; they need only to open the door and he will come in and they will commune together.

XII

Curriculum For First Day--To Be Or Not To Be

By Kate McCrone

[Note: *Kate McCrone edits a publication for deaf and hard-of-hearing high schoolers at Gallaudet University in Washington, D.C. Her curriculum on religious pacifism in action,* **We Minister With Christ,** *was published this spring. Kate is on the board of William Penn House, Washington's Quaker conference center. She and her two daughters live in Annapolis Maryland, and attend Annapolis Meeting.*

Last year I was privileged to take part in writing an ecumenical curriculum for Protestant denominations to use in religious education classes. The curriculum, in the format of a magazine entitled "Journey," will be published by the Christian Board Publications in St. Louis, Missouri, this spring.

I was grateful to be asked to speak a little about that experience and what such a curriculum means for Quakers. It is important to evaluate such a process and its product, and to decide if such endeavors are worth pursuing in the future.

Many Quakers--and I include myself in this group--are resistent to an idea of an ecumenical First Day curriculum. Some object to the idea that we should "dilute" Quaker principles into a colorless and meaningless ecumenical blend; others that individual revelation is difficult if not impossible to share--let alone teach; still others object to separating our youngest members in "First Day Classes" entirely. Let our kids join in our Meeting for Worship, they reason, and learn with us. Let them enrich us with their presence and be enriched by our presence and the Presence that so fills our gathered meeting.

Actually, the biggest proponents of this last, at least in our meeting, are people without kids. As a person who has tried to explore my own relation with God, as a parent of increasingly less small children, and as a casual reader of Piaget, I can't help but wonder if Meeting for Worship doesn't demand something that children before they are 12 years old are not ready to bring to it.

Although some Quaker adults report moments of connectedness and spiritual growth from attendance in meeting as youngsters, for many the experience most of the time seems to be akin to being adrift, without a motor or destination. It is at best boring, at worst frustrating. When I asked the kids in our Meeting about the virtues of attending Meeting for Worship, their response was unanimous: they didn't want to do it; they wanted to come to First Day School. These were kids from 10 to 7 years old; I don't think their sentiments should be discounted.

For me, the ecumenical nature of curriculum does not dilute Quaker ideas. Its assumption--that what unites us a people of different faiths is more important than what separates us, and that this shared aspect of faith is in fact the most important part of it--seems to me at once positive and Quakerly. As "the most radical of Protestant denominations," as the theologians persist in calling us, Quaker testimony is at the core, not the periphery or inference of Christian belief.

Episcopalians, Presbyterians, Lutherans had to give up the word "sacrament" in the ecumenical curriculum. But only by changing the basis of Christian writings could a curriculum subvert Quaker teachings. Thus my daughter observed one day that she was confused about the word Christian because as far as she was concerned "some of the best Christians were Jews."

So what about the curriculum itself? My 14-year-old daughter who occasionally looks after the younger kids in our meeting already has the formula for a successful class:

"They need a little reading; a little discussion; a project; and some food," she said.

I would only add that they also need other kids. All of the above is better with a little company.

But this is only format--not subject matter. It is no wonder that a people who rely on the "inner light" and "God within" stumble over any specified course for its discovery and nurture. We are often at odds on what we believe--let alone what we teach, let alone how to teach it.

In an article in *Friends Journal*, Barry Morley once tried to answer the question about what Quakers believe by naming three things--one God, continuing revelation, and that of God in every person. Thus with this one premise, incontrovertible for most Quakers, we are privy to a precious 2000 year heritage of Jewish and Christian thought.

And it seems to me that the enormity of this easily warrants the organized structure of learning experiences that gets the awful appellation that people have hated ever since they hear it first in third grade of "curriculum." Although some kids successfully learned to read from the King James Bible, most kids learn fastest and easiest with simpler material. Similarly, it eases the learning process to do multiplication before division and division before algebra.

But few people discover God through tomes on history and philosophy. And religious education is different than secular education. Do we need the Old Testament before we study the New Testament? Can't we even look at each parable and each psalm as its own entity? And in fact don't we believe that a person isolated from Christian thought in any form can listen as effectively to the God within as the most learned scribe? Isn't each individual's connectedness and participation in the Spirit, regardless of any earthly circumstance, at the heart of our Quaker belief?

So where does a curriculum fit a program when the only knowledge worth having is already imparted freely to all? When one can glean insights from whatever place in the Bible one happens to open to? When insights just as overwhelming and valid have been gleaned from nature, from paintings, from music, from the most innocent prayer?

A curriculum can nevertheless be helpful. For one thing, it assures the involvement of more than one mind in planning any one or any series of First Day classes. In the curriculum that I worked on, one group of people came up for the outline of the semester, "We Minister with Christ"; another group wrote an outline; I fleshed out the outline with stories; and my editor refined and added to what I did. And the next step, the most important, is what the teacher does with what we collectively came up with.

A curriculum can also help teachers--who have a lot to do working on format, the activities, the eats--with ideas; for example, by providing a unit on minorities, and with technical assistance, for example giving the wording of a Bible verse and stating explicitly where it may be found. It can provide ready-made material--a brightly-colored book that students can write in, for example. It can also reinforce teachers--affirming that for toddlers, pasting sheep on pastel pastures is not always an inappropriate activity.

Most importantly, a curriculum can also provide a common ground for discussion, not only across classes--of Quaker kids, Christian kids, kids--but also across generations. It helps assure a shared familiarity with the ideals, history, and spiritual explorations that are part of western civilizations. When someone proclaims "my cup runneth over," they will share in the interpretation enriched by generations of use and lifetime familiarity.

For a curriculum that purports to be Christian, the Bible-- whether viewed as a rich source of history and myth or divine revelation--is a resource text extraordinaire. The kids know this instinctively. Once asked to substitute at the last minute for a group of elementary-school-age kids, I had them take turns reading the first lines of Genesis--from the King James version no less.

The youngest was only in kindergarten and the words he knew were few, far between, and monosyllabic. Nevertheless he took his turn. The four other children listened silently as he--with a little help--stumbled through his part. Then we stuck pieces of suddenly-trimmed coleus from the YMCA kitchen into styrofoam cups, covered their stems with water, talked about life and God, and proclaimed it was good.

When the youngest boy's dad asked him what we had done that day, his answer was "we did 'in the beginning'." To my delight, I listened as father and son discussed the creation story.

God speaks to us in many ways, through nature, history, art, philosophy, music, math. For some people the body of thought and human experience that comprises the development and articulation of their religion will lead to spiritual growth. For these people, that growth may begin in First Day class.

XIII

Plenary Concert:
Music on Biblical Themes

by Patricia McKernon

[Note: One of the three plenary presentations at the Conference was a concert by Patricia McKernon. It's too bad we can't reproduce her wonderful singing, which by the end brought the sedate Quaker crowd to its feet in a noisy standing ovation. But here is her program, with annotations, followed by her discography of selected Bible-oriented music for children. Patricia McKernon has a day job in publishing, but her true calling is the making of beautiful, original music. She has issued two tapes, River of Light and New Moon; and as this book went to press, she was in the studio preparing a third album. She lives in Golden Valley, Minnesota, and attends Minneapolis Meeting.]

When the Spirit Says Sing	Traditional
Rasslin' Jacob	Traditional
Rainy Day Blues	K. and R. Eddy
Turn Around	K. and R. Eddy
Roll Away the Waters	Bob Franke
Things That Shall Remain	Steve Rose
St. Paul's Song	Pierce Pettis
Turn, Turn, Turn	Pete Seeger

A Moment Between Times	Patricia McKernon
Blessed Quietness	Ferguson and Kirkpatrick
How Blest	Ruth Rocchio
Twenty-Third Psalm	Traditional
Done Found My Lost Sheep	Traditional
Jesus Loves Me	Linda Worster
Take My Hand, Precious Lord	Thomas Dorsey
Take These Hands	Patricia McKernon
I Bid You Goodnight	Traditional
Encore: River of Light/Spring Forth a Well	Casebolt/Traditional

Discography

"Sing When the Spirit Says Sing," "Rasslin' Jacob," and "Twenty-Third Psalm" are not recorded, to my knowledge. For notated copies, write to me at 4340 Sussex Road, Golden Valley, MN 55416.

"Rainy Day Blues" and "Turn Around," by Kathy Wonson Eddy and Robert Eddy, are on *A Ceremony of Women's Songs*, available in album, tape, and sheet music through Quaker Hill Press, 36 Highland Avenue, Randolph, VT, 05060.

"Roll Away the Waters," by Bob Franke, is on his album called *Brief Histories*. It's published by Flying Fish Records, 1304 W. Schubert, Chicago, IL, 60614, and is available in folk music stores.

"The Things That Shall Remain" is by Steve Rose, and is on his album called *Rolled Away*. Write to Patricia for an address.

"St. Paul's Song," by Pierce Pettis, on his album called *Moments*, is distributed by Small World Records, 601 Meridian Street, Huntsville, AL 35801.

"Turn, Turn, Turn" is by Pete Seeger. The words and guitar chords are in *Rise Up Singing*, available through Sing Out Corporation, P.O. Box 5253, Bethlehem, PA 18015. (The song was recorded by the Byrds.)

"A Moment Between Times," by Patricia McKernon, and "Jesus Loves Me," by Linda Worster, are on their *River of Light* tape. (Linda Worster also sings an early version of "Take These Hands.") Sound Mind Records, P.O. Box 8828, Minneapolis, MN 55408.

"Blessed Quietness" and "Done Found My Lost Sheep" are on a tape called *Sharon Mountain Harmony*, published by Folk-Legacy Records, Box 1148, Sharon Mountain Road, Sharon, CT 06069.

"How Blest" is by Ruth Rocchio, and is on her tape called *Waterfall of Light*. It's published by Moonbird Music, 19 Asbury Street, Asheville, NC 28787.

"Take My Hand, Precious Lord," by the gospel singer Thomas Dorsey, is recorded by Lisa Neustadt and Jean Redpath on their album called *Anywhere is Home*.

"Take These Hands" is sung by Patricia McKernon on her *New Moon* album. Sound Mind Records, P.O. Box 8828, Minneapolis, MN 55408.

"I Bid You Goodnight" is recorded by Bill Staines on his *Bridges* album. It's available in folk music stores.

"River of Light/Spring Forth a Well" is sung by Patricia McKernon and Linda Worster on the *River of Light* tape, from Sound Mind Records, P.O. Box 8828, Minneapolis, MN 55408.

XIV

Children's Bible Music: A Discography

Dear Friends,

When I envisioned this discography, I had no idea how much music I would find and how little was written about it. I wasn't able to listen to everything, so the information here is not complete. I gleaned it from catalogs and demonstration cassettes.* Where you see comments, you'll know I've heard a tape. Where you see none, you'll know I've gotten the information from a catalogue.

Because of the wealth of material, I've included the titles of cassettes that are not just about Bible verses, but also ones that contain songs on Biblical themes and songs of praise.

You may not be familiar with the term split track. It means the songs have been recorded in stereo, with the instruments on one side and the voices on the other. This makes it possible for you to turn off one speaker and use the tape as accompaniment for your own- -or better yet, your children's--singing.

I recommend calling the music companies listed here and asking for their catalogues. I also suggest that you find a Christian bookstore that has demonstration cassettes and listen to the recordings before you buy them. There's some very good Bible music out there, but you may have to listen to a number of tapes before you find what you want. I hope that this discography gives you a way to begin.

Patricia McKernon

4340 Sussex Road, Golden Valley, MN 55416

*Special thanks goes to Praise Unlimited! bookstore in Columbia Heights, Minnesota, for demonstrating goodness, longsuffering, and other fruits of the spirit during this project.

BENSON COMPANY

365 Great Circle Road, Nashville, TN 37228   800-444-4012

Destination Promised Land.

Gettin' Together. Songs of praise/fun times.

Pat Boone's Favorite Bible Stories for the Very Young. Lamb and Lion Records, distr. Benson. Each side of each tape has a story narrated by Pat Boone and a song version of the story.
Vol. 1: Creation and Eden.
Vol. 2: Noah and Joseph.
Vol. 3: Daniel and Jonah.

Pro Kids. Songs about God's love; kids' concerns.

Sing-a-Song-Along. Split track. Originals. Praise/spiritual virtues.

20 Songs for Kids, Vol. 1.
20 Songs for Kids, Vol. 2.
20 Songs for Kids, Vol. 3.
20 Songs for Kids, Vol. 4.
Original songs. God loves me/Jesus loves me.

NOTE: Benson Company only sends catalogs to bookstores.

BRENTWOOD MUSIC

316 Southgate Court, Brentwood, TN 37027   800-333-9000

Fundamentals of the Faith (cassette and book)
Kid James Series
> Kid James is a character who explains scripture in plain language.
> *Jonah/Joseph Kid James*
> *Moses/Good Samaritan Kid James*
> *Noah/Ruth Kid James*

Kid James Triple (the above three cassettes in one package
at a discount price)

Kids Sing Praise Series:
Kids Sing Praise [Vol. 1]. Standard kids' Bible and
religious songs. Split-track. Songbook available.
Kids Sing Praise Vol. 2. More standards. Split-track.
Songbook and videotape available.
Kids Sing Praise (video)
Los Ninos Cantan Alabanzas

Love-A-Byes--Christian lullabyes

Mother Goose Series:
Mother Goose Gospel, Vol. 1. Nursery rhymes rewritten
with a Christian twist. (For example, the Muffin Man song
becomes "Do you know the Son of God, the Son of God,
the Son of God . . .") Songbook available.
Mother Goose Gospel, Vol. 2. Songbook available.

Wake Up, You Sleepyhead!

The Great Late Potentate: A Children's Musical for Christmas. 1983
New Spring Pub. Co., a member of Brentwood Publishing Group
(ASCAP). Companion materials available from Brentwood Records,
8005 Church Street E., Brentwood, TN 37027. (800) 333-9000. A
Christmas musical.

KING COMMUNICATIONS

P.O. Box 24472, Minneapolis, MN 55424 (NOTE: This series is
distributed by Word, Inc., P.O. Box 2518, Waco, TX 76702-2518
1-800-622-9673.)

G. T. and the Halo Express "God's Word for Today's Kids" series.
Bible verses verbatim in song. Endorsed by Billy Graham. Songbooks
available.
Vol. 1. God's Love. Videotape available.
Vol. 2. God's Plan of Salvation
Vol. 3. God's Protection
Vol. 4. Winning the Great Race of Faith

MARANATHA! MUSIC

P.O. Box 31050, Laguna Hills, CA 92654-1050   800-245-7664

Kids' Praise Series:
>   *The Kids' Praise! Album*
>   *Kids' Praise! 2*
>   *Kids' Praise! 3*
>   *Kids' Praise! 4* Videotape available.
>   *Kids' Praise! 5* Videotape available.
>   *Kids' Praise! 6*
>   *Kids' Praise! 7*
>   *Kids' Praise! 8*
>   *The Best of Kids' Praise!*
>   *Charity Churchmouse on the Front Line*

>   *Psalty's Mighty Mini Musicals*--praise songs on the
promises of the Bible
>   *Kids' Sampler/Cassette Only*

>   Accompaniment cassettes and songbooks available for all
>   tapes.

Colby Series:
>   *Colby 1 (Make a Joyful Noise)*
>   *Colby 2 (Colby's Missing Memory)*
>   *Colby 3 (Save Colby's Clubhouse)*
>   *Colby 4 (God Uses Kids)*
>   *Afterschool Concert (Colby's Hot Hits)*--praise/fun.

Nannybird Series--for very young children:
>   *What's the Matter Nannybird*
>   *Nannybird's Birthday Surprise*
>   presents "a lesson on solving problems and the realization
>   that Jesus really does care about our feelings."

Kids' Singalong Series:
>   *The First Sunday Singalong*. Bible and praise standards.
>   Split track. Videotape available.
>   *The Second Sunday Singalong*. Split track.

The Third Sunday Singalong. Split track
The Fourth Sunday Singalong. Split track.
The Kids' Christmas Singalong

Bible Song Singalong [1]
--scripture verses (verbatim) put to music. Split track.
Songbook available.
Bible Song Singalong 2--more scripture songs. Split track.
Kids' Singalong Hymns--hymns. Split track.
Kids' Long-Play Praise--good-time standards and originals.
Stars and Stripes Singalong--songs of faith and patriotism.
Psalty's Non-Stop Singalong [Vol. 1]. Bible standards.
Psalty's Non-Stop Singalong, Vol. 2. More Bible
standards.
Camp Song Sing-A-Long--Bible standards. Distr. Word, Inc.,
P.O. Box 2518, Waco, TX 76702. 1-800-622-9673

Kids' Storyteller Series--for ages up to 13/14:
  Rachel's Secret
  The Math Test
  Helping Hands and Cold Pizza

  Battles and Bullies--"Michael's feelings about a local bully
  change when he hears the story of Paul's
  conversion."
  The Extra Mile--Miriam's courage in saving Moses is the
  example for a child who learns to be part of a family.
  Carpenter for President

Psalty's Sleepytime Helpers Series:
  Caper at the Castle
  Rough Ridin' Rodeo
  Kids' Praise Parade
  Blooper's Bloopers
  Baby Birdy Bomber
  "Uh-Oh' Art Projects
  Fear Fightin' Farley

Kids' Go Settes Series:
  Special Friends
  Can You Read

Farley McFirefly
Colbette
Charity
Glimmer
Chipper

Hi Tops. Soundtrack from the musical. Distr. Word, Inc., P.O. Box 2518, Waco, TX 76702-2518   1-800-622-9673
Jr. High/High school level. Videotape availble.

"MAVERICKS"

Below are children's tapes put out by artists or small companies. The list isn't exhaustive; it's what I heard at the Christian music store near me:

Agapaopolis: A Kids' Musical All About Love. 1985 Singspiration (ASCAP), a division of the Zondervan Corp. Praise/love.

Amy Grant's Heart-to-Heart Bible Stories. Sweet Publications, Fort Worth, TX. Bible stories narrated by Amy Grant, interwoven with personal stories from her own childhood.

And Then, I Sing. 1988 Broadman Press (SESAC). Distr. Genevox Music Group, Nashville, TN. Songs of praise/love/thanks, including some standard children's religious songs.

Angels Hovering 'Round. 1988 Rounder Records. Distr. Rounder Records, One Camp Street, Cambridge, MA 02140. Gospel songs from white and black traditions.

The Builders. 1987 Van Ness Press (ASCAP). Distr. Broadman Press, Nashville, TN. Songs, stories on faith, trust, obedience to God.

Camp Crazy. 1989 Diadem, Inc., 50 Music Square West, Nashville, TN 37230. Distr. Spectra, Inc., 1101, Cherry Ave., Nashville, TN 37203. Teenagers at Youth Camp, singing songs of praise and fun, incl. one song about Jonah. Junior High or High School level.

Christmas Comes to Lone Star Gulch: A Musical for Young Voices.
1989 Lillenas Pub. Co., Box 419527, Kansas City, MO 64141.
Christmas with a Western twist.

*Creation Sensation: How the World Really Began . . . According to
God.* 1988 Celebration Press, a division of MacKenzie and
Associates, Inc. Distr. Spectra Distribution, 1101 Cherry Avenue,
Nashville, TN 37203. (617) 254-7227. A musical view of creation
from the creationist perspective.

*Fat, Fat Jehoshaphat: A Children's Musical That Teaches the Power
of Prayer.* 1985 Ariose Music Group. Distr. Alexandria House, P.O.
Box 300, Alexandria, IN 46001.

God with a Capital G. 1987 Fred Bock Music Company. Distr.
Antara Music Group, Alexandria, IN 46001. Recorded by Shepherd
of the Valley Lutheran Church fourth grade class. Bible stories about
Baal, Ahab, and Elijah in song and narrative.

Good King Wenceslas: The King Who Knew the Joy of Giving
1986 Ariose Music. Distr. Alexandria House, P.O. Box 300,
Alexandria, IN 46001.

Gotta Grow (King's Kids). 1988 Evidence Records, a division of
Franklin House Publishing, Inc., P.O. Box 989, Franklin, TN 37065.
(800) 537-SONG. Split track. Original songs about growing mentally,
physically, socially, and spiritually.

Jesus and the Children. 1985 Joshua Morris, Inc. Pub. by Ideals
Publishing Corp., Nelson Place at Elm Hill Pike, Nashville, TN
37214. Bible stories narrated with orchestral accompaniment.

Sharon Mountain Harmony: A Golden Ring of Gospel. 1985 Folk
Legacy Records, Box 1148, Sharon Mountain Road, Sharon CT,
06069. Gospel songs in the Appalachian tradition.

Songs of the Vineyard. 1988· Vineyard Ministries International, P.O.
Box 65004, Anaheim, CA 92815. Distrib. Frontline Music Group
through the Benson Co. Original songs, praise/God's love.

Take Out Your Crayons. Sts. Peter and Paul School, 11 Ave. and 12

St., North St. Cloud, MN 56303. Original songs. Praise/love/fun.

Watchkins Adventures. 1987 UMA Entertainment Productions, 3102 Bee Caves Road, Austin, TX 78746. Songs about dependability, eager beavers, self-control, etc. Built around watchkin bears, who watch everything children do.

Wee Sing Bible Songs. 1986 Pamela Beall and Susan Nipp. Pub. Price/Stern/Sloan Pub., Los Angeles, CA. Bible song standards.

THE SPARROW CORPORATION

P.O. Box 2120, Chatsworth, CA 91311-6995   800-634-0038

Animals and Other Things--spiritual virtues exemplified by animals (e.g., rooster, early riser; beaver, steady worker)

Ants'Hillvania--stories and songs about ants as they exemplify spiritual virtues.
Ants'Hillvania II

The Bible the Amazing Book--songs and narrative conveying facts about the Bible. Videotape available.

The Birthday Party

Bullfrogs and Butterflies--born again/God is good/praise.
Bullfrogs and Butterflies, Part II
Bullfrogs and Butterflies, Part II

Children in Praise--Black kids, black gospel; praise/worship.

Follow the Leader

I Am God's Project

Kids of the Kingdom

Lullabies and Nursery Rhymes, Vol. I

The Music Machine
The Music Machine, Part II
Nathaniel the Grublet
Sir Oliver's Song
The Story of Little Tree
We Like Sheep
Wise Guys and Starry Skies

Agapeland:

Character Builders Series:
        Faith
        Gentleness
        Goodness
        Joy
        Kindness
        Love
        Patience
        Peace
        Self-Control

Watch Me Grow Series:
        Cotton Candy Castle
        Down Lollipop lane
        Chocolate Choo Choo
        Down Peppermint Lane
        Bubblegum Band
        Big Rock Candy Mountain

WORD, INC.

P.O. Box 2518, Waco, TX 76702-2518   800-622-9673

Word, Inc. is primarily a music distribution company. They carry cassettes, videotapes, and printed music.

They also have a record company that produces albums and cassettes. Here are three children's cassettes I listened to:

The Christian Mother Goose. 1982. Nursery rhymes rewritten with a Christian twist. For example: "Humpty Dumpty shouted Amen! God can put me together again."

Papa's Rainbow. 1987. Original songs on the rainbow theme. Praise.

Special Times with Special People: Holidays with Children. 1986. Original songs. Not strictly about holidays. Incl. songs about dad, first day of school, thanks for good things, and at least one patriotic song.

XV

The Bible As A Resource For Spiritual Growth

Ann Miller

[Note: Ann Miller taught Bible for three years in Philadelphia Yearly Meeting's pioneering Quaker Studies Program, and has more recently conducted Bible studies for three Yearly Meetings in the Indiana area. She also works as a spiritual director in private practice, and as adjunct faculty at the Earlham School of Religion. She was recorded as a minister in Chester River Meeting in Pennsylvania, and now attends Clear Creek Meeting in Richmond, Indiana.]

In this workshop we will look first at some problems in using the Bible as a resource for spiritual growth, particularly among Friends in the Unprogrammed tradition, and will work toward a Quaker approach to Bible study which might lessen these difficulties. Then we will apply this approach to a particular text, Mark 14:32-36, to see how it might speak to where we are in our own spiritual growth process. I am assuming a concern for both individual spiritual growth and corporate meeting growth, and that a group context for Bible study can deepen the spiritual life of the whole meeting.

In using the Bible as a resource for spiritual growth within our meetings, we meet an initial problem of resistance from some Friends and attenders. I believe that a major reason for this is that many in our meetings today have come to Friends as refugees from other religious traditions, in which they have experienced the Bible being used as a rule book, an outward authority over-against them, inhibiting their own spiritual growth.

If these feelings of resistance are unacknowledged, they can negatively color the discussion and drain energy from the whole group.   An opportunity to name feelings about Bible study can prevent projecting onto the leader unresolved issues around authority that grows out of past experiences with Bible teachers, preachers, priests. Also, the group formation process happens as we listen to each other's feelings and stories.

Therefore, to facilitate the Bible becoming a resource for spiritual growth I begin new Bible study groups with a period of worship-sharing around the following questions:

What was your previous experience with Bible study?
Did your previous experience of the Bible open you up or close you down?

Given the way in which the Bible has been used to wound, some people wonder why try to use the Bible at all. Why not just use Quaker classics, like Woolman's Journal? I believe it is important to experience the Bible as the larger story of which our individual stories, including our Quaker story, are a part. It is a collection of people's experiences of God from prehistoric times to the formation of the Christian church. Its stories and images contain the corporate memory that guards healing stories of salvation/wholeness. When we enter its stories contemplatively, we open ourselves to the same Source of healing in our own lives.

I have found it also helpful to discuss at the beginning some distinctives of a Quaker approach to Bible study. This can be useful both to long-time Friends and to newcomers who wonder if our approach will be just like Bible study in the churches they left. There are three key aspects of Quaker belief that effect our understanding of Scripture.

First, the source of authority for Quakers is the inward authority of the Spirit, not the external authority of a book. In this we differ from churches whose origin was in the Protestant Reformation with its affirmation of authority as "Sola Scriptura." Early Friends saw that the Spirit existed before Scripture and therefore is the prime authority.

Second, to understand Scripture we must be centered in the same Spirit that created the world and inspired the writing of all

Scripture. This Spirit comes to us as present teacher and guide.
George Fox spoke of this inward Teacher as the Spirit of Christ,
who spoke to his condition and who comes to inwardly teach us
directly.

This direct teaching and speaking to our experience is the
third key aspect for a Quaker approach to Scripture. It is not
enough to know what the words of Scripture say; we need to know
in ourselves the experience to which those words point. George
Fox's words continue to query us: "You will say Christ saith this, and
the apostles say this, but what canst thou say?"

The goal of Bible study that incorporates these key aspects
of Quaker theology is transformation, not information. Information
about the text is not disregarded, but information is not an
end-in-itself. How then can we listen to a particular text so that the
Spirit can guide us into the deeper meaning that lies beneath the
literal words on the page? How can we listen in such a way that we
can hear what the Biblical story has to say about our own story?
Through all the words in the text, how can we hear the Living Word
that speaks to our condition right now?

To try to answer these questions and in reflection on the
way early Friends understood the Bible, I have used for several years
the following:

APPROACH TO A QUAKER WAY OF STUDYING THE BIBLE

1. Open yourself to the Presence of the Spirit.

Sit in quiet prayer asking God to help you to still your mind
and emotions, to let go of your own concerns or pre-occupations that
you have brought into this time of Bible study. You may need to
pray about these specific concerns first, naming them before God.
When you feel stilled or centered, ask God for eyes to see and ears
to hear as you open the Bible to begin your study.

2. What does the Scripture say?

Here we try to take the Scripture back to its original time,
setting, and culture in order to try to hear what it would have meant

in its original context. We are trying to hear these words as if for the first time, instead of hearing what others have said that they mean. Aids in seeing/hearing this are Bible dictionaries, different translations of the biblical text, our own careful study of the structure of the text; and after doing our own work with the text, commentaries are useful.

3. "What canst thou say?"

Now we are ready to bring the Scripture forward to our own time. Begin by identifying where this text is alive for you now. Where is it questioning or speaking to you in your own situation? Then ask what this text has to say to us as a community of faith. What new challenges or words are we hearing for our community in this text because of the particular time and circumstances in which we are living?

We will now apply this approach to a particular text, Mark 14:32-36:

> *"And they came to a place which was named Gethsemane: and he saith to his disciples, 'Sit ye here, while I shall pray.'*

> *"And he taketh with him Peter and James and John, and began to be sore amazed, and to be very heavy;*

> *"And saith unto them, 'My soul is exceeding sorrowful unto death: tarry ye here and watch.'*

> *"And he went forward a little, and fell on the ground, and prayed that, if it were possible, the hour might pass from him.*

> *"And he said, 'Abba, Father, all things are possible unto thee: take away this cup from me: nevertheless not what I will, but what thou wilt.'"* (King James Version)

If you cannot read the New Testament in the original Greek in which it was written, it is important to study a text in several different translations or versions. Any translation is already a step into interpretation.

I will not be telling you about the passage but asking you questions that are designed to facilitate your discovering the meaning of the text for yourself as you listen to the Inward Teacher. (Readers: Group discussion follows each question. I invite you to bring together a group of Friends to discuss these questions with you.)

I. Opening ourselves to the Presence in us and in our midst.

II. What does the Scripture say?

The following questions are designed to slow the reader long enough to see what the text really says, instead of what others have said that this text means.

This passage is taken out of its broader context or setting in the whole Gospel of Mark. The wider context gives us clues for interpreting this smaller segment of the text.

What has happened up to this point in Mark?
What happens after this passage?

Chapter and verse divisions were not made until the Middle Ages. While they make locating passages easier, they were not in the original manuscript.

How do we decide on the smaller unit to be studied?
Why might we start with verse 32?
Why end with verse 36?

I am defining the unit of the text so that it isolates Jesus' Prayer in Gethsemane. Where else might you choose to begin and end? How would this affect the focus of the smaller unit?

The literary form of this unit is narrative. What is the function of a narrative? How does the narrative form affect the reader? Where does the action in this narrative take place?

Look carefully at how the sequence of events in the narrative as the story unfolds.

Who are the persons involved at the beginning of the narrative? (v.32)

What did Jesus want of his friends during this time?

Why would Jesus leave some disciples and take only three with him to another place?

Who are these particular three? (Clues for seeing the place of these three in Mark's Gospel: Mark 1:16-20; 3:13-17; 5:37; 9:2; 8:27-28.) Why might Jesus want these three with him at this particular time?

What happens when Jesus is alone with these three friends?

What seems to be Jesus' inner condition in vv. 33-34?

Do these feelings seem appropriate to the outer circumstances confronting Jesus?

Why would Jesus leave even these three and go away by himself?

Why would Jesus throw himself on the ground? What is Jesus asking God in vv. 35-36a?

What is the significance of Jesus addressing God as "Abba"? What does this suggest about his relationship with his own father?

(Addressing God as "Father" can be a significant problem, particularly for women and men who have had abusive or absent fathers. Sometimes our parent's or other caretakers behavior gets confused with God's; and then we fear that if we trust our future to God, God will treat us as that significant other did. If this has been your experience, instead of addressing God as Father, try naming God from your own past experience by filling in the blank: "In my experience God has been like a _____ to me." Now take the word you put in the blank and address God that way. Notice what happens with your fear.)

What is the meaning of "this cup" in v. 36? (For clues see how this metaphor is used elsewhere in the Jewish tradition: Psalm 23:5; 11:6; and 116:13; Mark 10:38.)

Does Jesus want to die?

Looking at the whole narrative, name the steps in Jesus' process of coming to pray, "Thy will be done."

We know the rest of the story. What difference did this time in Gethsemane make for Jesus?

III. "What canst thou say?"

Here we move from searching the Scripture to allowing the Word to search us.

Spiritual growth is a life-time process. One of the hardest steps on the journey is coming to be genuine in our prayer. Sometimes we move too quickly into praying, "Thy will be done." Other times we are hesitant to pray this prayer at all. The same person can experience each of these feelings at different times on the spiritual journey. Each of these feelings about praying for God's will to be done involves both a trust issue and fear. An important step into genuine prayer is, like Jesus, to name our own feelings and fears in God's presence.

What is the problem in moving too quickly into praying that God's will be done?

Who is it that we don't trust?

What is it that we fear when we move very quickly into this prayer?

What is the problem in remaining resistant to praying for God's will to be done?

Who is it that we don't trust when we are in this place?

What is the fear of here?

What are your own feelings about praying for God's will to be done in your life?

How does this story of Jesus' prayer speak to your own condition?

What new possibilities does this offer to you where you are in your own process of coming to pray, "Thy will be done"?

TO LEARN MORE ABOUT THIS APPROACH

Barclay, Robert. *Apology.* Proposition 3: "The Scriptures."

Boobyer, George H. *The Bible and the Light Within.* London: Quaker Home Service, 1973.

Cadbury, Henry. *A Quaker Approach to the Bible.* Guilford College Ward Lecture, 1953. (Available from Philadelphia Yearly Meeting Library)

Fager, Chuck. *A Respondent Spark: The Basics of Bible Study.* Kimo Press, 1984.

Lampen, John. *Twenty Questions About Jesus.* London: Quaker Home Service, 1985.

Morrison, Mary. *Approaching the Gospels.* Pendle Hill Pamphlet.

--------------. *Questions and Procedures For Group Gospels Study.* Available from Pendle Hill.

McMakin, Jacqueline. *Doorways to Christian Growth.* Winston Press, 1984.

Mulholland, M. Robert, Jr. *Shaped by the Word.* Nashville: Upper Room, 1985.

Reichardt, Dorothy. *Finding Our Way in the Bible.* Philadelphia Yearly Meeting Religious Education Committee.

Sharman, Henry Burton. *Jesus In the Records*. Association Press, 1926.

--------------------. *The Records of the Life of Jesus*. Harper and Brothers, 1917.

Wald, Oletta. *The Joy of Discovery In Bible Study*. Rev. ed. Augsburg, 1975.

------------. *The Joy of Teaching Discovery Bible Study*.

Wink, Walter. *The Bible in Human Transformation*. Fortress, 1973.

------------. *Transforming Bible Study*. Abingdon, 1980.

XVI

The Common Visions Of
The Hebrew And Christian Scriptures

Arthur Rifkin

[Note: Arthur Rifkin is a psychiatrist at Queens Hospital Center in Jamaica, New York. He is Clerk of Ministry and Counsel at Manhasset Meeting on Long Island, and has previously published articles in **Friends Journal**, *on pacifism and on Jesus.]*

The central message of both scriptures is the identity of loving God and our neighbor, and the highest form of love is to suffer for someone else. In the Christian Scriptures this message is crystal clear. In the Hebrew Scriptures it is not. The Hebrew Scriptures are more heterogeneous than the Christian Scriptures, first by sheer quantity, and second by diversity of style and content.

The most misunderstood story of the Hebrew Scriptures, I believe, is that of Cain and Abel. As commonly believed, Cain is punished with the "mark of Cain" for his brother's murder. The actual story is more complex. The morality of that time was vengeance by a clan. A murder had to be avenged by one or more murders by the victim's clan. Anything else was dishonorable, unethical. A person was protected by his clan. Without a clan, a person was helpless and fair game for murder.

After Abel's murder, God deals leniently with Cain. He spares his life but banishes him from his clan: "a fugitive and a vagabond shalt thou be in the earth." (Gen. 4:12) Cain says this punishment is unbearable. Why? Because as a fugitive, "every one that findeth me shall slay me". (Gen. 4:14) At this point a quantum leap in moral development occurs. "And the LORD said unto him, Therefore whosoever slayeth Cain, vengeance shall be taken on him sevenfold. And the LORD set a mark upon Cain, lest any finding him should kill him". (Gen. 4:15) God says that the law of the clan is broken: murder shall not be answered with murder. The mark of Cain is God's protection, saving Cain.

On another level the story shows that Cain's real punishment is not physical but social: he is excluded from society and, by extension, from God. Here in a capsule we see the central theme of the Hebrew Scriptures and Christian Scriptures adumbrated. The so-called punishment of God is no such thing; it is our rejection of God which is the cause and the punishment. Cain shuts out God by murdering Abel. How? Does God withdraw? No, to be close to God is to love your neighbor. To hate and kill your brother shows how distant you are from God's love. The realization of this is the worst punishment.

Why don't the Hebrew Scriptures say it plainly and not disguise the meaning in a story that is ambiguous? This is the fascination and frustration of the Scriptures. A story is more than its interpretation, just as experience is more than a description of it. We extract meaning from a story and from experience--not to do so is not to be human--but our extractions are imperfect no matter how "correct" they are.

Life is ambiguous, lived on many levels, not reducible to formulas. So is a good story. Asserting that God is love and to love God is to love your neighbor, as a bald statement, is anemic compared to the real situation in which we must act, with all sorts of mixed motives and with a partial understanding of what is truly happening. In any comparison of the two Scriptures we must face, courageously, the question of value. Aren't the Christian Scriptures superior, less bloodthirsty, presenting a God and heroes more purely exemplifying love and forgiveness? This is an oversimplification, based on two distortions.

First, the Hebrew Scriptures are not just an earlier version of the Christian Scriptures. The Christian Scriptures are the story of one man's life, a short history of what happened to a small number of believers (Christians) for a few years after Jesus' death, and some commentaries on the significance of Jesus' life and death. The Hebrew Scriptures cover a vastly larger picture: the history of an entire nation for thousands of years, much detail of religious practices, stories of many prophets (persons who tried to disturb the Hebrew nation by shaking it out of its misunderstanding of God) and stories and poetry.   Naturally, there will be much more heterogeneity in the Hebrew Scriptures from its larger size and variety of intentions.

Additionally, the same problems that disturb and revolt us in the Hebrew Scriptures are present in the Christian Scriptures, although attenuated by its lack of scope. Achan disobeyed Joshua's rule and took spoils from Jericho. God then punished Israel by causing Joshua's forces to lose a battle with the men of Ai. To make atonement the people killed Achan.   "And all Israel stoned him with stones, and burned them with fire". (Josh. 7:25) Who are "them"? It refers to Achan's children, animals and property. What kind of God is this, who wants innocent people and animals killed?

In the Christian Scriptures we have no battles and human sacrifices. They aren't part of the story, but we do have Jesus, described in greater terms than any Hebrew Scriptures hero, acting strangely. A non-Jewish woman begged Jesus for help. "'Have mercy on me, O Lord, Son of David, my daughter is severely possessed by a demon.' But he did not answer her a word. And his disciples came and begged him, saying, 'Send her away, for she is crying after us.' He answered, 'I was sent only to the lost sheep of the house of Israel.' But she came and knelt before him, saying, 'Lord, help me.' And he answered, 'It is not fair to take the children's bread and throw it to the dogs'". (Mt. 15:22-26)

So we have the apostle of love calling a woman, who is begging for his help, a dog because she is a gentile! I find this as shocking as any of the grisly stories of the Hebrew Scriptures in which God seems to desire suffering. For example, the prophet Samuel tells Saul, the first king of Israel, that God wants him to "smite Amalek and utterly destroy all that they have; do not spare them, but kill both man and woman, infant and suckling, ox and sheep, camel and ass". (1 Sam. 15:3) As if this weren't bad enough, when Saul kills all the Amalekites but spares the king and his animals, God is so angry that he tells Samuel that he repents of making Saul king.

When Samuel confronts Saul, Saul, in all innocence, says he disobeyed God only to serve him better; that he spared Agag, king of the Amalekites, and his sheep and oxen because they were the best and he wants to offer them as a sacrifice to God. Samuel is unimpressed, "and Samuel hewed Agag in pieces before the LORD in Gilgal". (1 Sam. 15:33)

What are we to make of this gross moral insensitivity in the Hebrew Scriptures and Christian Scriptures? My response is to do my best to understand the core message and not be distracted by the distortion of God's image created by the imperfect tellers of these stories.

It is ironic that the most publicly pious among us are those who consider the Scriptures inerrant. To do so is to blaspheme God. I don't hold God responsible for hacking Agag to pieces, or for insulting a gentile woman. I hold responsible those persons, representative of their culture, who lacked moral sensitivity to evils of violence and ethnocentrism when they wrote the Scriptures.

The larger message-within-the-message is that we do not learn God's will in some ethereal, disconnected way, but it comes to us in our language and culture (always, to some extent, distorted)--an insight to make us both humble and arrogant. Humble, since any understanding we have of God's will must be partial and distorted. Arrogant, since we, standing on the shoulders of those who preceded us, who struggled to achieve a greater measure of wisdom, can see farther in some respects than the religious geniuses of the past.

To illustrate this need to get the important points and not be misled by peripheral aspects, let's return to these stories:

When Saul protests his innocence to Samuel, saying he spared Agag and his property only to make a better sacrifice to God, Samuel answers: "Has the LORD as great delight in burnt offerings and sacrifices, as in obeying the voice of the LORD? Behold, to obey is better than sacrifice, and to hearken than the fat of rams. For rebellion is as the sin of divination and stubbornness is as iniquity and idolatry" (1 Sam. 15:22-23). This is a message we need always: that following God's call is difficult. We want to please

God in superficial ways, and to replace God's will with ours.

After Jesus insulted the gentile woman, he listened to her spirited reply. "'Yes, Lord, yet even the dogs eat the crumbs that fall from their master's table'". (Mt. 15:27) Jesus answers: "'O woman, great is your faith! Be it done for you as you desire.' And her daughter was healed instantly". (Mt. 15:28) The message here is that powerful faith overcomes ethnic and religious differences.

The Bible addresses our deepest questions: What is the purpose of it all? How am I to live? What about suffering? The abstractions--love God and your neighbor--need flesh to be meaningful and to deal with the problem of suffering. I take as the central theme in both Scriptures the answer to the issues of suffering, repentance and atonement: restoring our relationship to God. Or, rolled into one question: "How can I be close to God?"

In the Hebrew Scriptures the struggle is between legalisms and true worship. At Mount Sinai God makes a covenant with the Jewish people. At that level of understanding, a monotheistic conception of God was beginning. We see a mountain God gradually emerge as a universal God of all creation and all people. The mountain God becomes "portable" by being carried in an ark, then in a temple that does not need to be mobile because God's presence is not limited by space. After the destruction of the temple, and during the Babylonian exile, the temple is no longer necessary, and decentralized worship replaces it.

A countercurrent to this spiritual evolution is its dark side. Every symbol of God can be distorted into an idol. Here too. This development of the concept of God from a primitive, tribal, geographic God to a universal, spiritual one is paralleled by the idolization of rules. The advance from totem to ideas and behavior is a great one. To be a people of the Book is to extend God greatly, but this Book can be limiting, and authentic worship can become legalism.

Before continuing this attack on legalism, I should give it its due. The proliferation of rules and a complex liturgy has its value. Putting religious faith into action helps both faith and behavior. Faith with no behavioral aspect can be empty and weak. If our faith doesn't affect our daily life, of what worth is it? The seeming inutility and purposelessness of many of the commandments are a strength. Not eating dairy products and meat together is best justified, not on some pseudoscientific hygienic basis, but as a symbolic action to express holiness.

Symbols can take on a life of their own and lose their function as connecting links. When we follow dietary rules not to express our wish to be holy before God but to conform to our ethnic group, to accentuate our separateness, the symbol is a hindrance in our religious pilgrimage.

One of the great moments of the Hebrew Scriptures is Jeremiah 31:31-34. This is the announcement of a new covenant which differs from the first at Mount Sinai. This one is not a set of rules written on tablets. This covenant will be in our hearts. Further, there will be no hierarchy of teachers and students; no one will tell another how to be close with God, because all persons will be close.

This jewel of the Hebrew Scriptures does more than announce that God is spiritual, in our hearts, not in codes and books, or rituals. It tells us how this happens, and in this it binds the Hebrew Scriptures to the Christian Scriptures, where this theme is continued. What is the mechanism of God entering our hearts? Jeremiah's God says: "for I will forgive their iniquity, and I will remember their sin no more". (Jer. 31:34)

This is crucial. We love and cleave to God when we feel forgiven. There is no question here that we need forgiveness. That is assumed. What clearer way is there to show love than to forgive? The recipient of forgiveness knows love. Once we know God's love, we know God in our hearts.

This is the same vision we see in the Christian Scriptures. In the parable of the woman who was a sinner (Lk. 7:36-50), a sinful woman (a prostitute, by tradition) shocks the Pharisee with whom Jesus is eating. She enters, wets Jesus' feet with her tears, wipes them with her hair, kisses his feet, and anoints them with ointment.

This parable may be read as the woman's love for Jesus coming first and then Jesus forgiving her. I think this is not the best reading. It seems to me that the first event is that she feels forgiven by God, and to express her gratitude she shows her love to Jesus, who here is God's emissary. Why does she love much? Because she feels forgiven.

Within this parable is another: the creditor with two debtors. One owed five hundred denarii, the other, fifty. He forgave the debt of both, and Jesus says the one who owed five hundred denarii loved him the most.

Do these two parables mean we should sin and owe money extravagantly, so that when forgiven we will appreciate it more? This makes no sense. The sensible meaning is that the person who feels most forgiven is most appreciative and loves the forgiver most. We don't lack enough sins to require forgiveness; that isn't the problem. The problem is that we don't feel forgiven, which is what makes us closed to God.

We have this theme beautifully told in Luke (15:11-32) in the parable of the Prodigal Son--more fittingly called that of the Forgiving Father. The emphasis should not be on the prodigal. In fact, the story is ambiguous about him. He changes his mind and returns home, but not necessarily because he has truly repented. His return home seems motivated by hunger. While caring for swine and wishing he could eat even what they were, he "came to himself" and said, "How many of my father's hired servants have bread enough and to spare, but I perish here with hunger. I will arise and go to my father, and I will say to him, 'Father, I have sinned against heaven and before you; I am no longer worthy to be called your son; treat me as one of your hired servants.'"

This sounds more like manipulative behavior than true repentance. The focus of the parable is the father. Before the son can recite his prepared speech of contrition, the father runs to him and embraces him, showing not only forgiveness, but extreme delight. This is an ancient patriarchal family at a time of marked filial respect during which fathers didn't run to sons to embrace them. The message that Jesus is giving here is that God's forgiving love is as "excessive" and uncalled for as the father's in the parable, even if we are as dubiously repentant as the prodigal.

God's love and our love, the central vision of the Hebrew Scriptures and Christian Scriptures, appear in other parts of the Bible. In the Hebrew Scriptures, such a place is in one of Isaiah's Servant Songs. (52:13-53:12) God's servant is described as ugly, despised, but he "has borne our griefs and carried our sorrows...he was wounded for our transgressions...with his stripes we are healed ...the LORD has laid on him the iniquity of us all.... .It was the will of the LORD to bruise him....he makes himself an offering for sin."

We see several themes here. God's servant is not handsome or esteemed; he is punished for our sins; and he does this uncomplainingly ("like a lamb that is led to slaughter, and like a sheep that before its shearers is dumb, so he opened not his mouth"). At first this seems the opposite of a hero. Certainly there is no other hero in the Hebrew Scriptures like this. David, Saul, Joshua, Moses--the great political leaders--were successful warriors (or in Moses' case, indirectly led the Israelite forces to victory). David, the archetypal hero, is handsome, suave, successful, and a leader in many endeavors, exemplifying God's favor by being treated more leniently than most for his sins, and certainly showing many sins.

The Suffering Servant of Isaiah is the opposite of this. The contrast is striking. It is another quantum leap of spiritual progress in the Hebrew Scriptures that is equaled but not surpassed in the Christian Scriptures.

This servant, more than David, is the true hero and exemplifies the apogee of devotion and love. The lack of beauty and esteem means he lacks the superficial features by which we judge most persons. It is a judgment on us, not of the servant. We don't value people correctly. We are misled by superficial or phony virtues, from physical features to wealth, to athletic prowess, to business acumen, to prestigious professions, to academic success. Many of these characteristics are not bad.

Physical beauty, like all beauty, is to be valued; clever

business sense that brings wealth may also bring benefit to others (maybe not); and so on, but compared to what is most important these are well down on the list. What is first? As the poem says, "he has borne our griefs and carried our sorrows...he was wounded for our transgression...upon him was the chastisement that made us whole and with his stripes we are healed."

In some unspecified way, this servant has given of himself to help us. This is vicarious suffering, sacrificial suffering, for altruistic purposes. What specifics the poet refers to here are not clear, and not that important. Isaiah probably was using this as a metaphor for the suffering of the Jews in exile, and how the experience will cleanse them.

This principle, that vicarious, sacrificial love is the ultimate virtue, is a monumental advance. We know this from daily life, but don't know it well enough. We are duly impressed by the heroes of our time, be they politicians, entertainers, or athletic stars, and we lavish attention, money and our emulation on them. But, in deeper moments, we know that the real heroes are those who quietly, unostentatiously, give of themselves to help others. Most of these people are known to only a few, because they are unobtrusive, but we all know them--the self-sacrificing parent whose children know advantages the parents never had; the person who gives his or her life for another.

We see this in the esteem given to the few such persons who do achieve fame because they act on the stage of history. Albert Schweitzer certainly deserved fame as a theologian and musician, but he became beloved for what was seen as sacrificing this double career to be a physician in a woefully under-served part of the world. What attracted people to him? The medical care he gave was not unusual, and it is doubtful if many persons made themselves familiar with his theological or musical writings. No, it was the sense that this man had made a personal sacrifice to help others.

The two greatest men of the Twentieth Century, in my judgment, were Martin Luther King, Jr., and Mohandas Gandhi, who have been elevated to almost sacred status not only by their efforts to reform society, worthwhile as those efforts were, but because they seemed to personify the Suffering Servant and Jesus by being persecuted without succumbing to bitterness, withdrawal from the struggle, or loss of lovingkindness.

Just as the great heroes seem, at times, to be upstaged by lesser persons, so is the central vision of the Hebrew Scriptures and Christian Scriptures sometimes obscured by dramatic elements in the Bible. The miraculous story of the Jews's escape from Egypt; the thunder on Mount Sinai; Jesus walking on water and appearing to the disciples after his death; all these stories "grab the headlines" but are not the central vision.

We must not forget that the Bible was not written to be a source of dissertations for scholars, but to be a source of inspiration and instruction for the common person. To emphasize the central vision, all stops were pulled out to catch the reader's or listener's attention. In our day, many of these emphases don't ring true, leading people to discount the Bible or twist the stories with much imagination to fit the current theology.

The sensitive reader of today who wants to avoid the intellectual numbing of fundamentalism and yet not dismiss the Bible should seek and treasure the central vision. Otherwise religion, especially the Judeo-Christian tradition, deals only with the superficialities. With the central vision clearly in view, the remainder of the Bible (usually) serves to emphasize and document it. It is not easy to use the spoken or written word to instill the central message of love of God and neighbor. It is the challenge to the reader as well as the writer to bring this message to life.

XVII

Re-Telling Biblical Stories

Jean Semrau

[Note: Jean Semrau presently divides her time between Rio Hondo Community College in Whittier, California, where she is a campus minister, and work at a nearby church-related retiremont home. Formerly director of the Woolman Hill Conference Center in Massachusetts, she is a member of the Bay State's Mount Toby Meeting, but attends Claremont(CA) Meeting.]

Stories have been told and re-told as long as humans have had the power of speech. Unfortunately, some stories are written down in such a way that they are considered finished, or even absolute, and there are sanctions against changing so much as a word of them. Biblical stories, by virtue of being part of a "closed canon" of scripture, are among those considered by some people to be unalterable. I suggest that unless stories are re-told they are dead, or at least dying. It is by re-telling them and using them that we make them ours; that we breathe new life into them; that the word again becomes flesh.

Stories give us new windows through which to see our world. They also show us ourselves. A story draws us in, engages us, enables us to forget ourselves for a moment. And because of that self-forgetfulness, the message of a story can catch us, open us, convict us, move us in ways a lecture, sermon or other prose rarely can. And we usually remember a story: its characters, its images, its action, its power stay with us.

Like all good rabbis ancient and modern, Jesus knew the power of story. And, like the prophets, he knew how to dramatize a story in the living of his own life. Many of his stories as well as stories about him are alive and well in our culture and in our individual minds/hearts today. Some stories which have come to us in scripture seem obscure and "wrong" to us today; others are so familiar that we hardly bother to reread them. In either case, re-telling these stories can reclaim them and renew them, while moving us and changing our ways of seeing.

In a time of worship last spring, I was moved to tell a story that went something like this:

> A gardener went out to plant her vegetable garden. As she planted, some of her seeds fell onto the path, where the earth was packed and hard. Birds later ate all that seed. Some of her seeds fell on thin, rocky soil, where they sprouted quickly but soon died from too much sun and too little nourishment. Some seeds fell in a low spot where the soil was too wet. Those seeds rotted and never sprouted at all. Some seeds rooted in soil that looked perfect. But weeds sprouted there so fast that they crowded out the little vegetable plants. And some of the gardener's seeds were carefully planted in healthy soil. They grew, and each seed yielded a hundred new seeds.

The vocal ministry that followed the story was full of excitement and insight. One person was delighted to think that seeds she had always thought of as wasted had in fact fed birds and enriched the soil. Another person was amazed that the mere substitution of "gardener" for "sower" could so change his perception of the parable.

For me, that simple re-telling of the parable of the sower has in a very real sense grounded (!) my interpretation of it. No longer do I need to rely solely on the spiritualized interpretation which follows the parable in Mark 4, Matthew 13, and Luke 8. The story can still be about the "word of God"; it can also be about the economy and ecology of my own garden.

Shortly after the above incident, I was attending the Quaker Theological Discussion Group on sexuality and was again moved in meeting for worship to re-tell a familiar story:

On the streets of Washington, DC recently, an elderly homeless man was mugged. He lay in a doorway moaning, and many people passed by, but no one so much as looked in his direction. After some hours, a youngish man heard the moans and stopped, and looked, and really saw the older man. After a few moments he went over to him, did a little first aid, got some water for the man to drink, and then helped him walk down the block to a shelter.

The young man left money with the shelter staff to pay for whatever medical attention the old man needed, promised to stop in the next day, and went on his way. The young man was gay....I'd like to be able to say also that he was a Quaker....

Also last spring, I found myself facilitating some workshops for groups of Friends in New England. At one of them, on Gifts, we looked at the parable of the talents as though "talents" meant personal gifts. Each of three small groups presented to the larger group its version of that story. All three versions were contemporary, thought-provoking, faithful in spirit but not in language to the so-called original, and delightful.

From experiences like this, of facilitating Bible study on a particular theme, I have learned that the Bible is able to speak to us, today, in very specific and moving ways. Sometimes I have been moved to action, sometimes to anger, sometimes to tears; but invariably I have been *moved* by "searching the scriptures."

These recent experiences of re-telling biblical stories led me to offer an experiential workshop at the Friends Bible Conference: a workshop in which participants had the opportunity to re-tell some biblical stories.

At the Conference, Friends will be looking at how we can use the Bible as a spiritual resource. As I thought how we might focus our story-retelling in this context, I was led to look at stories in which Jesus used scripture as a resource for teaching and transformation. How did Jesus "search the scripture"? When, where, and to whom did he quote from scripture?

This workshop, then, focussed on how Jesus used scripture, as related in four passages from the book of Luke. My hope was that, as we gained experience in story-telling, we would also gain insight about our study and use of scripture itself.

Workshop Logistics

The crucial element in any study of scripture, it seems to me, is acknowledgment of the presence of the Spirit in our midst. When we are conscious of that presence, amazing things can happen! So we'll begin by acknowledging (or invoking, or giving thanks for) the Spirit among us. And we'll spend a few minutes in silence, centering ourselves and waiting.

We'll introduce ourselves briefly, and begin to think about story. We'll look briefly at how Jesus used stories, and how he used scripture in general. Then we'll narrow our focus to the book of Luke and look at four stories which involve Jesus' relationship to scripture.

The large group will be divided into four smaller groups, and each small group will study one of these stories (and stories-within-stories):

Luke 4:1-13 Jesus, quotes from Deuteronomy when he is tested in the wilderness

Luke 4:14-30 Jesus reads from Isaiah in the synagogue in Nazareth

Luke 8:4-18 Jesus quotes from Isaiah when he tells the story of the sower

Luke 10:25-37 Jesus tells the story of the good Samaritan to illustrate the basic teachings of scripture.

Then each small group will re-tell and/or act out their story. And the session will end with sharing and worship in the large group.

I've found it very rich to have each small group work on a different story around a particular theme. At a workshop on base communities, each small group was given one of six passages about Jesus at Bethany, his "base community." (With or without re-telling, the juxtaposition of those six stories is fascinating.) Other engaging themes include images of God, women, money, healing, obedience, food, peace, compassion, and justice.

It's also fun for all small groups to work on the same story. I've found that each interpretation is so different that participants are invariably amused, surprised, and humbled. One group might decide to tell the story through animals' eyes; another group might re-tell it in contemporary slang; another group might dramatize two differing biblical versions; another might re-write the ending of the story; another might change the characters, or add a new character to the story; others might simply share insights from their study of the passage. The possibilities are as limitless as our creativity.

Whatever design is used, it's important to "frame" the exercise carefully. Assign (or let participants choose) small groups first. Then explain what is to come. If each group has a different passage, I suggest a short period of silence before the small groups leave; then I ask that someone in each group read its passage aloud in worship before beginning discussion and study. If all groups are studying the same passage, I read it aloud, slowly, once or even twice, in a spirit of worship.

Then the groups (or, in some cases, individuals) study the passage for 20-25 minutes, using more than one translation, if possible. Toward the end of that time they plan how to present the passage to the larger group. The large group reconvenes, and each group has about 5 minutes for its presentation. A time for "de-briefing" and worship-sharing follows.

When this "frame" is solid--clear instructions, adequate time allotted for each activity, surrounding atmosphere of worship-sharing--people feel safe enough to experiment and free to be wonderfully creative. That creativity breathes life into each story and makes it new. Makes us new.

Selected Bibliography

Bell, Martin, *The Way of the Wolf: The Gospel in New Images*. NY: Ballantine Books, 1970.

Brown, Robert McAfee, *Unexpected News: Reading the Bible with Third World Eyes*. Philadelphia: Westminster Press, 1984.

Buber, Martin, *Tales of the Hasidim* (2 vols). NY: Schocken Books, 1948.

Buscaglia, Leo, "No Room at the Inn," in *Seven Stories of Christmas Love*. Leo F. Buscaglia, Inc., 1927.

Cardenal, Ernesto, *The Gospel in Solentiname* (4 vols). Maryknoll, NY: Orbis Books, 1984. (See also Scharper, below.)

Carroll, James, *Wonder and Worship*. Paramus, NJ: Newman, 1970.

Greeley, Andrew, "Confessions of a Storytelling Priest," *Storytelling* (Summer, 1989), pp. 7-10.

Johnson, James Weldon, "The Creation," in *God's Trombones: Seven Negro Sermons in Verse*. NY: Viking Press, 1927.

Jordan, Clarence L., *The Cotton Patch Versions* (Matthew, Luke, Acts, John, etc.). Americus, GA: Koinonia Publications.

Kazantzakis, Nikos, *The Last Temptation of Christ*. NY: Simon and Schuster, 1960.

Levi, *The Aquarian Gospel of Jesus the Christ*. Marina Del Rey, CA: DeVorss & Co., 1964.

Lewis, C.S., *The Magician's Nephew*. NY: Collier Books, 1955. (A re-telling of the creation story.)

Scharper, Philip and Sally, eds., *The Gospel In Art By the Peasants of Solentiname*. Maryknoll, NY: Orbis Books, 1984.

XVIII

Children And The Bible:
Experiencing, Discovering, Interpreting

Mary Snyder

*[Note: Mary Snyder is the author of **Religious Education In The Home and Small Meeting,** published by Friends General Conference. She teaches English at the University of Wisconsin-Stout, and attends Eau Claire/Menomonie Meeting, where she publishes the meeting newsletter.]*

Just as George Fox found the Bible a basis for coming to better know God, so we as Friends today continue to turn to the Bible for inspiration. Sometimes the Bible speaks to us strongly. Usually where one or two are gathered, it speaks to us in a variety of ways. We value and celebrate such variety in an experiential approach. As we introduce our children to the Bible, then, we are clearly seeking similar qualities. We wish to open the possibility that the text may speak to them at their experiential level without teaching things that they will have to unlearn at some later time.

When the Bible, itself, is so complex, how can we possibly help children experience and discover realities that lay behind the text? Today I would like to answer this question by demonstrating two approaches; one for children ages 3 to 7, and another for 8 on up.

When working with the youngest, we can take some hints from several experts. Jean Piaget emphasized that "play is a child's work"--that children learn through doing. Maria Montessori brought

Piaget's theories into practice by designing beautiful manipulative equipment and outlining specific ways to use the equipment. It was Sofia Cavaletti, a Montessori teacher in Rome, who first applied these ideas to religious education.   She developed the following procedures for introducing a Bible story to children ages 3 to 7:

1. Before presenting the story, package small wooden figures representing péople and animals in an appealing box. This material is to help the child experience and explore. A copy of the story and other necessary props should also be included in the box.   The figures, themselves, should not be clearly defined.

2. Tell or read the story.

3. Ask questions about the story without answering them. Work in a meditative manner. You are opening the possibility that the text may speak directly to children. RESIST YIELDING TO THE TEMPTATION TO EXPLAIN.

4. Next, carefully open the box of materials and present each child with one or several figures to hold.

5. Take the story script from the box. As you reread the story, ask the children to move their figures in correspondance to the text.

6. If the children want to do the story again, redistribute the figures. Ask an older child to read if one is able to do so.

7. Lead the group in putting away materials. Point out where this special box will be kept. Invite the children to return to the box and recreate the story individually or in small groups. Recognize that as the children rework the story, a most important moment happens. "It is the time of the conversation with the inner Teacher when the child reconsiders, without the adult what has been presented and enters into its meaning." (p. 68, Cavelletti).

8. Offer other media to the children through which they can work their interpretations of the story. Pencils and paper for writing or copying; crayons, paint, paper, and clay for art; simple scarves and headcoverings for dramatic play.

In our meeting, we implemented these ideas with the
Christmas story since figures to enact the story are easily available.
During the workshop, we will work primarily with the shepherds
using the following queries for step 3, the community meditation:

"It is very surprising that in this story a baby was
born outside of the inn. How do you think Joseph and
Mary felt when there was no room in the inn? How do you
think Mary and Joseph felt when their baby was born? What
were the shepherds doing? Where were they? How do you
think they kept watch? How did they feel when they saw the
angel? Have you ever seen an angel? How do you think you
would feel? Do you think God sends us messages with
angels?" (I'm not sure if I have seen an angel or not.
Sometimes I have been with people who seemed like angels.
But I do not know if there really are angels.)

"Why do you think God sent angels to tell about
this baby? Do you think Jesus will help the shepherds
when he grows up? Can you think of other people Jesus
might help when he is older? Do you think God sends
messages with every new baby? How beautiful this story is
with the baby, the angels, and the shepherds!"

I have personally developed this approach to the Christmas
story. You may want to work with other stories. Sofia Cavelletti
suggests that the story of the good shepherd is both comforting and
critical for a child's religious development. Whatever stories you
choose, you are building a store to which children may return again
and again--physically, mentally, and spiritually.

After the age of seven, most children are ready for different
kinds of exploration. Their ability to read opens many ways to
investigate the structure and context of the Bible. Again, there are
several elements which an adult may consider when planning to
introduce a biblical story, poem, letter, or event to older children.
The following steps for older children need not be followed in order:

1. Recreate the experience of biblical characters in their
time through imaging, art, and drama. Help young Friends

experience the story in context. Ask them to put themselves in the place of that person at that time.

2. Explore what this story might have meant for people then. Find out why young Friends think wanderers in the desert found this story important enough to tell for generations.

3. Explore what this passage might still mean for people today? Here, older children often have tales to tell from their friends, neighbors, or Jehovah's Witnesses who have come knocking at the door.

4. Ask children what they learned from the story. Stress that this individual experience is important for Friends. As we change, our ideas may change. It is important here for you, the adult, to share what this story or verse has meant for you in the past and what it means now.

5. Physically work out various interpretations through art and drama activities. Offer these as opportunities to make choices, to know by doing, and to become really involved with the Bible.

We will turn again to the Christmas story, this time experiencing it on a more interpretive level appropriate for children over seven. Each workshop participant will receive a complete lesson plan from the *Jesus, Who Was He?* curriculum which will be available from Friends General Conference in 1991. (The lesson plan follows this text.)

As we experience a familiar story twice, I hope it becomes clear that involvement is what these two approaches are all about. Not only do children become involved with the Bible, but we all become involved with one another. Together we listen to ancient words. Together we explore, discover, and find importance. Together, we grow in the Spirit.

Resource:

Cavalletti, Sofia. *The Religious Potential of the Child*. New York: Paulist Press, 1983.

SAMPLE LESSON PLAN:

Session I PROPHECIES

From *Jesus, Who Was He?* an unpublished curriculum by Mary Snyder.

GOALS

*Review (or introduce) the structure of the Bible.

*Work on finding chapter and verse in the Old Testament.

*Look at some promises Jewish people feel God made to them through the prophets.

*Introduce the concept of a Messiah.

TO THE TEACHER

If your students have not studied Old Testament, this lesson may be their introduction to the structure of the Bible. It is not unusual to discover fairly mature young Friends who have never heard of the Old and New Testaments, the broad variety of literature and authors of the Bible, nor the division by book, chapter, and verse.

Questions are suggested in this lesson to help students review what they may have studied previously or learn this material for the first time. You will be able to informally evaluate what your students have learned in the past through the process of questioning and recording on your journal page.

This lesson also introduces the concept of the Messiah promised to the Jewish people. It is important to realize that then and now people think about the Messiah in many different ways. In the first century, some Jews expected a strong military leader--one who, with military might like David, would deliver them from the humiliation of foreign rule. Others waited for a superhuman much like a Roman or Greek god who would bring divine deliverance from the Roman occupation.

At the same time, still other Jews sensed their people were again slipping into evil, immoral ways of straying from Jewish law, following the customs of other lands, defiling the temple, being unfaithful in prayer, and listening to false prophets. These Jews expected a Messiah in the form of a new prophet to set their society straight.

Although they couldn't agree on form, everyone waited for this Messiah. The time was close. Daily rumors spread through markets. Every leader of any revolt was regarded with fervent hope. The prophets of old had given guidelines as outlined in this lesson. The scene was ripe with expectations. The prophecies which the class will read in this lesson were well known by every Jewish person including Jesus himself. With this lesson, you are setting the stage.

IN ADVANCE

Reread the planning section at the beginning of this curriculum. Duplicate journal pages for the semester, if you have not already done so. Prepare 3 by 5 cards. Write one of the following chapter and verse references on each card:

> Isaiah 9:6-9
> Micah 5:2
> II Samuel 7:12-16
> Jeremiah 23:5
> Isaiah 7: 14
> Isaiah 11:1

Gather typing paper, markers, and pencils for making advertisements and/or listing names for the Messiah. Have a file folder for each student. Read *The Prophetic Stream* by William Taber, a Pendle Hill Pamphlet for additional background.

IN CLASS

Comments on worship: If you and the children have just come from meeting for worship, invite a brief discussion on the quality of worship, how children felt during worship, and what silent or spoken messages were received. (Sometimes because of preparation for a lesson, you as teacher may be inspired to say something about the children's program from the silence. This ties meeting for worship with what is happening in the First Day School.)

Touch bases: Introduce anyone who is new. Briefly find out what is happening in the childrens' lives. Play a name game if students do not know one another.

Lesson theme: State clearly what you are going to do. "Today we are going to find some promises about the Messiah that the Jewish people feel God made to them through the Old Testament prophets."

Ask questions: Any of the following may be appropriate for your group:

"What is the Old Testament?" (Answers will vary. Stress that the Old Testament is Hebrew Scripture which contains stories of the ways in which people felt God was working in their lives long ago. Some of the people in the Old Testament are called prophets.) If the students are unfamiliar with the Old Testament, give them some time to page through and look at the names of books. Discuss which books are named for prophets.

"Does anyone know what a prophet is?" (The word prophet means "fore-tell" or "forth tell". Talk about the prophets as leaders and moral reformers.)

"What is the New Testament?" (The New Testament starts with the stories of Jesus.) "Some people believe that Jesus was the Messiah. Remember that we are going to find some promises about the Messiah? We had better know what the word 'Messiah' means. Does anyone know?" (Hebrew for "Anointed One" as in anointed with oil. Christ in Greek. An expected savior or liberator of a people or a country.) From whom did the Jews in the times of Jesus wait for liberation? (Romans)

"Look at the table of contents. What do you see? Why is the Bible arranged in this way?" If your class is more experienced: "Can you name some of the prophets? Do you know any of the things these prophets said? There are prophecies in the Old Testament that tell about the coming of a Messiah. Let's find some of the things that the prophets said a long time before Jesus was born."

Give each child a card with the chapter and verse of a prophecy written on it. If your group is smaller than six, use only the first three. A cross section can be obtained from them. If the group is larger than six, ask the children to work in pairs. Pair a young child with an older one to facilitate participation.

If the students have not handled the Bible before, tell them the name on the card is the name of a book. The first number tells the chapter which is just like the chapter of any other book except that chapters in a book in the Bible do not start on a new page (to save space?) The number after the colon (two dots) tells you the verse--tricky since most books we read don't have an indicator for verse.

"To find the right book, look again at the table of contents. When you have found the book, look for the big chapter number in the margin, then the small verse number in the chapter."

Read and discuss: Ask children to read what they have found. As each section is read and discussed, start making a list of names for the Messiah. The list may be kept by the teacher on a large paper or on separate sheets of typing paper by each individual. Individual sheets may be put into individual booklets at the end of the course. Note where each name is found and by whom it was spoken in either case. Ask the young Friend who found each passage to read, then ask the connected questions.

A child is born to us! A son is given to us! And he will be our ruler, He will be called, "Wonderful Counselor," "Mighty God," "Eternal Father," His royal power will continue to grow: his kingdom will always be at peace. He will rule as King David's successor, basing his power on right and justice, from now until the end of time. (Isaiah 9:6-9)

"What are some names given to the Messiah in this passage?" (son, ruler, counselor, God, Father)

"On whose throne will this kingdom be established?" (David's)

"What does that mean? What kind of kingdom do you think people in the days of Jesus expected?"

The Lord says, "Bethlehem Ephrathah, you are one of the smallest towns in Judah, but out of you I will bring a ruler for Israel, whose family line goes back to ancient times." (Micah 5:2.)

"What is the Messiah called in this verse?" (ruler of Israel)

"What town is mentioned as a special place?" (Bethlehem)

"When you die and you are buried with your ancestors, I will make one of your sons king and he will keep his kingdom strong. He will be the one to build a temple for me, and I will make sure that his dynasty continues forever. I will be his father, and he will be my son. When he does wrong, I will punish him as a father punishes his son. But I will not withdraw my support from him as I did from Saul, whom I removed so that you could be king. You will always have descendants, and I will make your kingdom last forever. Your dynasty will never end." (II Samuel 7:12-16)

"This is the promise God made to David through the prophet Nathan when David is disappointed to learn that he will not be the one who builds the temple. What is the promise that Nathan felt God made to David?"   (David's throne will go on forever.)

"What do you think people at that time thought such a promise meant?"

"The Lord says, 'The time is coming when I will choose as king a righteous descendant of David. That king will rule wisely and do what is right and just throughout the land. When he is king, the people of Judah will be safe, and the people of Israel will live in peace. He will be called "The Lord Our Salvation." ' " (Jeremiah 23:5)

"What names does Jeremiah give the Messiah?" (Righteous Branch, King)

"What does the prophet Jeremiah repeat that others have already said?" (descendant of David, peace)

"...Well, then, the Lord himself will give you a sign; a young woman who is pregnant will have a son and will name him 'Immanuel.'" (Isaiah 7:14.)

"What name is given to the Messiah here?" (Immanuel which means "God within us.")

"Who will be his mother?" (a young woman)

"Will the Messiah be a boy or a girl?" (son)

The royal line of David is like a tree that has been cut down; but just as new branches sprout from a stump, so a new king will arise from among David's descendants. (Isaiah 11:1)

"How is this like the other prophecies?"

ACTIVITY

Write an ad. One way everyone knows something today is through ads. Ask the students to be modern prophets with an old message. The message will be spread by making an ad to post in the meetinghouse, include in your meeting newsletter, or keep for a booklet to be assembled at the end of the course.

"Choose one prediction from the Old Testament and decide what you want to say to advertise it. Perhaps you will want to write a slogan such as 'Prepare for Immanuel' or 'Bethlehem is Special'. Can you think of other ideas? You will probably want to choose a few words from your prophecy. What words would you like to choose? Now, make a page ad from your ideas using markers on typing paper."

As students write their ideas, ask them to cite where they found these ideas in the Bible. If there is time, also do an oral TV ad on the same subject.

CLOSING

Pick up and put away materials from the activity as a class. Gather for a closing circle. Perhaps hold hands in silence for a moment if your group is able to hold hands. Or, simply stand in a silent circle.

Restate the theme of this lesson. Ask the children to share what they have learned today out of the silence.

CHECKING

Pack up and clearly mark materials for the next teacher if you are teaching with a partner. Save ads. Either put them up on the classroom wall or save them for the next class meeting if you have no permanent space. Record what you did on the check sheet for the class journal. In the space after each child's name you may wish to informally note the amount of experience that child has had with the Bible.

In addition, you may want to make note of the following:

Do you know the name of each child who attended class?

Do the children know each other?
How is class attendance?
Should you encourage more children to attend by sending
          postcards?
Telephoning?
Writing a newsletter article?
Did the class enjoy making prophecy ads?
Do students like to draw?

Start a file folder of each person's work. If each student is keeping a list of names for the Messiah, put individual lists in file folders. These lists will be used later and may eventually become part of a book assembled by each student.

XIX

Friendly Bible Study

Joanne and Larry Spears

[Note: Larry and Joanne Spears are pillars of the Bismarck, North Dakota Meeting. Both are graduates or Union Theological Seminary in New York. Larry, in addition, is an attorney on the staff of the state supreme court, and Joanne is at work translating the Bible in nonsexist language for children, a project described in the essay following this one.]

History

Early Friends used the Bible as a source of guidance for experiencing the presence of God in their worship and in their lives. George Fox and early Friends lived with the Bible. Their writings are filled with Bible quotations, reflecting their commitment to careful reading and study of the Bible as a source of authority in their lives.

Present Condition

Among Friends today there is a wide range of views of the Bible, from those who see it as an interesting historical document to those who see it as God's Word. An increasing number of Friends feel the need for study of the Bible. They seek an effective study method which reflects Quaker values and tradition and draws them to the core of the Bible message.

Many people remember Bible studies as occasions which encouraged sermonizing and authoritarian statements and discouraged questions. For these people, time spent in Bible study is remembered as fruitless for their spiritual lives and frustrating to the integrity of their own search for truth. Those who are struggling with life and religion, working through childhood religious understandings which have become inadequate to adult life, need the support and direction that a group study can host and a candid study method can provide.

For many, the struggle to find or retain the core of faith, separate from childhood distortions and disappointments, is intense. It is for those people who have been away from Bible Study and who sense a need to turn in its direction that the following method for a Friendly Bible study is shared.

Test for Sound Bible Study Methods

We should apply Quaker insights, understanding and standards to any Bible study method. Any Bible study method should support four important aspects of our tradition:

First, a Bible study method should recognize personal experience as a central part of our spiritual lives.

Second, a Bible study method should recognize the equality of all believers in the study process. It should remove the centrality of an authority figure as leader, thereby affirming that the Spirit works through everyone out of the open silence of even the few seekers gathered together.

Third, a Bible study method should recognize the availability of continuing revelation of God in our spiritual lives.

Fourth, a Bible study method should affirm the connection of the Biblical witness to our lives in our present world.

These elements should be central tests to apply to any Friendly Bible study.

Friendly Bible Study Method

The process of Bible study suggested here--the method --meets each of these tests and is simple to use. This method provides a structure for effective communication. The method suggested here has been arrived at through years of experiment. It is a tool that enables people to initiate and take part in productive exploration of the Bible and their lives.

It takes effort and practice to see the benefit of any Bible study method. But it is our experience that people invariably find that the sharing which grows out of this study method results in new understanding and deeper insight than may come from the use of many other methods. We suggest the use of this format before trying variations.

Eight Steps to a Bible Study Group

Starting a Bible study group can be a simple matter of following eight easy, specific steps:

Gather a group together.
Choose a book of the Bible.
Study only a few verses each week.
Review the questions.
Read the passage aloud.
Start in silence.
Share the answers.
End in silence.

STEP 1: Gather together at least three, but not more than six, interested people with any religious or spiritual background. No prior study of the Bible is needed by anyone. Members need not have ever picked up the Bible before to participate fully in this Bible study.

A person with extensive biblical background can be helpful to the Bible study process, but should not be seen as an authority figure. A group reflecting a diversity of viewpoints provides a stimulating variety of both spiritual experience and understanding.

Ask each person to make a commitment of one hour per week (regularly every week) for six weeks to study the Bible. The study should not begin until every member can make a commitment to attend all of the six study sessions.

Each Bible study should last one hour. Prompt starting assures completion in one hour. Ask each person to bring at least one translation of the Bible to the study session. A variety of translations is helpful to group understanding.

Ask that no one bring any book except the Bible and a notebook. Other references may be consulted after the study, but these books distract members from the Bible itself during the group study. No reading is required prior to the group study. Members may be stimulated to read further to search out solutions to particular problems which the study raises. They may or may not want to report back briefly to the group. However, no study or time outside the group is needed or expected.

By using several different translations of the Bible, it will quickly become apparent that translators are human. A translation cannot reproduce all the meaning of the original text in English. On finer points and on some surprisingly major points, there can be significant differences between one translation and another of the same text. The English words chosen to translate the Hebrew or Greek words are important.

Bible study in which members read from different translations makes the members more sensitive to the choice of English words and the change in meaning when alternate words are used. The English words of a translator point to the meaning of the original text which in turn is an effort to point to truth as an author understood it.

This alone is a liberating insight to many, and it shifts the study effort from an antagonism between the reader and the text to a cooperative partnership between the text and the reader to understand the truth underlying the text.

Have paper and a pencil available for each person. Many will find a notebook useful to maintain their papers for future reference. All writings are private except as their contents are shared orally with the group.

STEP 2: Decide as a group which book of the Bible the group would like to use to begin the study. One of the first three gospels of Matthew, Mark or Luke, or a letter of Paul, like I or II Corinthians or Philippians, is a good choice. In the Old Testament, the Psalms or one of the prophets, like Jonah, Amos, or Hosea, is a good starting point.

Do not start with a difficult book such as I, II or III John, Revelation, Daniel or Leviticus. It is our experience, however, that after some practice this method can be used successfully with any book of the Bible.

STEP 3: Choose just a few verses at the beginning of the book, to be followed each week by the next few verses. It is very important not to skip around among favorite passages. As the Bible study continues through the weeks, discussion will develop as themes emerge which link each session to the discussion in previous sessions.

One paragraph, or one stanza of a Psalm, will usually be three to six verses. It is dangerous to spiritual understanding to try to cover too much material. The goal of Bible study should be deeper understanding of our spiritual life tradition.

This method reflects the view that there is greater insight available through focusing full attention on small amounts of study material than on large amounts of material. Remember that each verse or section is an extract from a larger work. Each section does not necessarily give the true flavor of the whole content or reflect the major underlying themes. References can always be made to the complete book as each section is studied.

Being sensitive to group indications that a particular text is not consistent with their personal experience may indicate passages which need to be set in a larger context. It is essential to take a small number of verses for each Bible study session.

At first glance, there doesn't seem to be very much to discuss in just a few verses. We are culturally conditioned to cover as much material as possible to complete an assigned task. Resist this temptation. Bible study group members often feel frustrated when each member talks about different parts of a long passage. A common focus on a small section provides a focus for deeper insights.

STEP 4: At the beginning of the first few sessions each person needs to write down the five questions (listed below) which are to be answered in the silent period each time you meet (see Step 6). In the first session, and to a lesser degree in the following sessions, each question should be explained as in the text below.

When participants understand the questions, they will need to write down only the abbreviations (MAIN POINT or "Mn Pt," in question 1) as a reminder of the question. After two or three weeks, group members will be so familiar with the questions that they will not need to be reminded of the questions. Each person can answer at whatever level of background they bring. Assure everyone that there are no single answers which capture the totality of any passage.

Bible study is like the group of blind people describing an elephant, each from a separate viewpoint of experience. This Bible study method contributes the viewpoints of each person to our understanding of a common reality. Stress the value of hearing each person's views and seeing the passage through each person's eyes. Each view is important to the study.

The five questions addressed in each Bible study are:

1. What is the author's main point in this passage? (MAIN POINT)

This question helps each member focus on what the author says. It often helps to state the question again in another form: "What is the author saying about God?" Each person must address the text directly in a relationship formed between reader and author.

This is not the time to share the ideas of a commentator, minister, priest, or other authority figure. The search here is for the main point the author was making in this passage and the author's understanding of God working in our world. It is easy to respond with what we would like for the author to have said.

It is easy to express our own ideas on the subject. However, the target of the question is what the author actually said. To help those who may be unsure and timid about Bible study, remind the group again that a variety of responses can help the group see the whole of the passage more clearly. After one or two sessions, this will be easily understood and liberating to most participants.

2. What new light do I find in this particular reading of this passage of the text? (NEW LIGHT)

This question provides opportunity for the working of the Spirit in our silence. This question reminds us of the continuing revelation in our lives from both unfamiliar and familiar passages. The focus here is on each member's new insight, observation, or understanding during this particular reading of this passage on this particular occasion.

Each reading can bring some new or renewed insight. That insight may be small or great. This answer may grow with more and more points as the group works through the passage with other questions.

The new light may be something that is seen now, but had never been seen before. It may be a new understanding of a word or phrase. It may be a new way of seeing a particular problem that this passage triggers in a member's mind. It may be the last in the sequence of questions answered in the silence. It may grow with more and more points as the group works through the passage with other questions.

3. Is this passage true to my experience? (TRUTH)

The focus here is on comparing the message of the Bible passage with each person's experience in life. Our spiritual journeys are "experimental" as we search toward fuller understanding. Our personal experience and our community experience are sources of authority which we bring to the study to understand and supplement the Biblical text.

For those who come from other religious traditions, this question may come as a shock. Few of us have lived in other traditions in which we have been allowed to question the "truth" of the Bible. Yet we are accustomed to answering this question, if not with the Bible, with other written materials. This question is often a freedom experience and consistently will open up new insights for everyone in the group.

Recognition that our present understanding of the passage is not consistent with our experience may require reassessment of the meaning of our experience, deeper study of the meaning of the Bible passage, or recognition that our individual spiritual journeys, as with those of the Biblical authors, are searches in the dark in which full clarity is not given at every moment.

4. What are the implications of this passage for my life? (IMPLICATIONS)

The answer to this question may provide implications for living at any of several levels of spiritual life. The center of the question is, "What difference, if any, does the passage make for my life?" There is a reaching from the text back to our lives in this question. It brings the role of ethics and daily living practices to our attention. This holding together of faith and action is central to our tradition.

5. What problems do I have with this passage? (PROBLEMS)

Here we identify problems of language in the text, of interpretation, of meaning, or of applying the text to our lives. These problems may generate interest in seeking answers from other sources during the days before the next Bible study.

Problems can be identified without being solved. This question reminds us that study of a passage is a continuing process. Like life, understanding is never complete at any one time. It is a continuing dialogue between the text and life.

STEP 5: At the beginning of the Bible study, after being sure each person has understood each question and before starting the study, ask one person to read aloud the passage to be studied. Let all ears hear the sound of the passage. Have all members follow the text in their translations. If translations differ substantially, ask that a contrasting translation of the passage be read aloud. This will often stimulate thinking and insight if the passage seems particularly difficult or without significant meaning.

STEP 6: Move into group silence. After minutes of quiet, individuals begin at their own pace to reread the passage silently and to write answers to each question. This is the time for the group to work in the silence. Each person centers in silence, then moves to rereading and writing when ready.

The duration of the silence is similar to that in worship sharing groups. Take time to settle into the stillpoint and linger there until each member starts the silent reading of the passage and answering the questions.

STEP 7: After 15 or 20 minutes of silence and the completion of written answers, or as soon as everyone seems to be ready or nearly ready with written notes addressing the questions, explain the sharing procedure. In turn, around the circle, individuals read aloud their response to one question at a time. After each person's response to the first question has been shared, pause for a moment of silence. Then move around the circle again sharing the responses to the second question and so on until everyone has responded to each question.

This is the sharing of our insights. The accumulating benefit of these insights around the circle is consistently remarkable, sometimes extraordinary. There should be no extensive discussion during this time of sharing. There should only be short comments or questions for clarification of the individual responses for the remainder of the group. Clarity is important.

At all times, in all groups, the movement around the circle should be preserved. Everyone must have opportunity and time to speak to every question in turn so that the combining wisdom and insights are sensed by the group. Smaller groups can be less firm than larger groups in structuring the sharing of responses to each question without digressing.

Remind everyone that all answers are accepted and helpful. Each person may "pass" at any time on any question, with only the caution that something that seems like the obvious or the trivial to one person can be a wonderful new insight to another.

The only leadership needed by the group is one person who determines the time to begin oral sharing. This person should also maintain the movement around the circle. Keep moving around the circle so that everyone has a chance to answer every question in sequence. Movement around the circle must be fast enough to keep to the one-hour time limit. It is important that everyone feel confident that the study will not take a whole morning, afternoon or evening--one hour only.

Encourage each person to write something on the paper in response to each question. If, after serious consideration, there seems to be nothing to write for any one of the questions, a "pass" is always acceptable. Sometimes we are so unclear that even a tentative response seems impossible. No one needs to feel pressured to have an answer if there is none for that person at that time.

With experience using this Bible study method, the members will see that insights will grow during the sharing. People who join the Bible study with no feeling of insight will find the passage opening to their understanding through the insights shared by others. As the discussion proceeds, new insights will occur which far exceed the sum of the initial individual insights. An apparently superficial comment can be the key to great openings for others in the group.

STEP 8: End the study with a short period of silence. It may be the occasion for breaking silence with a message or simply providing the conclusion in the stillpoint with which the Bible study began.

At the end of six hours over a period of six weeks each person must be free to discontinue or continue the Bible study. Each person should make a conscious decision. It is best not to begin this kind of study as a "Lenten Study" or "Advent Study." Choose a time when there is not an obvious seasonal end in order to permit natural continuation if the group wants a continuing Bible study.

It has been our experience that after six studies, one hour per week, with every member participating every week, most people find the study so helpful they want to continue. Where the group decides to continue Bible study, they should always meet regularly even if only three members can attend a particular session.

Skipping sessions, even for very good reasons, breaks the pattern. Like other spiritual disciplines, no matter how good the results, it may be hard to get going again if there are too many interruptions. The expectation must be that every week there will be a one-hour Bible study and the group always meets, even if, after the initial six weeks, some must occasionally miss an hour.

Conclusion

People are seeking to renew their roots in the tradition of the Bible. A Bible study method can be consistent with the testimonies of the Quaker spiritual tradition. This is an extraordinary Bible Study method in its results. Through Bible study our lives are deepened and renewed.

For further information about this Bible study method, please contact: Joanne and Larry Spears RES Corporation 1824 Catherine Drive, Bismarck, North Dakota 58501 (701) 258-1899.

XX

Translating The Bible For Children
Using Inclusive Language

Joanne Spears

Why a Bible Translated for Children?

Parents and grandparents want their children to know the Bible and its wisdom at an early age. But the Bible was written for adults and translated for adults. Children need Bibles which have been translated at their readability and vocabulary level.

For 300 years it has been widely recognized that the Bible should be translated into the thousands of languages of the peoples of the world. At the same time there has been a general acceptance of giving our own children only Bible paraphrases, or retold Bible stories, based on English versions of the Bible translated for adults.

Too often, translations for adults have been given to children in third or fourth grade during a ceremony which is intended to tell the children that the book given to them is of special value. Yet these Bibles are translated at a reading and vocabulary level beyond that of the receiving child. Children are immediately disappointed and frustrated because they can not understand the Bible. Too often they conclude that the Bible is not relevant to their lives.

We do not expect our children to read or understand Shakespeare in fourth grade. Yet we expect children to benefit from a Bible which has a readability and conceptual level above their own. As long as parents, teachers, and churches want young children to have the Bible, we should find a way to give them translations prepared especially for children.

Bible translations are not rewritten Bible stories. Rewritten Bible stories always carry a much greater amount of the teller's personal theology than does a translation. Bible stories are usually rewritten to make a particular point, too often a particular moral point, rather than to communicate the theological point of the original author.

These story tellers rarely reflect the work of Biblical scholars. These stories lead people to think, incorrectly, that they have learned the contents of the Bible itself. They become accustomed to paraphrases and condensations and have no desire to study the actual Bible. If they do study the Bible from this background, they come to the Bible with preconceived ideas about what it says and, therefore, never actually understand the Bible as its authors intended, or in a way that helps them grow into a mature faith.

Why Inclusive Language for Bible Translations?

Non-sexist language is not gender biased. Non-sexist language is sex-inclusive language, which includes both males and females equally when referring to people who are not specifically identified by sex in the text.

Inclusive-language translations are more accurate.

The first and primary reason for an inclusive-language translation of the Bible is that it is the most accurate way to translate the Bible into English. Current scientific research is demonstrating, as graphic artists have long shown, that by depicting an overwhelming majority of Biblical characters as male, one creates the reality of the Bible. The masculine words "he," "him," "his," and "man," although often meant by writers and translators to be generic and inclusive, are today imaged by virtually all persons of all ages as specifically of the male sex.

Sex-biased translations distort Biblical reality.

Because translators of the Bible have traditionally used the masculine gender as the generic and inclusive gender, English-speaking people throughout history have depicted Biblical characters with male images as the rule and female images as the exception. The frequent use of capital letters on male imaged words "He," "His," "Him" when referring to God or Christ add to the concept that maleness is of greater importance. The historical Jesus was a male. The Christ of all time is not.

Children's first concepts of God and their religious heritage are formed before they are able to distinguish between generic and sexual use of nouns (lord, king, man, men) and pronouns (he, his, him). Children's first experiences of the Bible should be inclusive because this develops the most accurate understanding of the Bible.

If their deepest understanding of their religion is to include an inclusive God who cares for and relates to female and male equally, and an inclusive religious heritage which includes strong women and men and weak men and women, attention to translation accuracy is essential.

Religious sexism harms social structures.

To address the sexism in our religious symbols is one way to improve our social structures. There is a need for a greater awareness of the relatedness of our social structures and our religious symbols. Increasingly people are recognizing the destructive nature of sexism. Today the scope and depth of the effects of sexism are becoming clearer.

A clarified understanding of God and of our religious heritage as inclusive, one that values male and female people equally, is a necessary part of this process. This can be accomplished by more accurate translation of the Bible into English.

There is a danger that important religious symbols will be abandoned if they are not inclusive. Our children, boys and girls, are growing up in a world with a new awareness of the sexism that has long been part of our culture. Children, growing up in or out of the Church, will learn that the deepest symbols infected by sexism are religious symbols.

Since the Bible is the primary source of powerful religious symbols of our culture, an effective way to help young children is to provide inclusive, not gender-biased, Biblical and religious symbols for them as they grow in their awareness of the world around them.

Our language shapes our understanding of life.

No matter what our religion is, it is the basis for our actions. When our religious language gives greater importance to males, our understanding of life will also include an understanding of males as having greater importance. Our Twentieth-Century religious language is unfair to boys and men by encouraging them to feel themselves to be superior to girls and women. Our Twentieth-Century religious language is unfair to girls and women by leading them to feel themselves to be inferior to boys and men. When God is imaged as male, then male is believed to be superior to all that is female.

These inaccuracies in religious language distort our understanding of God and the Biblical message. Psychologists have long known that the way we refer to ourselves, to one another, and to God, and how we understand and interpret these references, has critical importance for our thoughts and actions. The inaccuracies in present Bible translations distort the text and wrongly communicate that all people, regardless of sex, are called to be sons of a father God, brothers in the faith, to be saved by a male Christ, and to be led by a male Spirit. These false ideas of male centeredness, due to the wrong use of English masculine words used in present English translations of the Bible, are not supported by an accurate understanding of the Biblical texts themselves.

WORD OF MOUTH

WORD OF MOUTH is a newsletter to share the ongoing work of accurately translating the Bible for children using inclusive language. The Bible is a primary source of powerful religious symbols. The first experience of the Bible often forms the deepest images in a child's spiritual life. Therefore, it is important that children first receive the Bible in a form they can understand and that the translation is as accurate as possible.

A child's first experience of the Bible needs to be inclusive, if the deepest understanding of a child's religion is to be of an

inclusive God and if the Biblical message is to be equally available
to girls and to boys. It should accurately reflect the roles of men
and women in the Biblical record. It should be accessible to a
child's ability to read or hear with an understanding of the
vocabulary used in the text.

WORD OF MOUTH translations provide this accessibility
of the Bible to children. Many people have asked to have copies
of the WORD OF MOUTH translations of the Bible. These are
translations expressly for children--not paraphrases. They incorporate
modern research findings regarding the readability levels of children.
People have been eager to obtain copies as they are available and
have wanted to know more about the project.

WORD OF MOUTH is a newsletter which is available to
answer these requests. WORD OF MOUTH articles cover many
topics, including accurate translations from Hebrew and Greek, the
use of inclusive language for children, articles on the canon and how
it was formed, guidelines for evaluating currently available
"Children's Bibles," and the history of translations and the
procedure used to assess readability levels of literature for children.
The name of the newsletter, WORD OF MOUTH, reflects the way
in which people have heard about this work and also the oral
tradition by which scripture was first communicated, sometimes for
centuries, before it was reduced to writing for preservation.

We look forward to sharing this work with people who are
interested in ideas of inclusive language and of translating for
children. We value comments and suggestions about the translations.

If you want to support this work, please subscribe to WORD
OF MOUTH and critique the translations, making comments and
suggestions as they come to you in WORD OF MOUTH. To
receive one volume (four issues) of WORD OF MOUTH, send
$15.00 to Religious Education Services (RES), 1824 Catherine,
Bismarck, North Dakota 58501. Please make checks out to RES
Corporation.

XXI

Who Is Sophia? And Why Is She Important?

By Cynthia Taylor

[Note: Biographical information follows this essay.]

The Bible is rich with multiple names and images of God. Some of this heritage offers us models of God as a mighty hero, a judge, or a king whose energy is masculine, transcendent. Yet some of it, less well known, offers an undeniably feminine and immanent image of God.

Unfortunately, some of the strongest pictures of the Divine Feminine are "hidden" in books that many of us have never read or even knew existed. As modern feminists (people of either gender whose commitment is to the full equality--economic, social, political, religious--of all persons) become interested in bibilical scholarship, these hidden texts are being studied more carefully.

We confirm Elizabeth Cady Stanton's 19th Century awareness that cultural limitations on women have strong roots in the biblical interpretation. (See *The Women's Bible* by Elizabeth Cady Stanton & the Revising Committee, 1895--republished 1974 by Coalition Task Force on Women and Religion, Seattle, WA). Stanton thought there would be no change in women's position in society until

> "another revision of the Protestant Bible shall strike from its pages all invidious distinctions based on sex....Not until women make an organized resistance against the withering influences of canon law, will they rid themselves of the moral disabilities growing out of the theologies of our times." ("Has

Christianity Benefited Woman?", *North American Review*, May 1888.)

Meeting Stanton's ideas in the mid-seventies--nearly one hundred years later--was apocalyptic for me. Talking with Catholic feminists who were equally concerned with the Catholic Bible and its effect led me next into wondrous new territory--the Apocrypha.

Apocrypha actually means "hidden books"--those Judeo-Christian scriptures which for many reasons were judged unworthy (for many reasons) of being included into the canon. It is to these apocryphal, or deutero-canonical books that we turn to find one of the most frequently used female names for God's power: SOPHIA, the Greek name for Divine Wisdom.

In Hebrew her name is Hokhmah. She is co-creator of the world, guardian and teacher of hidden mysteries, messenger and lover of God, a stream of pure glory, an everlasting light, an image of God's goodness, the one who makes all things new, the very "breath of God." (Proverbs 8:27-31 and Wisdom 7:25-26)

Biblical feminists are reclaiming the Bible as a tool for understanding ourselves, human culture and our vocation as change-agents for the future. We work to see past, rather than through the distorting lenses of patriarchy; we strive to look toward the True Source. Gradually more of us see that Sophia is not an obscure figure from history, not simply an archaic idea, but one vital way of comprehending God's nurturing power, God's never-ending motherhood of life.

"Wisdom" or Sophia, in the first eight chapters of Proverbs (within the canon) is also the name for a way of knowing, a capacity for discernment and clear perception. She is not an independent goddess, not a remote carry-over from Canaan's cults, but a complex synthesis of images which requires some sophisticated thinking, a real stretching of our everyday notions about God and theology.

When the sages of Israel speak of Sophia as the shelter and starlight of pilgrims (Wisdom 10:17-19), or the mother of all good things (Wisdom 7:10-11), we need poetic, eastern ears--not our usual western, scientific logic--to hear their meaning. We must listen with our third ear, our *inward receptivity*, seeking divine help to know God as the "all encompassing womb" which mystics have experienced.

We might learn something good from the non-intellectual theology, including iconography, of Greek or Russian Orthodox churches. Perhaps Western culture has not noticed Sophia because we have drifted away from that deeper, eastern way of knowing, thus making her more and more distant. But Sophia is increasingly important to biblical feminists, and I believe she has something significant to offer Friends, if we are ready to admit that "the present system is breaking down, that we must find ways to break through to a different kind of future." (*The Chalice and The Blade*, Riane Eisler, Harper, 1988)

Modern Quakerism has drifted, along with the dominant culture in which it exists and with which it must daily trade or interact, into unprecedented individualism--with its insideous rank-ordering of persons and hierarchical ways of thinking (the dominator model of technological development).

This drift, like every addiction, must first be admitted before it can be changed. We have to think that we can be transformed by God before we will know renewal as children of God. Then, I have found, we are enabled to live our testimonies.

But for the Quaker testimonies on equality and peace and unity to be fulfilled, we must make this transition as communities--knowing God as the one doing the converting--in order for our testimonies to become fully communal, less individualistic ways of thinking and behaving. We will gradually--together, in community--become capable of greater waiting upon God for broader and deeper, communal understanding of God's will and greater sharing of resources (the partnership model based on the power of linking rather than of ranking).

As we grow toward greater spiritual depth, knowing God as intimate Friend and Lover, more women and men are already called to see what the less familiar Judeo-Christian scriptures have to say about *mutuality* by taking a closer look at the eternal partnership between Divine Wisdom and the Almighty Creator, between Sophia and Yahweh. (Note: For more on mutuality as essential to Divine energy, read *The Divine Invasion*, by Philip Dick [Simon and Schuster, 1984, out of print but available in some libraries] a science fiction fantasy about the names, faces and methods of Sophia/God.)

But here I am, speeding!

Let us move backwards briefly, restarting this exploration of SOPHIA with some ancient history; then spend a brief time examining how the canon developed; finally returning to some implications of Sophia for Friends today.

In 586 B.C.E. (before the common era) Jerusalem was captured by Nebuchadnezzar II, king of Babylon. Part of the population was deported, remaining in exile--the Babylonian captivity--for over three generations. A genuine shift in understanding of God and God's ways followed this political chaos. The Jewish sages learned the hard way--experientially--that their God was not a local deity, limited to particular geography or demanding animal sacrifices.

During this time the institution of the synagogue developed. This is still a powerful concept in Judaism and its offspring: that the faith community creates its own place for collective meetings with God, retelling their story, and keeping covenant alive.

Mostly educated Hebrews enduring foreign captivity, speaking and writing two or three languages, these captives worked quietly to be successful in a bustling cosmopolitan world very different from provincial Palestine. Writings which appeared after this captivity reveal that they began to experience God as ever-present, working "behind the scenes", nurturing their hopes and dreams for the future, advising them about life and keeping them spiritually secure.

Through religious disciplines and communal exhortations, they felt aided in spiritual awareness or discernment of Divine Guidance. While many of their compatriots completely adapted to the Babylonian way of life, some remained faithful to the Law and yearned for home, weeping by the waters of Babylon. (Psalm 137) Abraham Leon Sachar writes:

"They began to understand the deeper significance of the prophetic messages. Yahweh was not dependent on temples and sacrifices. He was a god of the heart, as near in Babylon as in Palestine..." (*A History of the Jews*, Random House, 1964, p. 79)

During this exile the monumental Second Isaiah was written (Chapters 40-66); these chapters reveal an important deepening of Israel's awareness of God's constant presence, commissioning God's people to lift up their heads and hearts toward a new dawn. We also find in Second Isaiah some important female images of God: "As a mother comforts her child, so will I comfort you." (Isaiah 66:13; see also 49:50)

The prophet Baruch, writing in Greek about the same time, made a causal connection between the suffering endured in captivity and Israel's having "forsaken the fountain of wisdom....they have not recognised the path that she treads." (Baruch 3:12, 21)

Following this period, returnees brought back to their homeland a keen sense of destiny and of justice. Talmudic writings of the First and Second Century B.C.E. used the term *Shekinah* to express the indwelling presence and glory of God. Like Hohkmah (Wisdom in Hebrew), Shekinah is feminine and present from the moment of creation. In my mind, Sophia and the Shekinah are one.

In their book *Sophia: The Future of Feminist Spirituality*, (Harper 1986) Cady, Ronan & Taussig declare that

"There is more material on Sophia in Hebrew scriptures than there is about almost any other figure. In all of these books only four persons have more written about them than Sophia. Only God (under various titles), Job, Moses and David are treated in more depth."

For more history of the Wisdom Literature, see the explanatory chapter in the Jerusalem Bible, the leather covered edition which is not paperback. (Note: For more on the connectedness between heaven and earth, spirit and body, which Sophia's wholeness offers see *The Great Mother*, by Eric Neumann, Princeton University Press, 1963).

Things really warm up among biblical scholars when they look into the Christian Scriptures for evidence of Sophia. This is where some see heresy, where orthodoxy rubs shoulders with Gnostic tradition. Yet more of us are seeing that Jesus and Sophia are the same, as are Christ and the "Comforter" whom Jesus promised to his disciples.   This latter aspect of God's energy is the Holy Spirit, which was present with God from the beginning of time (Genesis 1:1,2). This *ruach* (Hebrew for God's breath) is also feminine. This is Sophia, who said about herself:

> *Yahweh created me when his purpose first unfolded,*
> *before the oldest of his works. From everlasting I*
> *was firmly set, from the beginning, before earth came*
> *into being. The deep was not, when I was born, there*
> *were no springs of water. Before the mountains were*
> *settled, before the hills were, I came to birth; before*
> *he made the earth, the countryside, or the first grains*
> *of the world's dust. When he fixed the heavens firm,*
> *I was there, when he drew a ring on the surface of*
> *the deep, when he thickened the clouds above, when*
> *he fixed fast the springs of the deep, when he*
> *assigned the sea its boundaries--and the waters will not*
> *invade the shore--when he laid down the foundation*
> *of the earth, I was by his side, a master craftsman,*
> *delighting him day by day, ever at play in his*
> *presence, at play everywhere in his world, delighting*
> *to be with humans. (Proverbs 8:22-31, Jerusalem*
> *Bible)*

Paul emphasizes in I Corinthians 1: 23-25 and 2: 6-8 that Jesus is God's Sophia. Christ incarnates Sophia; they are one. Of course, few of us have ever been taught this amazing truth! But once we know the ancient and parallel texts, it is not hard to see that John was writing about Jesus/Sophia in the first chapter of his gospel; John has simply given the Word of God a new name!

In the gospels of Matthew and Luke, Jesus even speaks the words of Sophia (he knew ancient texts): Matthew 11:25-30, Luke 11:49-51 and 13:34-35. Compare also James 3:13-17 with Wisdom 7:22-30 and Psalm 102:25-27; John 14:15-17 with Wisdom 6:17-20; Matthew 11:28-30 and John 6:35 with Ecclesiasticus 24:17-22.

The attempt to find categories or metaphors through which Jesus' significance can be explained is called Christology. This study (of the nature, person and actions of Jesus Christ) was the primary task of early church theologians, bringing them hard up against Gnosticism and its related difficulties.

Without going too deeply into formal Christology--a rewarding journey, one I have taken and highly recommend--I want to remind Friends that there are many images and analogies used by all New Testament writers and *by George Fox* (see latest T. Canby Jones publications, including his adult curriculum, CHRIST IS...) to explain the meaning of Jesus' life, ministry, crucifixion and resurrection.   He is known as teacher, healer, shepherd, lamb of God, seed of God, high priest, son, prophet, Light of the world. Why not also as Sophia?

Authors Cady, Ronan, & Taussig (*Sophia: The Future of Feminist Spirituality*) state emphatically that "Jesus in John takes his character from Sophia.   The picture of Jesus in John as self-proclaiming teacher sent from heaven by God with whom he creates and communicates is the picture of Sophia." (p. 47)

I urge you to read this book and make your own decision. Before they published this book, Susan Cady and Hal Taussig gave a workshop on Sophia in November 1985 for Philadelphia area Methodists.   Someone told me about an unusual retreat for Methodist women and invited me.   In that situation my friend was a messenger of the Spirit! It was quite a liberating weekend for my heart, and a deep challenge to my mind! I have been studying and pondering ever since.

The studying necessarily has taken me into an unexpected area: learning more about how the Bible was pieced together.   In other words, what constitutes the canon--who decided its limits, by what criteria, and why?

Bernhard Anderson in *Understanding the Old Testament*, writes that while devotion to the Torah (also called The Pentateuch, both of which refer to the first five books of the Hebrew scriptures) was the unifying factor in Judaism, there was also great richness and diversity in what the faith community used as scripture in worship.

The fall of Jerusalem with the destruction of the Temple in 70 C.E. (Common Era; formerly known as A.D.) and the circulation of Christian "messianic writings" caused a crisis in Judaism, leading to a special called meeting at Jamnia in 90 C.E. Long before this event, however, "the Law and the Prophets" had been the standing expression for the scriptures--even though a third category had been shaping for a while, called "The Writings." The Psalms are an example of this collection, already used in worship.

Jamnia, or Jabneh, on the coast of Palestine was an academy of Jewish studies established after the war with Rome, 66-70 C.E. In 90 C.E. rabbis gathered there for a special meeting to settle on criteria for acceptance of books as authoritative. Three principles prevailed:

1.) a book had to be in harmony with the written Torah;

2.) it had to have been written before the exile, since they assumed that prophetic inspiration ended in the post-exile period, just after the time of Ezra. All books written during the Hellenistic period were excluded;

3.) books written in Greek were unacceptable, as Greek was not used during the period of prophetic inspiration.

About some books, e.g. Song of Songs, Ecclesiastes and Esther, many rabbis had serious questions--some still do. Anderson warns that Jamnia was not "an ecclesiastical council which arrived at official decisions binding upon the community." In fact, "those writings were preserved and used devotionally which spoke authoritatively to the community of faith." (Anderson, op. cit. p.597-600)

Most probably, the formation of a Jewish canon was triggered by the sudden growth of Christian churches claiming equal authority for their writings. The rabbis perceived a threat to the centrality of the Law.

The story of the development of a Christian canon, or official list of books of the Bible which were authoritative for

Christians, is equally conflictual. The issues were many, including protection against numerous heresies.

As we learn from reading Paul's letters, teachers and teachings or doctrines abounded. Just as we find now in the Religious Society of Friends, there was considerable variety of opinion about many points of both faith and practice! Then as now, some of the differences hinged on language and its subtle meanings. Concepts of deity ranged from a remote, indifferent "principle" to an active, living creator who heard and cared about every word or sigh uttered by every individual.

But some of the differences were in cosmology, how humans understood the creation and its meanings. There were so many contradictory epistles and gospels available that it must have been exceedingly difficult for religious educators to know what to give to new converts for their growth in the faith.

Demiurges, aeons, mediators, emanations and new theories multiplied overnight, like wire coathangers in closets. Salvation was available through any number of complex pathways. In resistance to the several heresies, bishops and scholars published official lists of books that would provide reliable sources of truth for the rapidly growing churches; there were just too many converts to rely upon the oral tradition alone.

Several heresies thrived, and their stories are fascinating (see *Creeds in the Making*, by Alan Richardson, SCM Press, 1958). But for our purposes of understanding Sophia, one in particular must be mentioned: Gnosticism--the way of knowledge ('gnosis' in Greek). Because it denied that Creation was good, and that the Incarnation was real (Jesus wasn't human and didn't really feel the crucifixion), it was not acceptable to those for whom Christianity was a faith rooted in Judaism and its concept of a just, almighty, covenant-keeping God.

Gnosticism also had a Sophia (see *The Gnostic Religion*, Hans Jonas, Beacon Press, 1958 pp. 176-199); she became more esoteric and more complicated, dangerously anti-Yahweh and no longer to be trusted as a reflection of God's commitment to justice and shalom.

The gnostic tradition is not dead; portions of it still appeal to many moderns, but its nihilistic attitude about nature could destroy all life on earth! By the end of the second century, three criteria had developed for judging that a book was worthy of the new faith:

1.) fidelity to the earliest preaching of Jesus' gospel;

2.) correspondence to the Old Testament prophecies;

3.) apostolicity, or a clear foundation in the work of the apostles.

The original nucleus around which the Christian canon seems to have been formed is the body of letters from Paul and portions of Luke-Acts. It took several hundred years for the church to become organized; it took just as long to decide on its official biblical texts.

The final decisions were made in North Africa in 393 and 397 C.E., with Augustine and Jerome playing large roles in establishing the Old and New Testaments and the Apocrypha. The latter were dropped from the Protestant Bible after the Council of Trent in 1545-63. The discoveries of the Nag Hammadi or Coptic Gnostic library in 1945 and of the Dead Sea Scrolls in 1947, have shed much light on the problems facing the early church fathers in deciding what to include. To examine some books not included in the canon, see the *Nag Hammadi Library*, recently translated into English and now in paperback.

Quakers have an old testimony to the continuation of God's revelations; for some the very idea of canon will be a total desertion of Quaker principles. But Friends are constantly drawing up lists of books for newcomers and students of Quakerism! So we cannot fault the early church educators for trying to bring some order into their chaos. What are the ten books you would take with you into isolation (a desert island or a space journey, i.e. a very long trip far from libraries)?

Some Universalists claim that their scriptures are all the holy books of all the world religions. As one who tried that for nearly fifteen years, returning to the foot of the cross from the orient, I rejoice in discovering that my core library is not so large. The availability of many resources is always an important freedom, but it will not necessarily reflect what keeps one going through thick and thin.

Not only for the sake of simplicity, nor for my shoulders during address changes, but for my soul I've found less to be necessary. When the Christ-Child's manger, cross and resurrection are within, the Word or Breath of God--the Inward Teacher--will instruct from life itself.

With joy I have found written evidence for my own mystical and life experiences, including my visions of the divine feminine, within the Judeo-Christian scriptures. I more fully "grok" George Bernard Shaw's answer to the query above. His list of books consisted of the Bible, a one-volume complete works of Shakespeare, and the remainder in blank notebooks!

I am unconvinced that Quakers are finished with the Bible.

There is too much in it to learn, to ponder. It is too vital for understanding the Quaker classics, my own faith journey, our communal knowing and acting, our relating with other people and societies.

The central point of modern Sophialogy is the relationship between God and the world. Sophia brings to us a new awareness of this divine-human relationship. However, I would not say she is the twin sister of Jesus (a question I was asked in one of my workshops). Jesus for me is Sophia, the same beacon who leads me to make knowing and being known by God my primary relationship. She tempers my grasp of the Unknown, the central mystery of the faith, i.e. how Christ lives now, resurrected and incarnated in hearts open to receive him/her.

However, my relationship with God will suffer if I limit it to one metaphor or model. I only diminsh and confuse myself if I get stuck on one. Sometimes it is appropriate to use the image of judge and guilty one (sometimes I stand convicted); or of a wrestling match (I have indeed experienced that anguish); or of a shepherd and sheep (yes, I sometimes do stupid things and need my shepherd's care). Sophia leads me beside still waters and comforts my soul.

Nor do God and I relate only as physician and patient (although when I hurt deeply, I return gladly to God for healing). When I feel particularly vulnerable, my prayer may be that God as loving father (or as Big Mama) will protect and help me. In addition to these ways of relating, many times I feel that this is a relationship between lovers who care for each other deeply and are committed to mutual growth and support. This is why the Song of Solomon has been included in the category of Wisdom Literature; God and the soul are spouses, eagerly awaiting each other, tenderly meeting each other, working as partners in love for the world.

Never can we assume that this espousal means that we must leave the world. Nor must we deny either nature or our "flesh" as good. To be incarnated with God is a glory, an honor and gift for humanity! We can love and be loved by God and still affirm our interdependence with special humans, loving them deeply, feeling our lives irrevocably interwoven with them.

God's love gives us wisdom and insight into being more loving with one another. In *WomanChrist*, a mystical and Jungian approach to Sophia, Christin Lore Weber writes that "Our spirituality needs to be one of becoming more and more sensitive to Wisdom and of living in accord with her. We are creation. We are the movement of Wisdom....Wisdom is the heart of God....Our deepest consciousness is God-consciousness; our deepest subjectivity is divine." (p. 168)

For those of us who have had this experience of being kissed by God, of *knowing* God and *being known* in intimate embrace, we recall desiring private time together (prayer) and longing for each other as would two lovers whose work has separated them for a time; of being awakened at night by God as a spouse asking for us to listen to something important, spoken in soft whispers.

Sophia as God's breath is an opening provided by Grace. She is Grace, working through or as Christ/Messiah to show humans that mutuality is exactly what has been in the mind of God since before the world began.

Out of this understanding, we *could* form new ways of living in community, where decisions are made in concert with God and where other intimates (friends of God) help us to grow closer to God. As a body, gathered in love and tenderness, expecting to be kissed by God and yet "fearing" God (i.e. approaching with awe), we will seek to know God's truth and to discern God's will. We yearn for this tenderness and communion with God and with each other.

But a word of warning seems in order! We must know that not everyone wants this fellowship. The search for Sophia, according to Proverbs 14, divides people into two groups: the wise and the foolish, the virtuous and the wicked, the prudent and the schemers, the humble and the arrogant.

These are the same divisions which Jesus used, to the annoyance of many who thought they were wise and he, foolish. There are still rigid, sanctimonious critics around, behaving like the sour pharisees that wanted Jesus out of the way. They would tell us that we have it all wrong, we'd better toe the old mark, pretty quick.

Something frightens them into thinking that mutuality is the opposite of morality. They (we?) assume that too much intimacy, ecstasy, and passion must be wrong, that "all hell will break loose" if people get so filled with delight in God and life that they overlook the Law. For biblical feminists that is a false dichotomy. Sometimes the sour critic lives within, and only Sophia/Christ can rout its fear-based arrogance.

While some male scholars have seen Wisdom literature as overly focused on the individual and his/her relationship with God, feminist biblical theologians are clear that for Sophia to be relevant now, she must be about a full and wider morality, about a transformed sight and hearing that includes higher ethical desires for justice and peace, for all of creation.

Both the individual perspective and the historical, communal comprehension of Divine action in human history are necessary to bring about a just society. We are relational beings, agents and recipients of Love; relational or "I-Thou" issues are feminist issues.

Early Quakers had a similar grasp of the connection between an apocalyptic experience of Christ as Present Now and openly shared spiritual fellowship with others in a new order of living. They were not content to let the experience of Christ's immediate presence remain a private possession. (See Doug Gwyn's *Apocalypse of the Word*, Friends United Press, 1984 p. 205.) They formed close, caring groups in which their ministry to one another and to the world was of a whole, as they strengthened, enabled and equipped one another to hear and obey the voice of their Lord-- heard within and verified corporately.

Radical dependence upon that voice took them joyfully into prison, to the Caribbean, to Turkey, to places they would not have dreamed of going on their own, to carry out God's plan that all creation shall be united in truth and love and peace. Their lives and faith are still persuasive.

What kinds of places are many Quaker meetings today? Are they close and caring groups, where our energies are restored by love and our ministries are empowered, where our complete dependence on God is encouraged? It could be from the "womb- love" of our meeting that we go forth, sent by the Eternal One who is always with us, steadying our course.

A few of us have experienced this, and long for more. Within this close sharing and relating, this "communion" as lovers and help-meets of God, we receive the strength to keep on going in a world that looks so grim, so filled with greed and hatred and cruelty. Quaker feminists know that few Friends' meetings have been such places; we have needed retreats and women's meetings in which we hope to find Sophia again, to hear her comfort and to acknowledge her challenge.

A few men have wished us well, seeing that love means letting go, wondering at their own fuzzy lenses and long enjoyed privileges. Still, too many Friends are resisting, puzzling over language and what this "goddess-fuss" is all about.

They do not see that something was and still is broken. They would have us hurry to get through this uncomfortable phase, to arrive at a destination of gender-less god concepts, attributing the

feminist phenomenon to irrational thinking, to early childhood
psychosexual trauma, to any number of social maladjustments.

One point we must give them, when they bring it up. It is
true that impersonal models of God are safeguards against the
limitations of all images. As one of my teachers of philosophy said,
"All analogies limp." We know that a rich body of mystical
literature points in the direction of non-anthropomorphic images or
metaphors.

Yet it is also true that we humans like metaphors. We
create them at every chance to help us express our inward being and
outward relating. However, one of them, the model of God as
Father, has become more than a problem. It has been altered from
its original, nurturant meaning. It has changed from being a once-
helpful model; it is now an all-powerful idol whose use is too often
abusive.

Insistence on fatherhood as the only or best model makes
it an idolatry! Finding solidarity with those who are oppressed,
becoming agents of love, we will refrain from hitting people with
anything. Choosing life over death and peace over war, affirming
creation as good and participating as caretakers of the garden, we
will use it sparingly. We'll put our energy with the "impoverished"-
-listening carefully to what is being said, then correcting our sight.

Sophia as a model gives me the opportunity--indeed, the
responsibility--to act justly, to love mercifully and to walk with
humility and reverence. And thus it is true that Sophia cannot be
the final model; to make her such would only be another idolatry.
As Sallie McFague notes in *Metaphorical Theology* (Fortress Press,
1982) the human spirit needs the freedom to use many models of
God. McFague wisely writes that "all our language about God is
but metaphors of experiences of relating to God." (p. 194)

Friends know this truth, and yet keep slipping into the
dominant culture's patterns and ways of speaking, subtly trying to
get familial peace through avoidance of conflict. When we signal
to someone that we wish they would hurry up and heal--get through
with languishing and self-indulgence--or that we don't believe their
pain is real, we become part of the problem, supplying salt to their

wounds. Rather, let us ask, what can we do? Let's listen with affirmative nods and patience, eyes filled with love and attention.

And let us take seriously in our meetings the number of new people who come to us looking for what Sophia represents: divine wisdom, divine light, wholeness, God's glory, an image of God's goodness. The needed healing will only come slowly. We--the spiritual offspring of a wise people who gave Christianity the vital new model of God as friend--may have a long haul as a faith community in helping ourselves and our world recover from the trauma inflicted by wrong use of god models. Even if "father" has no negative connotations for me, when my sister cries out, how dare I deny her sorrow or leap over our unity as children, friends, lovers of God?

And one more query must be put to Quaker feminist thinkers. It can only be said woman to woman: *what is our goal?* Do we allow for, make space for the pluralism we want? Do we see that we, too, could go too far from our human center, creating another idolatry?

In the long run, Sophia cannot replace Yahweh. Neither can she be separated from Yahweh. The male and female energies need each other to complete the vision, interdependent in every way. Sophia could--but she will not stand alone, a separate goddess of nature or culture.

Neither dare we. We are connected to *diverse families*, to sons and nephews, to daughters and nieces, to parents, spouses and friends, to our meeting communities by promises and vocations, by needs and aspirations. They need us and we need them, however flawed or imperfect.

I see us becoming more, not less intertwined as we grow spiritually. We live in the tough and ugly world in the midst of which Sophia has always lived. "Sophia calls aloud in the streets, she raises her voice in the public squares; she calls out at the street corners, she delivers her message at the city gates." (Proverbs 1: 20,21)

Not a description of a meek, mild woman! Nor one

delivering a popular message! She never forsakes her own, however, and will be available to those who have eyes to see and ears to hear. I pray that more Friends are listening. In the long, slow task of bringing more love, more justice, more peace to a tired, bleeding world we modern Friends need Sophia's commitment to the long haul and to community as much as we need her daring.

BIBLICAL PASSAGES WHERE SOPHIA MAY BE FOUND:

Job 28; Proverbs 1:20-9:18; Wisdom 6:1-11:4; Ecclesiasticus (Sirach) 1, 4:11-20, & chapter 24; Baruch 3:9-4:4; John 1:1-18.
Bible quotations in this essay are from the Jerusalem Bible, 1966

About myself and my personal experience of Sophia:

In 1960 I earned a B. Sc. in chemistry, with a minor in education, from Ursinus College and then worked for a while in biochemistry and cell biology, believing that a career as a physician was in front of me. The birth and nurturance of four sons, the death of one of them, and the many questions inherent in parenting--drew me toward Religious Education as my vocation. My childhood was rich in biblical studies from several traditions including Congregational, Lutheran, and Mennonite--where the Bible was a peace-maker's tool.

Between 1973 and 1976, I trained in the Unitarian-Universalist accreditation program for religious educators. Hungry for even more knowledge about belief systems and their power, I earned an M.A. in Philosophy with a concentration in Religious Studies at the Unversity of New Mexico.

After a sudden divorce, a two year return to bio-medical research, and a year as a technical writer and editor in the semiconductor industry, I had an opportunity to spend nearly a week alone in New Mexico's Jemez mountains. I needed this time, to be sure that God really was calling me back to educational ministry. My meeting confirmed my leading, and I moved to Philadelphia to become the Religious Education Coordinator for Friends General Conference from June, 1983 through September, 1989.

A distant member of Albuquerque Monthly Meeting (New Mexico) and a sojourning member of Newton Monthly Meeting (Camden, New Jersey), I'll return to New Mexico in early 1990 to begin work as Joint Service Projects Coordinator for InterMountain Yearly Meeting and the American Friends Service Committee.

Slowly, I have become braver about telling Friends that I was "mystically startled" during a visit to Findhorn in 1978. Gradually I have gained confidence and words to talk about who it was that greeted me as personal spiritual guide: Christ as a woman!

And there have been other times, luring me to learn more over the years about this guide's power for healing and transforming both the inner and outer world. In the summer of 1986, I began leading short workshops on Sophia and Wisdom Literature at InterMountain and Illinois Yearly Meetings. In 1987, I was invited to lead a group of English Friends in this same exploration in London, at Friends House, Euston Road. In the fall of 1988, I led a full weekend workshop at Powell House on Sophia. In each place, Quakers--women and men--found Sophia important for widening their concepts of deity. And I learned more about her compassion.

My personal hope is that Friends will continue to study this concept and soon share with each other how Sophia is working in our lives, what insights from our own hearts give evidence of Sophia's presence. Perhaps we'll inquire of each other how Sophia makes a difference in our understanding of God's plan for all of creation to live in peace and harmony, carrying mutuality to new levels.

To find Sophia in the Judeo-Christian scriptures, it is important to use a Bible that contains the deutero-canonical books (apocrypha). The Jerusalem, New English, Today's English Version (Good News) Bibles all have versions with these books. To check, look for the Book of Baruch--if that is not in the Bible, then it is what is known as the Protestant canon and will sharply limit your vision of Sophia. The Catholic tradition has used Sophia to fortify Mariology, while the Protestant tradition has completely ignored her.

BIBLIOGRAPHY

I recommend several books in this essay, but three are especially important: *Sophia: The Future of Feminist Spirituality* by Susan Cady, Marian Ronan, and Hal Taussig (Harper & Row, 1986). *WomanChrist* by Christin Lore Weber (Harper, 1987). And *The Divine Feminine*, The Biblical Imagery of God as Female, by Virginia Ramey Mollenkott (Crossroad, 1984).

Other books mentioned include:

The Women's Bible by Elizabeth Cady Stanton & the Revising Committee, 1895--republished 1974 by Coalition Task Force on Women and Religion, Seattle, WA.

The Chalice and The Blade, Riane Eisler, Harper, 1988.

The Divine Invasion, by Philip Dick, Simon and Schuster, 1984.

The Gnostic Religion, Hans Jonas, Beacon Press, 1958.

Apocalypse of the Word, Douglas Gwyn, Friends United Press, 1984.

Metaphorical Theology, Sally McFague, Fortress Press, 1982.

XXII

Plenary Address:
The Bible And Continuing Revelation

Elizabeth Watson

[Note: A well-known writer, speaker and Quaker minister, Elizabeth Watson has been living in North Easton, Massachusetts, and attending Easton Meeting.]

Margaret Fell tells of George Fox preaching at Ulverston, near her home in 1652, and quotes him as saying:

> Then what had any to do with the Scriptures, but as they came to the Spirit that gave them forth? You will say, Christ saith this, and the apostles say this, but what canst thou say?

And she comments:

> Then I saw clearly that we were all wrong....And I cried in my spirit to the Lord, 'We are all thieves, we are all thieves, we have taken the Scriptures in words, but know nothing of them in ourselves!' (1)

Sometimes knowing Scripture in words can lead to knowing it in ourselves. I grew up in an old-fashioned Sunday School that gave stars for memorizing Bible verses. There have been times in my life when I have been too sick to read, and have drawn strength and courage from the wealth of Biblical passages stored up in childhood.

During a long life I have found many different ways to read the Bible, each one adding new understanding and constituting continuing revelation. My love affair with the Bible began early. I dearly loved my grandfather, a Bible-thumping Methodist preacher. He made the Bible stories come alive, and set me to reading them for myself. At that time I accepted his faith that God had quite literally dictated all this to Moses and other worthies.

I early came to appreciate the Bible as literature. And all my life I have read it meditatively, finding inspiration and words to live by. Sometimes such reading has yielded new insights from familiar passages.

In high school I learned to read the Bible historically and developmentally, as the record of the growing concept of God in the experience of the Hebrew people: from the tribal deity of wrath and vengeance, to the God of justice, and finally to the God of mercy, forgiveness, and love.

In college I learned how the different documents and traditions had been woven together, not always consistently. Also, I was a Greek major. I still like to go back to the Greek text when working on New Testament themes. I regret that I never learned Hebrew.

In September 1936, I first crossed the threshold of Chicago Theological Seminary and paused before words attributed to Pastor John Robinson, carved into the stone of the entry:

The Lord has more truth and light yet to break forth from his Holy Word.

These words seemed a good omen as I began my Seminary training. I was not yet a Quaker, and had not heard the phrase, continuing revelation, but I was already committed to the concept.

Across the street from the Seminary is the University's Oriental Institute, housing the magnificent finds of various archeological expeditions. Class sessions were sometimes held there, and archeology added another dimension to Bible study. Although my interest in the Bible continued, the excitement for me was in theology, and I made that my major.

George and I settled in Chicago and raised our family in the University neighborhood, and I continued to keep up with what was going on in my field.

This has been a tremendous century to be a student of the Bible, for there has been unprecedented ground-breaking scholarship in many areas. In the 1940's the Dead Sea Scrolls were found, and later the Gnostic Gospels at Nag Hammadi in Egypt, both adding greatly to our understanding of Jesus. Archeological digs continue to yield new knowledge of Biblical times and more accurate dating of parts. Linguistic studies have also shed new light. Indeed, Paul did not write all the epistles attributed to him, and probably did not write all the gynophobic passages for which we blame him.

New English translations have proliferated, adding understanding, although none have quite the majestic flow of the King James version. Many of us follow with interest Joanne Spears' translation using a vocabulary for children and translating generic words in Hebrew and Greek into inclusive English. Other inclusive language translations are in process.

In the last quarter century, I have found four additional ways to read the Bible:

1.   through the lens of Liberation Theology, making a "preferential option for the poor" and oppressed.

2.   through the lens of Creation Theology, assessing the Bible's role in our deepening ecological crisis.

3.   through the lens of Feminist Theology.

4.   through the lens of mythology, remythologizing parts of it I had earlier demythologized.

I want now to look at a familiar story in Genesis through these four contemporary lenses, detaching the story of Jacob from the longer multi-generational story of the matriarchs and patriarchs. We will begin with Jacob's birth and end with his reunion with Esau many years later. Our story is in Genesis, chapter 25 through chapter 33.

We can date the story more or less accurately. We know that the Children of Israel were in Egypt four hundred years, from roughly 1700 BCE to 1300 BCE. This places our story some time in the 1800's BCE, in the Middle Bronze Age. Egypt, the dominant power, was in the Middle Kingdom, and the great pyramids were already a thousand years old. Hammurabi had already established his great civil code in Babylonia. And the Hebrews were still a small nomadic tribe, making the transition from hunting and gathering to herding.

Their wanderings had taken Jacob's grandparents from Ur, then on the Persian Gulf in present-day Iraq, up the Tigris and Euphrates valley to Haran in Mesopotamia. Some of the tribe stayed in Haran, but Abraham and his group moved southwest into Canaan, the so-called Promised Land. By the time the old man Jacob emigrated to Egypt with his family, the tribe still did not have much of a toe-hold in Canaan. All they owned was the cave Abraham had purchased from Ephron the Hittite for Sarah's burial vault.

I. THROUGH THE LENS OF LIBERATION THEOLOGY.

I have called this Jacob's story, for that is how the Bible sets it forth. Actually it is the tale of two brothers, twins, and it begins in utero. Already the sibling rivalry is so intense that their mother, Rebekah, despairs that she will survive her pregnancy. She consults an oracle who tells her that her sons will be founders of rival nations, and that the older will serve the younger. Finally they are born, about as simultaneously as twins can be, with Esau emerging first, and Jacob hanging on to his heel. (Jacob means heel, and he turned out to be one in both senses of the word.) By the law of primogeniture the first-born inherits everything, and Esau is technically the first-born.

Even at birth they are different. Esau is red and hairy. (Esau means red.) Jacob is smooth-skinned and fairer. Esau grows up to be a hunter, while the Bible describes Jacob as a tent dweller, one who kept herds and flocks. (His making lentil soup suggests he may have practiced a little agriculture.) Rebekah loves Jacob, and Isaac, their father, loves Esau, which does not help the sibling rivalry.

One day Esau returns from a long, unsuccessful hunting, worn out and famished, and finds Jacob making lentil soup. One would think Jacob would offer some to his hungry brother, but Esau has to ask for it. Jacob takes advantage of Esau's exhaustion and bargains for his brother's birthright in return for the soup. Esau agrees; he is so weak from hunger that he feels he will die if he does not eat at once.

Some months later Isaac, now old and blind, thinks he is about to die. He asks Esau to hunt game and make a savory stew. When Isaac has eaten he will bless his first-born. Rebekah is eavesdropping and schemes to deceive Isaac into blessing Jacob instead. Later Esau returns, learns what has happened, and is so angry that Jacob must flee for his life.

Let us look at the story thus far through the lens of Liberation Theology, which had its origins in the Second Vatican Council in 1962. There Pope John XXIII make the connection in our time between peace and justice, and the bishops first considered a "preferential option for the poor." Through Liberation Theology the Bible has been opened up in rather amazing ways, particularly in Latin America.

Priests began literacy programs and translated the Bible into native languages. In small house churches, called base communities, little groups of the newly literate read the Gospels together and learned for the first time that Jesus is on their side, not on the side of the rich and powerful. Gospel stories became contemporary, a parable of their own lives and struggles, and Jesus became their friend and companion.

Sharon Cohen says that to the proponents of Liberation Theology

> the central message of the Bible is human liberation.... Rather than asking, 'What does this text mean?' the Liberationist might ask, 'How can this text speak to us if we read it in the context of a broader biblical message of liberation?' (2)

Let us begin with the obvious injustice that twins should be treated so differently--that one gets everything and the other nothing. We noted that Rebekah was told that the second-born would rule over the first-born. God apparently favors second sons. Indeed, grandmother Sarah insisted that Abraham's first-born, Ishmael, be banished after her son Isaac was born. Abraham hesitates, and God tells him to "do as Sarah tells you!" (Genesis 21:12) Still earlier God favored the offering of Abel, second-born of Eve and Adam, over Cain's offering, and again, the terrible rage of the first-born.

Savina Teubal, in her book *Sarah The Priestess,* suggests that we are seeing here a shift from ultimogeniture (inheritance of the last-born) to primogeniture. (3) Younger sons Isaac and Jacob, aided and abetted by their mothers, did inherit, although their fathers accepted primogeniture. Ultimately inheritance of the first-born won out, as witness the royal houses of Europe.

If Rebekah had it straight from God that Jacob was to inherit, why did she not let it be a self-fulfilling prophecy? It is bad enough for Esau to lose because God willed it, but insult is added to injury with the niggardly refusal of Jacob for a bite to eat, and the deceit of his mother and brother in acquiring the blessing. Will no one speak for the injustice done Esau?

The Bible does not sound the cry of justice for Esau. The unknown writer of the book of Hebrews says:

> Let no one be immoral or irreligious like Esau, who sold his birthright for a single meal. For you know that afterward when he desired to inherit the blessing, he was rejected, for he found no chance to repent, though he sought it with tears. (Hebrews 12:16-17)

Paul, writing to the Romans, attributes to God the condemnation of Esau:

> It is written, 'Jacob have I loved, but Esau, I hated.' (Romans 9:13)

I recently read an article in *Bible Review* about the

midrashim that grew up around our story. Tradition has Esau the
father of the Edomites, mortal enemies of the Hebrews. In midrash
after midrash Esau is given full blame for anti-Semitism. (4)

And writing from the point of view of Jungian psychology,
John Sanford in *The Man Who Wrestled With God* sees Jacob as
one who achieved individuation, that is wholeness, autonomy. He
describes the young Jacob as "an intuitive person, aware of the
possibilities of life." [Possibilities of cheating his brother?] He then
characterizes the young Esau as "a sort of supermasculine character
...literal, down-to-earth," with a "what's for dinner?" mentality. (5)

How could the God of Justice condone all the deceit and
treachery against Esau? Will no one speak for Esau?

Laurens van der Post was the first person I heard speak out
forcefully for Esau, in a lovely little book called *A Mantis Carol.*
It is now out of print, and if you ever see a copy in a second-hand
book sale, buy it. The story actually opens at Pendle Hill. Van der
Post sees Esau and Ishmael as prototypes of hunters and gatherers.
For thousands of years all our ancestors were hunters and gatherers.
Then many made the transition to herding. Jacob is a herder, we
noted. For much of the human race, herding gave way to
agriculture. The Hebrews entered this stage when they took Canaan
after the exodus from Egypt.

With agriculture came civilization and on every continent
hunters and gatherers have been mostly hounded out of existence
or relegated to the fringes of society in the least desirable places.
Van der Post writes movingly of Esau as the spiritual ancestor of
the Bushmen of the Kalihari desert, and also of the Maoris of New
Zealand and the Aborigines of Australia. Only a handful remain to
carry on their traditional and ecologically sound way of life.

Hunters and gatherers of our own continent, whom we
misnamed Indians, welcomed the Pilgrims and enabled them to
survive that first dreadful winter. Within a few years the Indians
were transformed in the minds of the settlers into instruments of
the devil who were to be hunted down.

Jacob's greed and deceit are now writ large in our civilization where the bottom line takes precedence over people and our fragile environment. Many of you must have seen the movie *The Gods Must Be Crazy.* I ask you: who was sane in that story? The frantic city-dwellers? The warring tribes? The anthropologists? Or the Bushman, trying to get rid of the Coke bottle?

Dick and Sarah Preston, members of Hamilton, Ontario Meeting, are an anthropological team who have worked with tribal people in Canada. Several years ago at Pendle Hill Dick wrote a paper on Esau. Listen to Esau, his voice filtered through Dick's sensitive awareness and imagination:

> I will be freed from the domestication wrought upon humans by the animals they domesticate. For by keeping animals...men then regulate their lives to the needs of the animals for fodder, milking and the like. And worse, they regulate their souls to the possession and protection of their wealth in animals. So humans become the domesticates of their animals ....My father feels this in his deep mind, and so he loves me for the smell and feel of freedom. This is what his ancestors, the patriarchs, abandoned for the sake of security and for the vanity of having more than life's needs in their possession....
>
> My father's home is an oasis in the wilderness, but I love the other side of his frontier. I walk cheerfully over the wilderness. The free beasts are my true community. We know each other intimately, and it is in the nature of life that some of them must give themselves as food, so that others can live. These make their lives a sacrament, their gift to sustain the life around them. This gift must be respected by those who receive their food and so are enabled to see more days before they too must give way. (7)

In becoming civilized we inheritors of Jacob have destroyed much of the wilderness, and we have lost something we need for survival. We have destroyed part of ourselves.

The tribal deity may have chosen Jacob to carry on the tradition of Abraham, but the God of Justice stands with the oppressed inheritors of Esau, their remnants struggling for their very existence.

As Thomas Jefferson said, "I tremble for my country when I reflect that God is just."

II. THROUGH THE LENS OF CREATION THEOLOGY.

Our story continues:

> Jacob left Beersheba and went toward Haran. And he came to a place and stayed the night. Taking a stone, he put it under his head and slept. And he dreamed that there was a ladder set upon earth, reaching to heaven, and angels ascended and descended, and the Lord stood above it and said, 'I am the God of Abraham and of Isaac....Behold I am with you wherever you go....' Jacob awoke and said, 'Surely the Lord is in this place and I did not know it.' He took the stone which he had put under his head and set it up for a pillar and called the place Beth-El, which means the House of God. (Genesis 28:10-19)

And the man who drove a hard bargain with his brother now bargains with God:

> And Jacob made a vow, If God will be with me and will keep me and give me bread to eat and clothing to wear, so that I come again to my father's house in peace, then the Lord shall be my God. (Genesis 28:20-21)

Creation Theology grew in the mind and heart of Matthew Fox, a Dominican priest and scholar. He writes prolifically, the two major books being *Original Blessing* and *The Coming Of The Cosmic Christ.*" (8) His thesis is that we are not born in original sin, but with original blessing--the blessing of being members of God's creation on this beautiful planet.

The first chapter of Genesis tells us that God created the world "and saw that it was good." We have been taught to see it as a vale of troubles, something to be endured bravely so that we can enjoy our real life in heaven after we die. Leaf through any

Christian hymnal and see how that is the message of most of the hymns.

Matthew Fox wants to restore our joy and full participation in God's creation. Paradise is here and now on this beautiful planet. He has founded his Institute of Culture and Creation Spirituality at Holy Names College in Oakland, California, and has invited to its faculty Native Americans, women knowledgeable in ancient wisdom and others with an earth-centered mythology. For this Fox has been silenced by the Vatican for the calendar year 1989.

Some years ago I represented Friends General Conference on a panel on the Source of Authority for Friends. There were also representatives of Evangelical Friends Alliance, Friends United Meeting, and Wilburite Friends. I asked the EFA representative if he believed in continuing revelation. "Yes," he answered, "if it doesn't contradict the Bible."

For myself, if continuing revelation calls into question something in the Bible, then I must weigh the evidence on both sides and make my decision on the basis of as much truth as is given to me. The world changes; human knowledge expands; and we know things our spiritual ancestors could not know. Their observations told them that the earth is flat and that the sun revolves around it. The insights of Copernicus, Newton, Darwin, and Einstein were not yet available to them. Their conceptualization of reality, their naming of the world, is often inadequate, and at times amounts to a misnaming of the world.

I now see our ecological crisis to be of such urgency and such magnitude that we must identify the causes and face them honestly. I see our crisis basically as a theological problem. Underlying Western civilization are attitudes giving us license to exploit the earth. They are an inherent part of our Judeo-Christian tradition, rooted in the Bible, particularly in Genesis. Even those who are not practicing Jews or Christians, even those who have never opened a Bible, are influenced at a deep psychic level by these myths. We must look at them honestly and consciously remythologize them.

The Genesis myths tell us that in the beginning God ordained that man (and I let that uninclusive word stand!) was given dominion over the earth and the other creatures. In our better moments we have translated dominion to mean stewardship. The concept of stewardship implies taking charge of things on behalf of other members of creation. It is now an outmoded concept.

Lewis Thomas, the biologist, puts the case:

Except for us, the life of the planet conducts itself as though it were an immense, coherent body of connected life, an intricate system, an organism. Our deepest folly is the notion that we are in charge of the place, that we own it and can somehow run it. We are a living part of Earth's life, owned and operated by the Earth, probably specialized for functions on its behalf that we have not yet glimpsed. (9)

But still we persist in trying to be in charge. We lack a proper humility. Even those on the right side fail to see this. *Scientific American* has just put out a special issue on the ecological crisis. It covers the field thoroughly and well, yet they call the issue "Managing Planet Earth."

We do not yet see that we are part of the living planet, that Earth is our mother, source of all that we need. We do not see the other species as our brothers and sisters from whom we may learn ways of being.

You are wondering what all this has to do with Jacob as he flees his brother's wrath, camps for the night in a lonely place, and feels the assurance of God's presence. Alas, it was Jacob's dream that saddled us with the unfortunate symbol of the ladder. Even as I write, a radio commercial for Toshiba intrudes on my consciousness. The oily voice says:

It is not easy to climb the corporate ladder, but the view from the top is so heady that it is worth the struggle....

We all see life as a ladder to be climbed: "We are climbing Jacob's ladder, soldiers of the cross." It may be the corporate, political, academic, or ecclesiastical ladder. (How ironic that the Christian Church became one of the most rigidly hierarchical institutions in the world, when Jesus himself did not think or act hierarchically. He called his followers "friends," as we well know. We can be grateful that our Religious Society of Friends is a bottom-up structure.)

Ingrained in us from childhood is the pressure to be the best, to get to the top. This implies climbing over the competition, knocking them off the ladder, if necessary. Deceit and greed are justified in getting to the top. Our history is full of scandals of those who cheated to win.

We all see the world hierarchically. At the top of the ladder is God, where Jacob saw him. Then "a little lower than the angels," is man; still lower, women, children, enemies, slaves. Lower still are animals, then plants, and at the bottom, earth itself. "Thou hast put all things under his feet" (Psalm 8:6b). "Fill the earth and subdue it and have dominion over the fish, over the birds, over every living thing." (Genesis 1:28)

Dominion over implies power over, and people who "know their places" and are not uppity. But people don't want to stay on the lower rungs of the ladder. Wars and revolutions have characterized our history.

For long ages Earth was so spacious, so large, so resilient that it could absorb our efforts at dominion over it. There was always a new frontier to move to. The physical frontiers are gone. We have travelled to the moon and have seen Earth as a tiny blue and white marble in the vastness of space. It is time that we know inwardly that we have reached the end of our stewardship of the Earth. Earth cannot survive much more of our management.

We need a new symbol. Interestingly enough, William Blake began a modification of the symbol in his drawing of Jacob's ladder. He shows it as a gradually rising spiral staircase.

A similar symbol is the circle, without beginning or end: Arthur's round table so that the knights would not have distinctions among them as they broke bread together! It is time we climbed down from Jacob's ladder and joined the intricate circle dance of interdependence. Instead of climbing Jacob's ladder, let us join in "dancing Sarah's circle," as many women are doing.

And that brings us to the next part of the story and the view through the lens of Feminist Theology.

III.   THROUGH THE LENS OF FEMINIST THEOLOGY.

After his dream, Jacob continues his journey and eventually arrives in Haran at the village well, just as Rachel is watering her sheep. He loves her at first sight. She takes him home and his Uncle Laban welcomes him. In Laban Jacob meets his match; Laban too is an expert in dirty tricks.

Jacob bargains with Laban. He will work seven years for Rachel as his wife. Laban agrees, but on the wedding night, he substitutes Rachel's sister Leah, and in the darkness Jacob makes love all night to the wrong woman. Jacob winds up working seven more years for Rachel.

Laban's affairs prosper in Jacob's hands, and after the fourteen years are up, Jacob continues to work for his father-in-law. Jacob again bargains with Laban. All the unblemished animals will be Laban's and all the striped and spotted ones, Jacob's. Laban thinks it is a good deal. However, by selective breeding Jacob manages to acquire great flocks of healthy spotted and striped animals, while Laban's flocks, although unblemished, consist of weaker, less vigorous specimens. It takes time for Laban and his sons to notice what is happening, but when they do, Jacob must flee again. God tells him to go home.

This is not only a tale of two brothers, it is also about two sisters: beautiful Rachel, the younger, and unattractive Leah, the elder, whose eyes were perhaps crossed.

Rosemary Radford Ruether expresses the point of view of feminist theology in the context of the Bible when she says:

> Whatever diminishes or denies the full humanity of women
> must be presumed not to reflect the divine or an authentic

relation to the divine, or to reflect the authentic nature of things, or to be the message or work of an authentic redeemer or a community of redemption." (11)

She is making a "preferential option" for women.

Phyllis Trible's position is:

> that traditional Jewish and Christian commentators have imposed their own chauvinistic interpretations upon biblical material. Trible asserts that there are, in fact, anti-patriarchal tendencies within Scripture itself that emerge when the texts are reread from a feminist perspective. This conviction inspires her to engage in a serious re-examination of familiar biblical texts....She see the fundamental hermeneutical challenge for contemporary feminists, 'to translate biblical faith without sexism.'

And I could not resist adding this:

> Depatriarchalizing is not an operation which an exegete performs on the text. It is a hermeneutic operating within Scripture. We expose it, we do not impose it. (12)

Can we depatriarchalize this story?

Let us look first at Rebekah, mother of Jacob and Esau. A generation earlier Abraham had sent a trusted servant to Haran to find an appropriate wife for Isaac among his own people. There is an earlier scene at the well. The servant arrives and Rebekah offers him a drink and then waters his camels. She takes the servant home and he asks for Rebekah as a wife for his master's son.

Rebekah apparently had some say about this arranged marriage:

> Her brother and her mother said, 'Let the maiden remain with us awhile....' But he said to them, 'Do not delay me....' They said 'We will call the maiden and ask her.' And they called Rebekah and said to her, 'Will you go with this man?' And she said, 'I will go.' (Genesis 24:55-58)

Isaac comes through to us as a passive man. A servant picks his wife. He has a gift for finding water, but when he digs a well, if another tribe disputes with him, he walks away and lets them have the well. He can always find water elsewhere.

Rebekah really runs the family. I can imagine her looking at her passive husband, and her first-born who loves the wilderness, and feeling that the whole tribe will fall apart if Esau inherits responsibility for it. She must manage things so that practical, enterprising Jacob will head the tribe. She thinks nothing of deceiving her husband.

As for Rachel and Leah, marriage to the same man only embitters their already intense sibling rivalry. God, at this point, seems to favor the first-born, Leah. Yahweh opens and closes wombs for his own mysterious purposes. Leah gives Jacob many sons and Rachel is barren. Leah reflects her resentment of her sister and the bitter knowledge that Jacob does not love her by giving names to her sons that have double meanings.

Years later, when Jacob must flee Laban's wrath, he calls Leah and Rachel and asks if they wish to go with him. This is the answer:

> Is there any portion or inheritance left to us in our father's house? Are we not regarded by him as foreigners? For he has sold us, and he has been using up the money given for us. All the property which God has taken away from our father belongs to us and our children. Now then, whatever God has said to you, do. (Genesis 31:14-16)

Their complaint that Laban has spent the bride price seems to imply that he owes them the equivalent of Jacob's fourteen years of work.

> So Jacob arose, and set his sons and his wives on camels, and he drove away all his cattle and livestock, to go to the land of Canaan to his father Isaac. (Genesis 31:17-18)

Rachel has conspired to get even with her father for spoiling her wedding night. She steals his household gods, and does

not tell Jacob.   When Laban catches up with them after several
days, Jacob can honestly urge him to search, saying that if he finds
the gods, whoever has them shall die.

> Now Rachel had taken the household gods and put them
> in the camel's saddle, and sat upon them.   Laban felt all
> about the tent, but did not find them.   And she said to her
> father, 'Let not my lord be angry that I cannot rise before
> you, for the way of women is upon me.'   So he searched,
> but he did not find the household gods.   (Genesis 31:34-35)

It is probable that whoever possessed the household gods
was legitimate heir to the family property.   In any case she had
defiled them by sitting on them when "the way of women" was upon
her.   What is going on here?   What kind of docile, submissive
victims of patriarchy are these?   Is Trible right that there is an
antipatriarchal tendency within our story?

For comment, let us turn to our own Elise Boulding and her
monumental book *The Underside Of History*.   Elise says:

> What led to the loss of status of the Israeli women?   When
> Sarai set out with her tribe from Ur of the Chaldees, in the
> 1900's BCE, she was setting out from a matrilineal society.

At this point, she inserts a footnote:

> ...I am taking the position that the Israeli tribes were
> originally matrilineal, since this fits my general reading of
> the history of this period.

Elise continues:

> True, the Israelites were already herders, but the woman's
> line was clearly recognized.   Right through the records of
> the later Old Testament books...there are descent listings
> recording the woman's line, so common in manuscripts of
> the period.   Perhaps the shift toward patriarchy started when
> the tribes were fighting their way into Canaan; a militaristic
> orientation works against a high status for women....The
> memories of women's earlier roles, and a continued status

for wise women, prophetesses, and judges carried on for a long time after the settlement in Canaan. (13)

At the end of the book of Ruth, the people at the city gate say to Boaz,

'May the Lord make the woman who is coming into your house like Rachel and Leah, who together built up the house of Israel.' (Ruth 4:11)

Try reading the story of Sarah and Abraham as if Sarah were head of the tribe. It explains some strange incidents. (God told Abraham to 'do what Sarah tells you,' in the matter of Ishmael, as we noted.) Try seeing Rebekah as head of the tribe. Perhaps Rachel and Leah were in a period of transition to patriarchy, but still retained some autonomy.

Sarah, Rebekah, Leah and Rachel all had a strong sense of personhood and were capable of taking charge and seeing that their children had advantages they felt due to them. They manipulated fathers and husbands to bring about what they thought important or just. They are our spiritual ancestors at least as much as Abraham, Isaac, and Jacob. For women today they are sisters, as they in their time struggled to keep their autonomy in a world in transition. Today we strive to move beyond patriarchy; they tried to prevent its institution.

When I was feeling my way into the story of Rachel in writing *Daughters Of Zion*, (14) I felt a strong desire in both sisters for a reconciliation. I saw it taking place as Rachel came to know that she would probably die giving birth to Benjamin.

Arthur Waskow has written a beautiful book called *Godwrestling*, in which he imagines a confrontation between God and Rachel over the Holocaust in our own day:

God says, 'I am a jealous God, and you were whoring after strange gods, and I'll have none of it.'...There appears our Mother Rachel and says to Him, 'You're a jealous God. All right. I was...jealous of my sister, who was given to Jacob although he was to be my husband. So jealous that

I knew ahead of time that my father was going to do that
trick, and I planned with Jacob...I told him signals he could
use to tell whether it was me or Leah....

'But when the moment came, I couldn't go through with it.
I told her the signals....You see, I couldn't go through with
my plan because I loved my sister. I was jealous of a real,
flesh-and-blood sister, and You are jealous of what: empty
idols, sticks, and stones! For such jealousy You will destroy
your people?' (15)

IV. THROUGH THE LENS OF MYTHOLOGY

And now having torn the story apart with my twentieth
century concerns and ways of perceiving, I want to end the story
larger than life, telling it as your story, and my story.   Joseph
Campbell has made us all aware of the power of myth, and this
story has been a source of self-understanding and strength at some
of the worst moments of my life. So Jacob, deceiver of his father,
cheater of his brother and father-in-law, Jacob who made love as
lustily with Leah whom he did not love as with Rachel whom he
loved, becomes in the end an archetypal figure.

And now to the end of our story. Laban overtakes Jacob,
and after accusations on both sides, they are reconciled. They part
with the familiar words, "May the Lord watch between me and thee
while we are absent, one from the other." (Genesis 31:49)

When Jacob travelled to Haran he was alone and travelled
light. Now he has wives, concubines, children, maid servants, men
servants, and many flocks with herders. The journey home is much
slower.

Finally one evening scouts report to Jacob that Esau is just
over that next line of hills, with four hundred men. The company
camps for the night by the Jabbok River, but Jacob cannot sleep.
Tomorrow will be the confrontation with Esau, and he is afraid. He
leaves his tent and wanders along the river bank, and it seems to
him that all night he wrestles with a stranger.   They are about

evenly matched, but finally the stranger throws Jacob and dislocates his hip. For the rest of his life Jacob will limp.

When the morning comes, Jacob sees that the stranger is an angel, and says to him, "I will not let you go unless you bless me." The angel blesses him and gives him a new name. From now on he will be known as Israel, one who struggles with God.

> And Jacob called the name of the place Peniel [which means the face of God] for he said, 'I have seen God face to face, and yet my life is preserved.' (Genesis 32:30)

> The sun rose upon him as he passed, limping because of his thigh. And Jacob lifted up his eyes and looked, and behold, Esau was coming. (Genesis 32:31; 33:1)

> And Esau ran to meet him and embraced him, and fell on his neck and kissed him, and they wept. (Genesis 33:4)

> And Jacob said, 'Truly, to see your face is like seeing the face of God.' (Genesis 33:10b)

At times all of us struggle with dark angels through a seemingly endless night. Broken relationships, loss of job, betrayal by someone we trusted, a sense of failure, grief for someone we love, a serious, perhaps life-threatening illness: the dark angels are many. And, like Jacob, we bear the scars of these encounters the rest of our lives, in our memories and spirits, if not in our bodies.

Like Jacob, we must mark an end to the experience, whatever it may be, by looking to the dawn, knowing that "the world is always turning toward the morning." (16) And although we may not know it until daylight, we find that the living God has struggled and suffered with us all through the long night.

Like Jacob, we must claim the blessing: learn what we need to learn from this encounter. We must rename ourselves. Perhaps we have called ourselves victims, but henceforth we will name ourselves survivors. And we must change our lives as well as our names. We may want to name the place of our encounter, seeing it as a place where we met God.

And then it may be given to us, as it was to Jacob, to look into the eyes of brothers and sisters whom we have perceived as enemies, and to see in them the face of God, and so to reach across the vast distances that separate us one from the other. Dare we envision a world in which all creation wears the face of God?

As subsequent history makes plain, the Jacobs and Esaus of the world were not permanently reconciled, but their embrace at Peniel stands before us, a light to the future.

So I return to the words of Margaret Fell with which I began:

We have taken the Scriptures in words and know nothing of them in ourselves.

And I commend to you the Bible as a living document. Set it beside your contemporary concerns, problems, opportunities, and see whether it can shed light for you. Wrestle with it, as Jacob wrestled with the angel. It is possible that God may speak to you from its pages. It is also possible that God may choose some more contemporary medium for the message. Believe in continuing revelation, whether it comes through the Bible, or through other sources. It is part of our Quaker heritage.

Invite the people of the Bible into your life, to be your companions as you face difficult situations. They too faced agonizing decisions. Question them; challenge them; wrestle with them. What happened to them when the story in the Bible ends? Read between the lines. Let the reconciliation of brother with brother, sister with sister, take place in you. Think of those who have wronged you, or whom you have wronged, and try to see them wearing the face of God.

Make your own preferential option for the poor, for women, for our planetary home.

And let us hear again George Fox speaking to us across the centuries, as Margaret Fell heard him:

You say, Christ saith this, and the apostles say this, [and I

would add, 'and the Bible saith that,'], but what canst thou
say? Art thou a child of the Light and hast walked in the
Light, and what thou speakest, is it inwardly from God?

FOOTNOTES

1. George Fox, *Journal,* 1694, p. ii. "The testimony of Margaret
Fox concerning her late husband."

2. Sharon Cohen, "Reclaiming the Hammer: Toward a Feminist
Midrash." *Tikkun: A Bimonthly Jewish Critique Of Politics, Culture,
And Society.* March/April 1988.

3. Savina J. Teubal, *Sarah The Priestess: The First Matriarch Of
Genesis.* Athens, Ohio, Swallow Press, 1984. p. 42 ff.

4. Pinchas H. Peli, "Responses to Jew-Hatred, ll *Bible Review,*
October 1989, p. 36-41.

5. John A. Sanford, *The Man Who Wrestled With God: Light From
The Old Testament On The Psychology Of Individuation.* New York,
Paulist Press, revised edition, 1987. pp. 13-14.

6. Jared Diamond, "The Worst Mistake in the History of the
Human Race," *Discover,* May, 1987, p. 64-66.

7. Dick Preston, "Flying into Imaginings: Esau's Story." Unpublished paper written at Pendle Hill, pp. 1-2.

8. Matthew Fox, *Original Blessing.* Santa Fe, Bear and Company,
1983. *The Coming Of The Cosmic Christ.* San Francisco, Harper
and Row, 1988.

9. Lewis Thomas, "Human Responsibility," *Phenomenon Of Change.*
New York, Cooper-Hewitt Museum, 1986, p. 1. Cited in Charlene
Spretnak, *The Spiritual Dimension Of Green Politics.* Santa Fe, Bear
and Company, 1986. p. 28.

10. *Scientific American.* Special Issue, September 1989, "Managing
Planet Earth."

11. Rosemary Radford Ruether, *Sexism And God-Talk: Toward A Feminist Theology.* Boston, Beacon Press, 1983. pp. 19.

12. Phyllis Trible, "Depatriarchalizing Biblical Interpretation," Elizabeth Koltun, Editor, *The Jewish Woman: New Perspectives.* New York, Schocken Books, 1976. Cited by Sharon Cohen, op. cit.

13. Elise Boulding, *The Underside Of History: A View Of Women Through Time.* Boulder, Colorado, Westview Press, 1976. p. 236. p. 273, n. 9.

14. Elizabeth G. Watson. *Daughters Of Zion* Richmond, Indiana Friends United Press, 1982. Chapter 3, on Rachel. See also, chapter 2 on Rebekah.

15. Arthur I. Waskow, *Godwrestling.* New York, Schocken Books, 1978, pp. 132-133.
16. Gordon Bok, song, "Turning Toward the Morning." Folk-Legacy Records, 1975.

Quotations from the Bible are from the Revised Standard version.

XXIII

Workshop Summary:

The Gospel According To The Women

Elizabeth G. Watson

We examine evidence in the four Gospels that there were women among the disciples of Jesus, turning first to Luke 8:1-3. Here we learn that along with "the twelve" were women, among whom were "Mary, called Magdalene," "Joanna, wife of Chuza, Herod's steward, and Susannah." And, Luke adds, "many others." We speculate as to how Joanna, a woman of the palace, came to be wandering the dusty roads of Galilee with an itinerant rabbi and a bunch of fishermen.

Turning to Luke 24, we read that after the death of Jesus women had come to the tomb on the first day of the week with spices to anoint his body. Luke says it was "Mary Magdalene and Joanna and Mary the mother of James and the other women." Joanna had made the long journey from Galilee to Jerusalem with the other disciples, and was present for the fateful events of Passover week.

Next we look at Matthew 20:20ff and see the mother of the sons of Zebedee asking Jesus if they might sit beside him when he comes into his kingdom. Jesus told her and the disciples that in God's kingdom the great would be servants. Did she turn away, feeling rebuffed and disillusioned, or did she understand what he was saying? Matthew 27:55-56 tells us that many women watched the crucifixion, among them Mary Magdalene, Mary the mother of James and Joseph, and the mother of the sons of Zebedee. Had she become a disciple, along with her sons?

In Mark 15:40-41, we note among the women watching the crucifixion Mary Magdalene, Mary mother of James and Joses, and Salome. Who is Salome? Is she perhaps the mother of the sons of Zebedee? We note also that Mark, like Luke, speaks of "many other women."

John has still a different list of women at the crucifixion. In chapter 19:25ff. He mentions the mother of Jesus, her sister, Mary wife of Clopas, and Mary Magdalene. Some scholars think that Clopas is probably the same as Cleopas, one of the two disciples on the road to Emmaus, in Luke 24:13ff. Painters have shown us two men on the road to Emmaus, but might not he be walking home with his wife?

Common to all lists of women is Mary Magdalene, and we note that all four Gospels indicate that Jesus appeared first to her after the resurrection and entrusted his message to her. We look for evidence in the Gospels that she was once a prostitute, but find none. We speculate as to why this label became attached to her. We turn to the Gnostic Gospels and learn that many thought she was the number one disciple, and that Peter was jealous of her. We ask ourselves if the women had written the Gospels, how might they differ from the four we know? What would they have seen as of prime importance in the message of Jesus?

If time permits we will look at Mary and Martha and wrestle with what seems to be Jesus' put-down of Martha. And we will look also at the Syro-Phoenician woman of Matthew 15 and Mark 7, whom Jesus insulted, and who turned the situation around. Was Jesus willing to let a woman open his mind to new possibilities? Was this a turning point in his perception of his message and mission?

And there are "many others," if we had unlimited time: the "Woman at the Well," the woman with an issue of blood, the woman with a crooked back, and the unnamed woman who anointed him with costly oil shortly before his death, whom the male disciples put down as extravagant. We hope the workshop will open to the participants this fascinating aspect of the Gospels, so that they will continue to read and speculate on their own.

XXIV

The Bible And Archetypes In Jungian Perspective

John Yungblut

[Note: A widely-known counselor, spiritual director and author, John Yungblut lives in Lincoln, Virginia, and attends nearby Goose Creek Meeting.]

Those who have been led to arrange this conference are to be congratulated. Friends have become increasingly illiterate when it comes to a working knowledge of scripture. We have largely lost a sense of being rooted and grounded in our Judaeo-Christian heritage. As a "religious society" we have also lost our myth. We have retained our central profession of faith, namely that "there is that of God in everyone," but we no longer feel the connection between this Quaker tenet and the Bible. Theologically we have lost our moorings and are adrift on a vast sea of abstract speculation.

The problem for many of us has been that in our youth the Bible was presented to us as a set of historical facts from which the fathers of the Church derived doctrines that were to be understood literally. Meantime, we have been conditioned in our scientific age to approach everything in the mode of empirical reasoning.

The deepest impulse in us is the religious one: to get everything together into one integrated whole. The word "religion" is from the Latin, "religio, religare," to bind into one sheaf or bundle. Applying this principle intuitively meant that in the interest of true religion we would have to abandon one or the other--our religious upbringing in credal form or our discipline in the empirical process of scientific investigation. The latter would more profoundly alienate us from our age, and few there be that try it.

Some attempt to live with a bifurcated mind, trying to make the best of both worlds. Others, paradoxically in the name of religion, have had to part company with the historic stream of orthodoxy, even with some of George Fox's basic theological assumptions. I suspect that most of us here converge at this point in our inward journeys.

A More Excellent Way

Thomas Berry, author of a remarkable new book, *The Dream of the Earth*, published by the Sierra Club, points out that since the Renaissance our culture has contained two communities, basically at odds with one another. A "religious" community that did not accept the necessity of integrating with its interpretation of its historic faith, fresh revelation from scientific research, and a "scientific" community that in pursuit of its principles of inquiry, forewent the relevance to its synthesis of anything numinous (that is, the mystical or the holy).

Happily, this general division is breaking down in our time. There are more and more scientists like Albert Einstein and Fritjof Capra who acknowledge the validity of mystical experience, and there are more and more theologians who are engaged in creative re-mythologizing.

It is no longer necessary to accept the impossible task of attempting to live in two worlds nor, in accepting fresh revelation, to feel obliged to deprive oneself of the life-giving riches of our religious heritage. There is, indeed, a more excellent way, religion's own way, in the classic sense--the way of assimilation, of binding everything together in one sheaf.

This requires the shaping of a new myth which in turn involves allowing our historic myths to continue to evolve. We are using the word myth here, not in the sense of legend or poetic fiction or falsehood, but in the sense of another definition offered by Webster: "a fabulous narrative about an event in the early period of a people by which they have come to know themselves, their god, and the rest of creation."

Myth or metaphor is the only language religion knows how to use with reference to interpreting its deepest truths. Many years ago Robert Frost pleaded for a principle of education which he described as "education by metaphor." Had we followed this counsel in our religious education, teaching children how to understand the doctrines of the Church metaphorically rather than literally, we would have prevented much misunderstanding and consequent feelings of guilt. There was no need to abandon our myth as long as we understood it as metaphor, as Joseph Campbell has admirably demonstrated in his televised dialogue with Bill Moyers, now published in book form, *The Power of Myth*.

Friends have from the beginning allowed for the principle of fresh revelation which must be assimilated from time to time if one is to have a viable, ongoing myth of meaning. Now, there are many forms of fresh revelation today, but there are two in particular which our own myth of meaning (as a Society of Friends and as individuals) must assimilate: the fact of evolution as the process of continuing creation and the accumulating wisdom emerging from depth psychology.

The revelation of continuing creation through evolution calls for radical changes of metaphor in the part of our myth of meaning which deals with the beginning of things and the process of change. And the fresh revelation of the nature and dynamics of the psyche as presented by Jungian psychology must of necessity radically alter our response to the Biblical query, "what is man that thou art mindful of him, or the son of man that thee visitest him?" Even the form of the query must be altered and presented in more inclusive language if it is to gain respectful attention in our time.

It was said in the citation accompanying the conferral of an honorary Doctoral Degree in Psychology on a recipient at the Tercentenary Celebration of Harvard: "Psychology--the newest of the sciences and the oldest of the arts." The truth that is conveyed by this statement explains why of all the sciences that require some kind of integration with religion the need for mutual recognition and assimilation between psychology and religion is the most pressing in our time.

This is why Jung's work is so important. He has served as

the greatest apologist for religion in that discipline in which religion has most needed an effective apologist, in the sense of advocate and interpreter: namely, psychology.

We shall presently see how Jung's concept of archetypes and the collective unconscious have provided us with a key with which to unlock and enter the treasury of our Bible with a new grasp of its relevance for today. He has said:

> we must read the Bible or we shall not understand psychology. Our whole lives, our language, and imagery are built upon the Bible. (1)

It could also be said that it is necessary to study the psychology of C. G. Jung if one is to understand the Bible in the light of fresh revelation that has come to us from this source. He has enabled us to approach the Bible in a wholly new way. In his book, *Psychology and Religion*, he explains:

> I am not...addressing myself to the happy possessors of faith, but to those many people for whom the light has gone out, the mystery has faded, and God is dead. For most of them there is no going back, and one does not know either whether going back is the better way. To gain an understanding of religious matters, probably all that is left us today is the psychological approach. That is why I take these thought-forms that have become historically fixed, try to melt them down again and pour them into moulds of immediate experience. (2)

For most of us here I judge that Jung is accurately describing our condition when he says there is no going back to that frame of mind which could accept the Bible as literal truth. But he has made it possible for us to reclaim the Bible by taking "these thought-forms that have become historically fixed," melting them down again and pouring them "into moulds of immediate experience." This more excellent way is to take the Bible out of its traditional context and try to understand it from a psychological point of view. In *Answer to Job* Jung says:

The statements made in the Holy Scriptures are also utterances of the soul...they point to realities that transcend consciousness. These "entia" (realities) are the archetypes of the collective unconscious. (3)

From this point of view, far from suffering any diminishment or loss of its numinous aura, the Bible assumes more stature and relevance than ever. We must begin to see the insights, the central figures in the very stories themselves and the dogmatic utterances as unconscious projections from the objective psyche of men and women. They reflect stages of growth from an evolutionary point of view, progressive visions of eternal truth, building, in a word, raised consciousness.

In *Answer to Job*, Jung seems to suggest that the raising of God's consciousness follows from, and is dependent upon, the raised consciousness realized in men and women. I think this goes too far. The creature does not create the creator, else we must search for a god beyond God, a god above God. Rather, we are to see evolution toward higher consciousness in homo sapiens as enabling men and women to grow in the knowledge and love of God.

The grandeur of humanity is in its capacity to keep on transcending its former condition, becoming ever more conscious in a universe in which there is ever more to be conscious of. The faith in which Job had been brought up had as one of its unquestioned tenets: "the good shall prosper and the evil suffer."

But this was not Job's experience. The misfortunes that befell him and the plagues of physical suffering that beset him were excessive on any fair basis of judgment. The punishment simply did not fit the crime. His closest friends taunted and tortured him with the suggestion that perhaps his secret sins were responsible, those held long forgotten or whose memories he had repressed.

But Job knew in his heart he did not deserve his miserable plight. Though he was tempted to abandon the God who so ill-accorded with the archetype that served to portray God for so long, in the end he held fast to his love of God. "Though he stay me, yet will I love him."

The Evolution of an Archetype

Through Job's reflection upon and his wrestling internally with the disparity between what he had been taught and his own personal existential experience, he arrived at an enlightenment, satori-like, which presaged a new vision of the nature and reality of God as radically transformed. As Jung has put it, "after Job Jesus of Nazareth was a psychological necessity."

God did not change, of course. The human perception of God changed. God's query of Job was quite appropriate: "Where were you when I fashioned the earth?" If Job could discern this query from God, answering to that of God in himself, this was proof against any danger of inflation. The archetype of God in the experience of the human psyche was radically and permanently altered. With the coming of Jesus of Nazareth, the whimsical tyrant who delighted in punishing his people when they disobeyed him became like a suffering servant, redeeming his people with love.

Sylvia Brinton Perera in her book, *Descent to the Goddess*, offers the following definition of archetypes. She says they are:

Irrepresentable in themselves but their effects appear in consciousness as the archetypal images and ideas. These are collective universal patterns or motifs which come from the collective unconscious and are the basic content of religions, mythologies, legends, and fairy tales. They emerge in individuals through dreams and visions. (4)

Before the discovery of the fact of evolution this concept would have been unthinkable. The collective unconscious, what Jung elsewhere calls the objective psyche, is the reservoir wherein is stored the distilled wisdom of the whole animal progression on the tree of life, and more specifically that which has accumulated in the human species and its forebears, the hominids, homo habilis and homo erectus in the last three million years.

This wisdom takes the ultimately indescribable shape of images and ideas and is miraculously transferred through the genes and manifested in the personal unconscious. The archetypes are to the psyche what the instincts are to the body. Their presence in the collective unconscious has preserved the benefit of trial and error as the human consciousness groped its way through guided chance to higher consciousness.

The instincts are habits achieved by the body, fashioned in the crucible of trial and error over eons of time. Similarly the archetypes are images in the unconscious memory of the psyche of its journey on the arduous evolutionary path it has traversed in arriving where it now is. They serve as guard-rails, whose experience and wisdom are available to the individual psyche through dreams and fantasies. They function to help keep us on our unknown future evolutionary course, to keep us "on thread," to use the homely image put forward by Irene Claremont de Costillejo in *Knowing Woman*. Jung puts it this way:

> In the deeper stratum we also find the a priori inborn forms of "intuition," namely the archetypes of perception and apprehension, which are the necessary a priori determinants of all psychic processes. Just as his instincts compel man to a specifically human mode of existence, so the archetypes force his ways of perception and apprehension into specifically human patterns. The instincts and the archetypes together form the collective unconscious. (5)

It is important at this point to recognize that the process of evolution as continuing creation has two characteristics. It is responsible for the "ongoingness" of life in the sense of reproduction to offset death. In this way the archetypes could be said to preserve the integrity of the species.

But evolution is also responsible for what we might describe as the "up-reachingness" of life. While life goes on it also reaches up in some mysterious way to transcend itself. The most helpful image, perhaps, is of an ascending spiral moving along the axis of what Teilhard described as "complexity consciousness," implying ever greater complexity in the presence of ever more remarkable integration. Raised consciousness Teilhard saw as the goal of evolution, the "suitable outcome" he so devoutly sought.

In the light of these dual aspects of evolution, ongoingness and the up-reachingness, there must be two kinds of archetypes, those that serve the ongoingness and those that serve the up-reachingness. Or perhaps it is simply that archetypes partake of the evolving process and themselves evolve.

It is my own conviction that Jung, while he certainly accepted the fact of evolution, and was helped by it to arrive at his idea of the collective unconscious, did not sufficiently discern the role of archetypes in the transcending or up-reaching aspect of the process.

Now, what we have in the Old Testament is the recording, journal fashion, of more than a thousand years of the external and internal history of the Hebrew people. Much of the external, political history is the most authentic account we have of the sequence in the vicissitudes of the semitic people over this span of time. But concurrently with this account of the external events the Bible is a journal of the internal reflections, insights and convictions of these people. They were all the while experiencing the interaction between the dynamics of the archetypes, deeply buried in the unconscious, and the external events.

In other words they were making projections upon the data both of legend (distant and therefore diminishing) and actual history from the unconscious. They had no grasp, psychologically, of what they were doing. So they told their stories and made their moral judgments as if the truth of their statements and conclusions were transparent. And, following in their train, we have brought the same "matter-of-fact" assumptions to our literal interpretations.

But something much more wonderful has been happening, which we are just now beginning to understand. Their psyches were informed by the archetypes alive in their collective and personal unconscious and they unconsciously identified real historic figures and ideas with archetypes. So what we are witnessing in the Bible is our historic Judaeo-Christian myth in process of formation with all the drama, passion and power inevitably involved.

Today we speak of genetic and cultural coding. The archetypes could be likened to genetic coding, which is species-wide. The distinctive Hebraic institutions, political, religious and economic reflect cultural coding. The cultural coding may seem remote and alien but the archetypes in the genetic code still ring a bell with us because we too are human.

At the same time, because evolution continues, archetypes also evolve and we must be ever alert to the coming of fresh revelation. This is the power that resides in archetypes: they not only enable the psyche to experience a strange "recall" that keeps it on course collectively, but also a transcendent pull that keeps it evolving toward higher consciousness, perhaps toward Point omega, as Teilhard named evolution's objective.

This is why Teilhard insisted that we must not only worship the God of the above, but also the God of the ahead. In our very genes we are coded not only to be human, but to become, making use of another of Teilhard's coined words, more highly hominized.

In the depths of our psyches and in the place where our psyches are linked with the collective unconscious, we may be experiencing what Paul called a travailing and groaning together until now in the crucial struggle of homo sapiens to become homo spiritus under the guidance of evolving archetypes.

This is the divine activity behind and beyond the whole story of the Bible. To discern its movements in the story is to become conscious of a whole new dimension in the story defined by the human psyche in its pursuit of the Holy Grail of individuation. In the light of the mystical insight of the immanence of God every approximation to genuine individuation means the realization of a new incarnation of God.

The Contribution of Edward F. Edinger

In *Two Essays on Analytical Psychology*, Jung defines individuation in this way:

> Individuation means becoming a single, homogeneous being, and, insofar as individuality embraces an innermost, last, and incomprehensible uniqueness, it also implies becoming one's own self. We could therefore translate individuation as "coming to self-hood" or "self-realization." (6)

No one has applied Jungian insights more effectively to understanding the Bible in this way than Edward F. Edinger, Jungian analyst and author. He deals with the old Testament story in *The Bible and the Psyche*, (7) bearing the subtitle "Individuation Symbolism in the old Testament" and with the New Testament in *The Christian Archetype* whose subtitle is "A Jungian Commentary on the Life of Christ."

In the book on the Old Testament, he offers in the preface, in addition to the above quotation from Jung, a further definition of individuation as "the process of the ego's encounter with and progressive relation to the Self." This is what we have been saying in other ways. The central figures in the Old Testament can best be understood as embarked on an inward journey in which the individuated self and the Self or God within are one destination.

Elsewhere Jung has said: "the archetype of the self and the archetype of the Self (God) are ultimately indistinguishable." Edinger writes:

> The Old Testament documents a sustained dialogue between God and man as it is expressed in the sacred history of Israel. It presents us with an exceedingly rich compendium of images representing encounters with the numinosum (the Holy). These are best understood psychologically as pictures of the encounter between the ego and the Self, which is the major feature of individuation. The Old Testament is this grand treasury of individuation symbolism. These venerable stories derive from countless individual experiences of the numinosum and their psychic substances has been augmented through the ages by the pious worship and reflection of millions. When these facts are realized, we discover once again that the Old Testament is indeed a Holy Book. It is quite literally the ark of the covenant in which resides the power and glory of the transpersonal psyche. We must therefore approach it with caution, honoring its numinous power. (8)

Edinger sees three major divisions in the twenty-four books of the Old Testament: the Law, the Prophets and the Writings. This grouping assists in our psychological understanding, as Edinger explains:

I see this arrangement as a balance: on one side are the historical books in which Jahweh deals with Israel collectively as a nation. At this stage, individuation imagery is carried by the nation as a whole, the chosen people. On the other side are the prophetic books, each one named after a great individual who had a personal encounter with Jahweh and was fated to be an individual carrier of God-consciousness. In the middle are the poetical-wisdom books, with Job at their head. Job is the pivot of the Old Testament story. That is why Jung focused his Bible commentary on Job. Here for the first time a man encounters Jahweh *as an individual* and not as a function of the collective. Similarly, Jahweh did not deal with Job as a representative of Israel but rather as an individual man. This book thus marks the transition from collective psychology to individual psychology--from group and church religion to the individuals lonely encounter with the numinosum.

After Job comes the wisdom literature, as though the individual's ego encounter with Self has generated wisdom, or as Jung puts it in Answer to Job, as though the demonstration of Job's greater consciousness has obliged Jahweh to remember his feminine counterpart, Divine Wisdom (Sophia).

The events of the Bible, although presented as history, psychologically understood are archetypical images, that is, pleromatic events that repeatedly erupt into spatio-temporal manifestations and require an individual ego to live them out. As we read these stories with an openness to their unconscious reverberations we recognize them to be relevant to our most private experience. (9)

Let us now see through a few examples how these psychological insights throw new light on the familiar stories.

If one follows Jung in seeing Adam as an image of the Anthropos, the original whole man, then he becomes a symbol of the self. Before Eve was fashioned from one of his ribs in the story, Adam was an androgyny--a union of opposites. Jung finds psychological implications in the temptation of Adam and Eve:

There is deep doctrine in the legend of the Fall; it is the expression of a dim presentiment that the emancipation of the ego consciousness was a Luciferian deed. Man's whole history consists from the very beginning in a conflict between his feeling of inferiority and his arrogance. (10)

To Jung's insight Edinger adds the suggestion that "eating the fruit of the tree of the knowledge of good and evil symbolizes the birth of consciousness with the dawning awareness of the opposites." (11)

In the story of Abraham's willingness to sacrifice his only son at the command of Yahweh we see a foreshadowing of the New Testament story of the sacrifice by God of his only son. Jung sees in this the unfolding relation between the ego and the self:

> It is the self that causes me to make the sacrifice; nay more, it compels me to make the sacrifice. The self is the sacrifice, and I am the sacrificial gift, the humble sacrifice. Let us try for a moment to look into Abraham's soul when he was commanded to sacrifice his only son. Quite apart from the compassion he felt for his child, would not a father in such a position feel himself as the victim, and feel that he was plunging the knife into his own breast? He would be at the same time the sacrificer and the sacrificed.

> Nay, since the relation of the ego to the self is like that of the son to the father, we can say that when the self calls on us to sacrifice ourselves it is really carrying out the sacrificial act on itself.

> We may also venture to surmise that insofar as the self stands to us in the relation of father to son, the self in some sort feels our sacrifice as a sacrifice of itself. From that sacrifice we gain ourselves--our "Self"--for we have only what we give. (13)

With reference to the story of Jacob and Esau, Edinger makes the point that the ego destined for individuation is born as twins. "This division into two has two aspects: ego and shadow, and ego and Self." When Jacob stole Esau's birthright and paternal blessing, Jacob's ensuing guilty conscience imparts to Esau a divine power over him. When Jacob meets Esau, he says: "I have seen thy face, as though I had seen the face of God." (Genesis 33:10)

Edinger interprets: "This means psychologically that a crime against the shadow is also a crime against the Self and may activate the Self in its avenging form." (14) In the apocryphal book, Wisdom of Solomon, we are told that it was wisdom that saved Jacob's life by being with him when he wrestled with the angel. As a result of his experience of transformation, Jacob receives his new name, Israel.

Again we see this kind of hermeneutic in Edinger's interpretation of aspects of the Joseph story. In Genesis 39:2 we learn that "Yahweh was with Joseph." Being his father's favorite as well, he was given a coat of many colors. The coat represents the self, but to wear it in an inflated way would be to confuse the ego with the self. His dreams also reflect a measure of inflation. He bears false witness against his brothers and is sold into slavery.

Another archetypal theme is introduced in Joseph's encounter with Potiphar's wife, an encounter between the soul and matter. Another potential conjunction of opposites: immorality versus courage and the promise of maturity.

Joseph's ability to interpret dreams reflects a state of sensitivity with respect to the unconscious. The opposites appear again: the dreams of the royal cup-bearer and the royal baker, one prophesying pardon, the other execution. Once again, in being called in to interpret Pharaoh's dreams, he is confronted with opposites: feast or famine.

Edinger comments:

In order to achieve a conscious relation to the Self one is obliged to integrate the opposites. since "Yahweh is with Joseph", he must endure the activated opposites...to the extent the opposites are reconciled, the inner authority of the Self takes control of one's life. The achievement of that inner authority is indicated by the fact that Joseph becomes the regent of Pharaoh. (15)

Edinger holds that "the encounter between Moses and Yahweh is one of the grandest individuation dramas of the Western psyche." In Moses Edinger claims we may perceive no less than the individuation of an individual--something that had been possible only with reference to the collective history of the Jews until now. It is easy enough to see in Moses the projection of the archetype of the wise old man.

Michelangelo has portrayed this image visually for us with consummate art. But Edinger goes farther and shows us how the figure of Moses fits the specifications of the hero archetype of universal mythology:

> The hero is a figure midway between the ego and the Self. It can perhaps best be defined as a personification of the urge to individuation. The story of Moses' birth follows closely the characteristic pattern of the myth of the birth of the hero. The chief features of this myth are: 1) the birth of the infant occurs under adverse circumstances; 2) the authorities seek to kill it; 3) the infant is exposed or abandoned, often in water; 4) it is rescued, usually by lowly people, and accompanied by marvels; 5) there is a double set of parents, royal ones and lowly ones. These features all apply to the myth of Moses' birth and refer psychologically to the vicissitudes surrounding the birth of the urge to individuation. The established authority (inner and outer) is always opposed. The individual is thus exposed to the experience of exile or alienation and receives help only from the "lowly" aspects of the psyche which are open to the transpersonal dimension. (16)

Legend has it that Moses was so brilliant that he seemed to anticipate what was imparted to him, after the manner of foreknowledge predicated by Plato. Edinger writes concerning the application of Plato's idea to Moses:

> This doctrine is an intuitive, philosophical anticipation of what we now know to be the collective unconscious or objective psyche. Applied to Moses, the process of learning by recollection means that individuation involves the discovery of one's innate wisdom and pattern of being. (17)

Edinger says of Moses' impulsive killing of the Egyptian slave driver, a crime for which he was sent into exile: "It is a primitive unmediated expression of individuation energy, the initial manifestation of his call." (18) He holds that Moses' encounter with Yahweh at the burning bush after being many years in exile is a classic image of an encounter with the self.

In response to Moses' query as to what he is to tell his people when he returns, Yahweh says "You must say to the Sons of Israel I am has sent me to you." The point that the fire does not consume the bush suggests to Edinger that it is transpersonal. It is not quenched by personal satisfaction. He refers to Jung's identification of a desire that can be described as a "thirsting for the eternal." He goes on to say:

> Libido is recognized as transpersonal when the ego succeeds in disidentifying from it. Then what one desires is no longer perceived as MY pleasure, MY power, MY ambition, but rather a task imposed by the Self. A task is what Yahweh imposes on Moses. Considering the symbolism of fire, out of which the assignment comes, Moses' task is to follow his libido. The fulfillment of this libido perceived transpersonally, is the sacred task of self-realization.

The advantage of a Jungian interpretation of scripture is that it enormously enhances the immediacy of its relevance to our lives here and now. The dynamics of the unconscious, the archetypes and their projections being universal and immemorial, were operative then as now.

Instead of an historical account of a succession of miracles in encounter with an external and transcendent God the stories become unconscious accounts of psychological principles, activated by the intuitive quest of the psyche for individuation. The self is the interior counterpart of Yahweh, the immanent God, God within.

We may once have identified with certain figures in the Old Testament and with imagination, engaged in role playing. But now, with the aid of the insights of depth psychology, we can find direct analogies with our own inner journey that are compelling and empowering. While we reflect on Yahweh's assignment of a task to

Moses and the response of the self within Moses, we are constrained
to ask what is my task, assigned by my Self, the accomplishment of
which would further my individuation?

Jesus and the Messiah Archetype

Over the past years, long before being introduced by
Edinger to some of the subtleties of the process, I have been at
work on my own Jungian understanding of the person of Jesus and
the Messiah Archetype which has been historically projected on him
by Christianity.

Archetypes are fashioned secretly in the unconscious as the
self gropes its way forward to the evolutionary goal of individuation.
When Israel was forced into exile, a great crisis confronted, not only
the self of the solitary Jew, but the collective identity of the nation
itself. The poignant question was how to sing the Lord's song in a
foreign land. The symbol of their religious unity, the temple, had
been destroyed. The personification of political unity in David and
his successor, Solomon, was no more. The Jewish psyche was "in
extremis." "Without the temple, and without a king can we any
longer be Jews?"

In this crisis the collective unconscious of the jewish people,
with the aid of the vision of individual prophets, forged a distinctive
image of the hero archetype, a messiah, a Son of David, a valiant
warrior, who would arise and crush the enemies of Israel. No sooner
had this archetype been confirmed by the corporate response than
variations on the theme began to evolve.

Another visionary saw the hero image in larger perspective.
The messiah would not only rescue Israel from bondage, but was to
be the savior of all mankind. Far from being a warlord, the new
messiah was conceived as a counsellor, a prince of peace. He was
no longer the son of David. He was named the "Son of Man,"
universal in his task, his saviorhood.

The concept of the Son of Man, by synchronicity, lends
itself to our need in the Twentieth Century in which everything must
be tested for its validity by the touchstone of the fresh revelation
emanating from the discovery of the fact of evolution: The Son of

Man, man's successor. Here we see an archetype itself in process of evolution.

A further clarification and modification came with the vision of yet another prophet, the author of the fifty-third chapter of the book of Isaiah. The messiah would come in the form of a "Suffering Servant," one who would redeem the world through redemptive suffering. He would indeed be "a man of sorrows and acquainted with grief." Such a vision was only possible after Job. Such a messiah was in psychological terms, an answer to Job.

Now the historic man, Jesus of Nazareth, whose childhood was nourished by these stories, was confronted by the need to appraise these images with active imagination and to select the images he could identify with in his own vision of the coming messiah. If Jesus were truly human, and for my part I have to begin with that assumption, then the insights of depth psychology must apply to him as well as every other man.

I remember laboring long and hard many years ago over whether or not Jung's insight that to identify fully with an archetype meant to become psychotic applied to Jesus as well. I decided it did and that Jesus' patent sanity was proof on psychological grounds that he did not identify himself as the messiah. If he were human, to do so would spell paranoia.

I was further persuaded by Albert Schweitzer's dissertation, *A Psychiatric Study of Jesus*, in which he effectively answered the claims of certain German scholars that Jesus was suffering from psychosis. Jesus himself gives testimony as to his sanity by saying, "Don't call me good. There is only one who is good: God." There are many other texts which demonstrate his sanity as a human being. He was always "present," never in retreat from reality. He thought of himself as healer, teacher, the greatest of the prophets because his prophesy encompassed the greatest reality, the Kingdom of God in which one could learn to dwell here and now.

He must have pondered what manner of man the messiah would be. Clearly he rejected the image of a warlord, crushing the enemies of Israel, in favor of the Son of Man image, a Prince of Peace, and the image of the Suffering Servant. But did he identify himself definitely with that archetype? We can only conjecture, but I think the psychological evidence is to the contrary.

However, immediately after his death his followers identified him with all three of the historic archetypal messiah figures. And the author of the fourth gospel added a new image, borrowed from Greek philosophy, the "logos," the word. The Church, as it grew in influence and power continued to enlarge his divine stature until he became the second person on the Holy Trinity.

The credal statements continued to elevate the divinity: "Very God of Very God, begotten not made, being of one substance with the Father by whom all things were made." For many he became indistinguishable from God.

When a young theological student was emboldened to deny the singular divinity of Jesus the infuriated professor shouted, "young man, no one is ever going to write an apostle's creed about you." No doubt the professor was standing on unassailable ground in making such a statement. It raises an important point. The fact is the Church did write an Apostles Creed about this historical figure, and the impressive thing is that the claims seemed plausible, the projections were acceptable, even to some of those who had known him in the flesh. So great was Jesus' charisma that it could support even so inflated a projection.

Beyond the hero archetype, beyond the messiah archetype, beyond the Son of Man, and the Son of God archetypes lies the archetype of the God-man. Many religions have made the ultimate query: If God were a man or woman, what kind of man or woman would he/she be? Jesus seemed to reflect and to embody this ultimate archetype.

There is yet another way to account for the continuing power of the classic Christ myth over the mind and imagination of men and women. Something still deeper seems to be plumbed in the human psyche by this numinous historic figure. We have distinguished earlier between archetypes that serve as guard rails to keep the human psyche on its course, to keep it characteristically human, what the Chinese call "human-hearted", and archetypes which may presage the next development in human evolution.

What if the unconscious dimly recognized in Jesus the man an evolutionary breakthrough, a mutation, a sport, a forerunner of man's successor, the Son of Man in this evolutionary sense, the first-born among many brothers and sisters (to use Paul's metaphor), a peduncle as it were of a new species, homo spiritus? Do we not see in his revelation of the Kingdom of God on earth the new environment in which this new being learned to live and to breathe with such excitement and intoxication?

What we would then be seeing in Jesus would be, in some sense our own potential, our own unrealized selves.

Jesus would then be activating for us the archetype of the second Adam and Eve, the new man and woman, buried deep in our own unconscious, leading us forward in our evolutionary inward journey to higher consciousness.

We should then have to re-mythologize our ancient myth to say something like this:

God so loved the world that he/she implanted deeply and darkly in matter itself the seed which by continuing creation through evolution would one day produce the Christ-life in one Jesus of Nazareth, thereby quickening the Christ seed in other men and women to their souls' salvation and fulfillment.

NOTES

[In these Notes "C.W." refers to Jung's *Collected Works*, followed by the Volume number.]

1. C. G. Jung, *The Visions Seminars*, Vol. 1, p. 18.

2. C. G. Jung, *Psychology and Religion*, in *Collected Works* (C.W.) Vol. 11, par. 148.

3. C. G. Jung, *Answer to Job*, *Psychology and Religion*, C.W. Vol. 11, par. 557.

4. C. G. Jung, C.W. Vol. 8, pp. 133-134.

5. Sylvia Brinton Perora., *Descent to the Goddess*, Inner City Books, 1978, p. 95.

6. C. G. Jung, *Two Essays on Analytical Psychology*, C.W. Vol. 7, par. 266.

7. Edward F. Edinger, *The Bible and the Psyche*, Inner City Books, Toronto, Canada, 1986, p. 9.

8. Ibid, p. 12.

9. Ibid., pp. 12, 13.

10. C. G. Jung C.W. Vol. 9i, Par. 420.

11. Edward Edinger, *The Bible and the Psyche*, p. 20.

12. C. G. Jung, C.W. Vol. 11, par. 397f.

13. Edward Edinger, *The Bible and the Psyche*, p. 41.

14. Ibid., p. 44.

15. Ibid., p. 45.

16. Ibid., pp. 45, 46.

17. Ibid., p. 46.

18. Ibid., p. 46.

XXV

The Not-So-Bad Good Book: A Meditation

Diane Bonner Zarowin

[Note: Diane Bonner Zarowin remembers that she stole her first Bible, out of her parents' bookcase, and thought sure Yahweh's wrath would soon fall on her; but she hastens to add that when it didn't, this did not induce her to become a doubter. Now she is an editor, a poet a feminist and a mystic--though not, she says, necessarily in that order. Also a self-styled "evangelical universalist," she attends Staten Island Meeting in New York.]

I believe that:

God speaks all languages; I don't;

God is personal, accessible, and active;

All of life proceeds, inexorably, from the divine, through the divine, and to the divine;

Each of us must invent God, that is, through self-discovered ritual, invite God into our lives.

I believe that the experience of God is our birthright.

Perhaps our only birthright.

* * *

If there is a God, where is she not?

* * *

How do we "invent" God? How do we "approach" that awesome throne room, let alone the ineffable throne, and when God asks:

"Whom shall I send?"

How do we answer, how do we prepare ourselves to answer, as did Isaiah (6:8):

"Here I am. Send me."

* * *

If there is a God, where is she not?

* * *

Moses, beloved of Yahweh: "I have set before you life and death, the blessing and the curse; therefore choose life". (Deut. 30:19)

Choose life.

To choose life is to live intentionally. To participate in intentionality. To become aware that we are creatures of instinct.

If only the divine is fully intentional, then only as we become more intentional can we participate in God's design.

To choose life is to be awake:
Jesus in Gethsemane: "My soul is filled with sorrow even to death. Remain here with me and stay awake". (Matt. 26:38)

To choose life is to remember:

Isaiah: "I shall not forget you. Look, I have engraved you on the palms of my hands". (49:16)

* * *

If there is a God, where is she not?

What is the Bible:

The Bible is the story of our search for God:

"As a deer longs for flowing streams, so my soul longs for you, O God. My soul thirsts for God, for the living God".(Psalm 42:1)

The Bible is the story of God's love for us, is God's whispered call of remembrance:

"I will entice you into the desert and there I will speak to you in the depths of your heart". (Hosea 2:14)

Above all, the Bible is a guide to life, a how-to book on choosing life:

"Be still, and know that I am God". (Psalm 46:10)

"You have been told what is good and what Yahweh requires of you: to do justice, to love mercy, and to walk humbly with your God".(Micah 6:8)

"Hear, O Israel: The Lord our God, the Lord is One. And you shall love the Lord your God with all your heart, and with all your soul, and with all your might. And these words, which I command you this day, shall be upon your heart; and you shall teach them diligently to your children, and shall talk of them when you sit in your house and when you walk by the way, and when you lie down and when you rise up". (Deut. 6:4-7)

* * *

If there is a God, where is she not?

APPENDIX: Quaker Quotes About The Bible--A Sampler

GEORGE FOX: ...[The priest at Nottingham] told the people that the Scriptures were the touchstone and judge by which they were to try all doctrines, religions, and opinions, and to end controversy. Now the Lord's power was so mighty upon me, and so strong in me, that I could not hold, but was made to cry out and say, 'Oh, no, it is not the Scriptures', and was commanded to tell them God did not dwell in temples made with hands. But I told them what it was, namely, the Holy Spirit, by which the holy men of God gave forth the Scriptures, whereby opinions, religions, and judgements were to be tried; for it led into all Truth, and so gave the knowledge of all Truth. For the Jews had the Scriptures, and yet resisted the Holy Ghost, and rejected Christ the bright morning star, and they persecuted Christ and his apostles, and took upon them to try their doctrines by the Scriptures, but erred in judgement, and did not try them aright, because they tried without the Holy Ghost.

[John L. Nickalls, ed., *The Journal of George Fox* (Philadelphia: Religious Society of Friends, 1985), p. 33.]

GEORGE FOX: And as concerning the Holy Scriptures, we do believe that they were given forth by the Holy Spirit of God, through the holy men of God, who, as the Scripture itself declares(2Pet 1:21) 'spake as they were moved by the holy ghost.' We believe they are to be read, believed and fulfilled--He that fulfills them is Christ--and they are 'profitable....' We call the Holy Scriptures, as Christ and the Apostles called them, and holy men of God called them, viz.: the 'words of God'....

[Letter to the Governor of Barbadoes, 1671.]

MARGARET FELL: ...I cried in my spirit to the Lord, "We are all thieves; we are all thieves; we have taken the Scriptures in words, and know nothing of them in ourselves."

(Upon hearing George Fox preach in her church): [Isabel Ross, *Margaret Fell: Mother of Quakerism* (York, England: The Ebor Press. 1984), p. 11, quoting from *A journal or historical account of...George Fox* (Leeds 1836). 6th edition. I,lxii.]

JAMES NAYLER: (Nayler was on trial, 1653.) Justice Pearse asked, 'What sayest thou to the Scriptures? Are they the Word of God?'

Nayler replied, 'They are a true declaration of the word that was in them who spoke them forth.'

One Higginson asked: 'Is there not a written word?'

Nayler: 'Where readest thou in the Scriptures of a written Word? The Word is spiritual, not seen with carnal eyes....'

[Quoted in Barbour and Roberts, eds., Early Quaker Writings,1650-1700. (Grand Rapids, Mich.: Eerdmans)

ROBERT BARCLAY: In the Scriptures God has deemed it proper to give us a looking glass in which we can see the conditions and experiences of ancient believers. There we find that our experience is analogous to theirs....This is the great work of the Scriptures, and their usefulness to us. They find a respondent spark in us, and in that way we discern the stamp of God's ways and his Spirit upon them. We know this from inward acquaintance we have with the same Spirit and his work in our hearts....Nevertheless, because they are only a declaration of the fountain, and not the fountain itself, therefore they are not to be esteemed the principal ground of all truth and knowledge...they are and may be esteemed a secondary rule, subordinate to the Spirit, from which they have all their excellency and certainty...the Spirit is the first and principal leader.

An Apology for the True Christian Divinity (1675)

ROBERT BARCLAY: ...I have known some of my friends, who profess the same faith with me, faithful servants of the Most High God, and full of divine knowledge of his truth, as it was immediately and inwardly revealed to them by the Spirit, from a true and living experience, who not only were ignorant of the Greek and Hebrew, but even some of them could not read their own vulgar language, who being pressed by their adversaries with some citations out of the English translation, and finding them to disagree with the manifestation of truth in their own hearts, have boldly affirmed the Spirit of God never said so, and that it was certainly wrong; for they did not believe that any of the holy prophets or apostles had ever written so; which when I on this account seriously examined, I really found to be errors and corruptions of the translators; who, as in most translations, do not so much give us the genuine signification of the words, as strain them to express that which comes nearest to that opinion and notion they have of truth.

[Robert Barclay, *An Apology for the True Christian Divinity* (Philadelphia: Friends' Book-Store, undated), p. 86.]

HANNAH WHITALL SMITH: So far as I can see, the Scriptures everywhere make it an essential thing for the children of God, in their journey through this world, to use all the faculties that have been given them. They are to use their outward faculties for their outward walk, and their inward faculties for their inward walk; and they might as well expect to be "kept" from dashing their feet against a stone in the outward, if they walk blindfold, as to be "kept" from spiritual stumbling if they put aside their judgment and common sense in their interior life.

Some, however, may say here, "But I thought we were not to depend on our human understanding in Divine things."

I answer to this that we are not to depend on our unenlightened human understanding, but upon our human judgment and common sense enlightened by the Spirit of God.

That is, God will speak to us through the faculties He has Himself given us, and not independently of them; so that just as we are to use our outward eyes in our outward walk, no matter how full of faith we may be, so also we are to use the interior "eyes of our understanding" in our interior walk with God.

[Hannah Whitall Smith, *The Christian's Secret of a Happy Life* (Old Tappan, NJ: Fleming H. Revell Company, 1970), p. 70.]

CAROLINE STEPHEN: ...I believe the doctrine of Fox and Barclay (i.e., briefly, that the "Word of God" is Christ, not the Bible, and that the Scriptures are profitable in proportion as they are read in the same spirit which gave them forth) to have been a most valuable equipoise to the tendency of other Protestant sects to transfer the idea of infallibility from the Church to the Bible. Nothing, I believe, can really teach us the nature and meaning of inspiration but personal experience of it.

[Caroline Stephen, *Quaker Strongholds* (Philadelphia, Henry Longstreth, 1891), p. 28.]

RUFUS JONES: But greatly as I loved the Bible and devoutly as I believed in my first years that it was to be taken in literal fashion, I am thankful to say that I very early caught the faith and insight, which George Fox and other Quaker leaders had taught, that God is always revealing himself, and that truth is not something finished, but something unfolding as life goes forward.

[Rufus Jones: *Finding the Trail of Life* (1926).]

WILLIAM WISTAR COMFORT: ...as the Holy Spirit existed before the authors of the Bible books were inspired, so it still exists today and forever, available for the inspiration, understanding and interpretation of new revelations, guiding us into all truth.

Friends, then, believe in a continuing revelation, a further unfolding of divine purpose as man is able to receive it. The Bible is important not as a fetish, but as a record of something still more important than itself: the Holy Spirit.

The Bible is of value to Friends not because what is in it is true, but because what is true is in it. The final reference must be to the Spirit or Word which inspired it, and which alone can interpret it, and that Word is eternally alive and at work.

[William Wistar Comfort, *Just Among Friends: The Quaker Way of Life* (Philadelphia, American Friends Service Committee, 1968), p. 22.]

HENRY CADBURY: Holding, as they did, that the revelation of God was not limited to Scripture, early Friends were not impressed by the arbitrary limits of the Bible canon. In using the Old Testament apocrypha they were not unlike other Protestants of their day, for the Protestant aversion to those books has increased more recently. Friends' curiosity about still other books, lost or professing early date, was a natural expression of their feeling that Divine revelation neither began with Moses nor ended with the Apostles.

...The dictionary is not the authority which dictates how words ought to be used. It is rather the record of how words are used and what they commonly mean. In like manner the Bible is not the dictator of our conduct and faith. It is rather the record of persons who exemplified faith and virtue. It does for religion that which the dictionary does for speech. Its value consists in its agreement with experience, or with truth, as Friends used to use the word. What is true in the Bible is there because it is true, not true because it is there. Its experiences "answer" to ours, that is, they correspond to ours....

...At best the Bible is a difficult book, often confusing, often ill edited, often obscure....

...It is much more important to know from the Bible how God reveals than what God reveals, if we want to share its experiences and not merely its expressions. In the same way one might rather aim to understand how Jesus thought than what he thought, if our wish is to learn to think for ourselves as he did.

To fail to make this approach is to be satisfied with the second best and automatically to exclude the very best. How much the Bible has to teach when taken as a whole, that cannot be done by snippets! There is its range over more than a thousand years giving us the perspective of religion in time, growing and changing, and leading from grace to grace. There is its clear evidence of the variety of religious experience, not the kind of straight jacket that nearly every church, even Friends, have sometimes been tempted to substitute for the diversity in the Bible....

...The Bible is the deposit of a long series of controversies between rival views of religion. The sobering thing is that in nearly every case the people shown by the Bible to be wrong had every reason to think they were in the right, and like us they did so. Complacent orthodoxy is the recurrent villain in the story from first to last and the hero is the challenger, like Job, the prophets, Jesus, and Paul.

[From *A Quaker Approach to the Bible*, The Ward Lecture, 1953 (Philadelphia, Philadelphia Yearly Meeting Library, 1978), pp. 12-15.]

WILLIAM TABER: ...For me, this unreality of the key Old Testament laws began to change when I began to read the Bible in what I sometimes call the Quaker way--that is, reading with both the analytical mind and the intuitive mind leaving plenty of space for the Holy Spirit to operate, to integrate. On the one hand such reading makes use of Biblical scholarship and all the light that modern science can provide; on the other hand, using this method, one reads softly, and deeply, and meditatively, with the intellect temporarily at rest. One simply savors and rests in the meaning instead of analyzing it; one just pauses from time to time to stare off into space and wait for what earlier Friends called "the inward motion."

[William Taber: *The Prophetic Stream* (Wallingford, Pendle Hill Publications, 1984), p. 8.]

YORKSHIRE QUARTERLY MEETING (1919): The canon of Scripture may be closed, but the inspiration of the Holy Spirit has not ceased. We believe that there is no literature in the world where the revelation of God is given so fully as in our New Testament

Scriptures; we go back to them for light and life and truth. But we feel that the life comes to us, not from the record itself, but from communion with him of whom the record tells. Through his own Spirit we commune with Him himself. In the words of Coleridge, "I meet that in Scripture which finds me."

[Quoted in *Christian Faith and Practice*, London Yearly Meeting.]

EVANGELICAL FRIENDS CHURCH, EASTERN REGION: With early Friends, we believe that all Scripture, both of the Old and New Testaments is given by inspiration of God, without error in all that it affirms and is the only infallible rule of faith and practice. It is fully authoritative and trustworthy, fully sufficient to all believers now and always....Thus, the declarations contained in it rest on the authority of God Himself, and there can be no appeal from them to any other authority whatever....The Holy Spirit, who inspired the Scripture, must ever be its true interpreter. Whatsoever any man says or does which is contrary to the Scripture, though under profession of the guidance of the Spirit, must be reckoned and accounted a delusion.

[*Faith and Practice, Book of Discipline*, 1980.]

FRIENDS GENERAL CONFERENCE: The Bible means a "library." It contains the records of the search for God by the Hebrews (Jews); and as they grew and changed, so did their ideas of God. The Bible contains myths, legends, poetry, laws, prophecies, history, biography, drama, short stories and novels, as well as the oldest riddle in the world, the oldest detective story and the oldest battle-hymn

....Of course, the Bible was written by many people over hundreds of years. Not all of it applies to our problems today; not all of it is about good men, but the more we read, the more fascinated we become and the more we want to read and study. If we do this intelligently, we will find the Bible truly a source of joy, help and interest all our lives and a pathway to God for each one of us.

[From *Graphic Outline for Study of the Old Testament*. (Philadelphia: FGC, 1953.)]

BALTIMORE YEARLY MEETING: Many differing attitudes toward the Bible can be found among Friends, but a few statements may find general acceptance:

a) In the experience of Friends, the Bible can be rightly understood only in the light of the Spirit which inspired it--the same Holy Spirit which is available to all.

b) Although the word of God is found in the Bible, inspiration may also be found elsewhere. The closing of the canon of Scripture did not signal the end of divine inspiration.

d) Detailed understanding of the Bible can be reached only through study of the time and circumstances of the writing, in the light of various commentaries and translations....

In the 20th century, Friends, like many other Christian groups, deplore the diminished knowledge of and interest in the Bible. Study of the Bible, especially in the light of modern scholarship, can be most rewarding. Meetings are encouraged to include Bible study in religious education.

[From *Faith and Practice*, 1988.